DRUMVOICES REVUE:
A Confluence of Literary, Cultural & Vision Arts

Fall/Winter 1992/93, Vol. 1, Nos. 1 & 2, ISBN 1-88807-01-0
Southern Illinois University at Edwardsville

--This Issue--
"Reports: Atlanta, East St. Louis, Paris, San Francisco"

CONTRIBUTORS

Jeanette Adams, Maya Angelou, Baron James Ashanti, Jabari Asim, Alvin Aubert, Amiri Baraka, Georgene Bess, Gwendolyn Brooks, Michael Castro, Doctor E. Pelikan Chalto, Henry Dumas, Kofi L. Dunbar, Cornelius Eady, Mari Evans, Leon Forrest, J. e. Franklin, Bob Holman, Darryl Holmes, Ja A. Jahannes, Ira B. Jones, Etheridge Knight, Earnest McBride, Debra F. Meadows, Janice Mirikitani, Carla Moody, Tess Onwueme, Raymond R. Patterson, Robert Earl Price, Eugene B. Redmond, Ishmael Reed, Luis Rodriguez, Darlene Roy, Jeffrey Skoblow, Christina Springer, Christopher Stanard, Richard Stimac, Erik Stinus, Francy Stoller, Zohreh T. Sullivan, Clyde Taylor, Seneca Turner, Derek Walcott, Charles Wartts, Jr., Tyrone Williams, Andrea M. Wren

Front Cover Photo: Inaugural Poet Maya Angelou, Winston-Salem, NC, April 1991.

Drumvoices Revue is published twice yearly, except for double issues like the current one, by the English Department of Southern Illinois University at Edwardsville in collaboration with the Eugene B. Redmond Writers Club of East St. Louis (P.O. Box 6165), Illinois 62202. Occasional monographs, chapbooks, pamphlets and special-focus projects will also be published in the *Drumvoices Supplement Series*. Example: *BREAK WORD WITH THE WORLD: A Commemorative Collection of Poems / Anecdotes / Commentaries*. Subscriptions: $6 per semi-annual issue; $10 per year. For information write Editor: *Drumvoices Revue*, Dept. of English, Box 1431, SIUE, Edwardsville, Il. 62026-1431. Tele: (618) 692-2060 or 692-3991. An SASE should accompany unsolicited MSS.

ACKNOWLEDGEMENTS

Reprints/First Prints: Gwendolyn Brooks for "Malcolm X." Reprinted from *Blacks*. Chicago: Third World Press. Copyright © 1945-1991 by Gwendolyn Brooks Blakely. Gwendolyn Brooks for "To An Old Woman, Homeless and Indistinct," from manuscript. Copyright © 1992 by Gwendolyn Brooks. Kofi L. Dunbar and the *East St. Louis Monitor* for "Kwanzaa '91: Gwendolyn Brooks in East St. Louis." Reprinted from the January 9, 1992 issue of the *Monitor*. Copyright © 1992 by Kofi L. Dunbar. Earnest McBride and *Jackson Advocate* for "'Magic Realism' Brings Men and Women Together at JSU Conference." Reprinted from *Jackson Advocate*, Jackson, Mississippi (Vol. 55, No.4, October 22-28, 1992). Janice Mirikitani for "For My Father," "Desert Flowers," "Salad," and "We, the Dangerous." Reprinted from *Awake in the River*. San Francisco: Isthmus Press. Copyright © 1978, 1982, 1984 by Janice Mirikitani. Eugene B. Redmond for "From the Chaosmos to Self-Knowledge." Reprinted from *Tornado Alley* (Vol. I, Issue I, December 1991/January 1992). Copyright © 1993 by Eugene B. Redmond. Clyde Taylor for "Keeping the Spirit Whole Under Wolves' Teeth." Reprinted from "Introduction" to *Griefs of Joy: Anthology of Contemporary Afro-American Poetry for Students*. Eugene B. Redmond, editor. East St. Louis: Black River Writers Press. Copyright © 1977 by Clyde Taylor. Derek Walcott for "A Far Cry from Africa," "Origins," and "New World." Reprinted from *Collected Poems*. New York: Farrar, Straus & Giroux. Copyright © 1962-86 by Derek Walcott. Derek Walcott for "Saint Lucia's First Communion," "Gros-Ilet," "For Adrian," "Menelaus," and "The Young Wife." Reprinted from *Arkansas Testament*. New York: Noonday Press. Copyright © 1987 by Derek Walcott. Derek Walcott for excerpts from *Omeros*. New York: Farrar, Straus & Giroux. Copyright © 1990 by Derek Walcott.

Photographs: AP/World Wide Photos for photograph of Malcom X, (March, 1964, Harlem). Bill Brinson of SIUE for back cover photograph. Loretta Dumas and the Henry Dumas Estate for photograph of Henry Dumas, circa 1953. Eunice Knight-Bowens and the Etheridge Knight Estate for photograph of Etheridge Knight. Sherman Fowler for photographs of Gwendolyn Brooks, Mari Evans, and Hillary Clinton/Tipper Gore at Jackson School. Eugene B. Redmond for photographs of Maya Angelou (including cover), Tina McElroy Ansa, Alvin Aubert, SIUE's Black Literary Guild, Homeless Brother, Michael Castro/Massey/Brandi, Xam Cartier & company, Katherine Dunham, Dunham dance students, Cornelius Eady, Student editorial assistants to *Drumvoices*, Leon Forrest and Ralph Ellison, Keya Ganguly/Gray/Stabile, Bill Harris and Clyde Taylor, Asa Hilliard/Lowery/Obenga, Maxine Hong Kingston, Annabelle Lee, Ruth Love and Alex Haley, Walter Mosley and Octavia Butler, Gyo Obata, Raymond Patterson and Barry Wallenstein w/son, Ishmael Reed, Luis Rodriguez, Darlene Roy/Singh/Wright/Davis, Ousmane Sembene, Jeffrey Skoblow, Gwendolyn Stephenson/Winters/Tapscott, Sekou Sundiata and Cornel West, Susan Taylor and Sonia Sanchez, Quincy Troupe & company at Duff's, Derek Walcott, Margaret Walker (Alexander), Joanne T. Gabbin/Joyce/Williams, Young Literati at Atlanta Literary Celebration '92.

Drumvoices Revue Fall/Winter 1992/93
(English Dept./Southern Illinois University at Edwardsville)

Founding Editor .... Eugene B. Redmond

Associate Editor .... Clyde Taylor

Assistant Editors .... Jabari Asim
George Barlow
Georgene Bess
Tess Onwueme
Jeffrey Skoblow

Senior Consulting Editors .... Maya Angelou
Amiri Baraka
Janice Mirikitani
Mari Evans
John A. Williams

Advisory and Contributing Editors .... Margaret Walker Alexander
Gwendolyn Brooks
Michael Castro
Robert Chrisman
Eugenia Collier
J. California Cooper
Toi Derricotte
Katherine Dunham
Jessica Hagedorn
Asa Hilliard
Joyce Ann Joyce
Jean Kittrell
Ruth B. Love
L.T. McGraw-Beauchamp
Jose Montoya
Raymond R. Patterson
Toks Pearse
Darlene Roy
Philip Royster
Isaiah Smithson
Gary Soto
Gerald E. Thomas
Eleanor Traylor
Ralph Cheo Thurmon
Quincy Troupe
Jerry Ward

SIUE Editorial Assistants .... Debjani Dasgupta, Michelle Foster,
Douglas Rudder, Richard Stimac, Christina Veasley

Special Thanks .... Alexandra Babione, Debbie Bacus (Steno Pool),
Linda Jaworski
A.C. and L.T. Mc-Graw Beauchamp of *Literati Internazionale*,
Technical Advising

SIUE Graphics for cover design

Table of Contents/*Drumvoices Revue*

Rite #1
DEREK WALCOTT: NOBEL LAUREATE
A POETIC RETROSPECTIVE: 1948-1990

Rite #2
CONFERENCES, SYMPOSIUMS, FESTIVALS, PALAVERS

Rite #3
CHANTS, BLUES, VISIONS, POEMS

Rite #4
WRITERS TALKING, WORDS WALKING

Rite #5
HUNGERS, FLOWERS, SIGHTINGS, BLOOD

Rite #7
ST. LOUIS AND OTHERWHERES: URBAN WORDSCAPES

Rite #8
'WHEREABOUTS KNOWN': APROPOS ANCESTORS

Rite #1

Derek Walcott: Nobel Laureate

A Poetic Retrospective: 1948-1990

Collected Poems

Arkansas Testament

Omeros

ORIGINS
[for *Veronica Jenkin*]

narrow path of the surge in the blur of fables. . .

– CESAIRE

Derek Walcott

I

The flowering breaker detonates its surf.
White bees hiss in the coral skull.
Nameless I came among olives of algae,
Foetus of plankton, I remember nothing.

Clouds, log of Colon,
I learnt your annals of ocean,
Of Hector, bridler of horses,
Achilles, Aeneas, Ulysses,
But "Of that fine race of people which came off the mainland
To greet Christobal as he rounded Icacos,"
Blank pages turn in the wind.
They possessed, by Bulbrook,
"No knowledge whatever of metals, not even of gold,
They recognized the seasons, the first risings of the Pleiades
By which signs they cultivate, assisted by magic...
Primitive minds cannot grasp infinity."

Nuages, nuages, in lazy volumes, rolled,
Swallowed in the surf of changing cumulus,
Their skulls of crackling shells crunched underfoot.
Now, when the mind would pierce infinity.
A gap in history closes, like a cloud.

II

Memory in cerecloth uncoils its odour of rivers,
Of Egypt embalmed in an amber childhood.
In my warm, malarial bush-bath,
The wet leaves leeched to my flesh. An infant Moses,
I dreamed of dying, I saw
Paradise as columns of lilies and wheat-headed angels.

Between the Greek and African pantheon,
Lost animist, I rechristened trees:
Caduceus of Hermes: the constrictor round the mangrove.
Dorade, their golden, mythological dolphin,
Leapt, flaking light, as once for Arion,
For the broken archipelago of wave-browed gods.
Now, the sybil I honour, mother of memory,
Bears in her black hand a white frangipani, with berries of blood,
She gibbers with the cries
Of the Guinean odyssey.

These islands have drifted from anchorage
Like gommiers loosened from Guinea,
Far from the childhood of rivers.

III

O clear, brown tongue of the sun-warmed, sun-wooded Troumassee
of laundresses and old leaves, and winds that buried their old
songs in archives of bamboo and wild plantain, their white sails
bleached and beaten on dry stone, the handkerchiefs of adieux
and ba-bye! O sea, leaving your villages of cracked mud and
tin, your
chorus of bearded corn in tragic fields, your children
like black rocks of petrified beginnings in whose potbellied
drought the hookworm boils, cherubim of glaucoma and gonorrhea!
White cemeteries of shells beside the
sea's cracked cobalt, poinsettia bleeding at your praying stations,
shadowy with croton and with "glory cedar,"
Whose gourds of cracked canoes hold the dead hopes
Of larvae,
live middens heaped by the infecting river, fetes of a childhood
brain sieved with sea-noise and river murmur, ah, mon enfance.
Ah, mon enfance! *Smothered in the cotton clouds of*
illness, cocooned in sinuous odours of the censer, buried in bells,
bathed in the alcohol of lime and yellow flowers, voyaging like
Colon on starched, linen seas; that watched the river's
snakes writhe
on the ceiling, that knew the forgotten taste of river water,
the odour of fresh bread and mother's skin, that knew its own skin
slowly (amber, then excrement, then bronze), that feared the
Ibo fifes
and drums of Christmas, the broken egg in which it sailed
at Easter,

festivals, processions voyages of the grave, and
the odour of rivers in unopened cupboards.

IV

Trace of our exodus across its desert
Erased by the salt winds.

The snake spirit dies, writhing horizon.
Beetles lift the dead elephant into the jaws of the forest.
Death of old gods in the ashes of their eyes.
The Plunging throats of porpoises simulating, O sea,
The retching hulks of caravels stitching two worlds,
Like the whirr of my mother's machine in a Sabbath bedroom,
Like needles of cicadas stitching the afternoon's shroud.
Death Of old gods in the river snakes dried from the ceiling,
Jahveh and Zeus rise from the foam's beard at daybreak.

The mind, among sea-wrack, sees its mythopoeic coast,
Seeks, like the polyp, to take root in itself.
Here, in the rattle of receding shoal,
Among these shallows I seek my own name and a man.
As the crab's claws move backwards through the surf,
Blind memory grips the putrefying flesh.

V

Was it not then we asked for a new song,
As Colon's vision gripped the berried branch?
For the names of bees in the surf of white frangipani,
With hard teeth breaking the bitter almonds of consonants,
Shaping new labials to the curl of the wave,
Christening the Pomegranate with a careful tongue,
Pommes de Cythère, bitter Cytherean apple.
And God's eye glazed by an indifferent blue.

VI

We have learnt their alphabet of alkali and aloe, on seeds of
islands dispersed by the winds. We have washed out with salt
the sweet, faded savour of rivers, and in the honeycombs of skulls
the bees built a new song. And we have eaten of their bitter olive.
But now, twin soul, spirit of river, spirit of sea, turn from the
long, interior rivers, their somnolence, brown studies, their long

colonial languor, their old Egyptian sickness, their imitation of
tea colour, their tongues that lick the feet of bwana and sahib,
their rage for funeral pyres of children's flesh, their sinuousness
that shaped the original snake. The surf has razed that
memory from
our speech, and
a single raindrop irrigates the tongue.

VII

The sea waits for him, like Penelope's spindle,
Ravelling, unravelling its foam,
Whose eyes bring the rain from far countries, the salt rain
That hazes horizons and races,
Who, crouched by our beach fires, his face cracked by deserts,
Remembering monarchs, asks us for water
Fetched in the fragment of an earthen cruse,
And extinguishes Troy in a hissing of ashes,
In a rising of cloud.

Clouds, vigorous exhaltations of wet earth,
In men and in beasts the nostrils exulting in rain scent,
Uncoiling like mist, the wound of the jungle,
We praise those whose back on hillsides buckles on the wind
To sow the grain of Guinea in the mouths of the dead,
Who, hurling their bone-needled nets over the cave mouth
Harvest ancestral voices from its surf,
Who, lacking knowledge of metals, primarily of gold,
Still gather the coinage of cowries, simple numismatists,
Who kneel in the open sarcophagi of cocoa
To hallow the excrement of our martyrdom and fear,
Whose sweat, touching earth, multiplies in crystals of sugar
Those who conceive the birth of white cities in a raindrop
And the annihilation of races in the prism of the dew.

A FAR CRY FROM AFRICA

From *In A Green Night* [1962]

Derek Walcott

A wind is ruffling the tawny pelt
Of Africa. Kikuyu, quick as flies,
Batten upon the bloodstreams of the veldt.
Corpses are scattered through a paradise.
Only the worm, colonel of carrion, cries:
"Waste no compassion on these separate dead!"
Statistics justify and scholars seize
The salients of colonial policy.
What is that to the white child hacked in bed?
To savages, expendable as Jews?

Threshed out by beaters, the long rushes break
In a white dust of ibises whose cries
Have wheeled since civilization's dawn
From the parched river or beast-teeming plain.
The violence of beast on beast is read
As natural law, but upright man
Seeks his divinity by inflicting pain.
Delirious as these worried beasts, his wars
Dance to the tightened carcass of a drum,
While he calls courage still that native dread
Of the white peace contracted by the dead.

Again brutish necessity wipes its hands
Upon the napkin of a dirty cause, again
A waste of our compassion, as with Spain,
The gorilla wrestles with the superman.
I who am poisoned with the blood of both,
Where shall I turn, divided to the vein?
I who have cursed
The drunken officer of British rule, how choose
Between this Africa and the English tongue I love?
Betray them both, or give back what they give?
How can I face such slaughter and be cool?
How can I turn from Africa and live?

NEW WORLD

From *Sea Grapes* [1976]

Derek Walcott

Then after Eden,
was there one surprise?
O yes, the awe of Adam
at the first bead of sweat.

Thenceforth, all flesh
had to be sown with salt,
to feel the edge of seasons,
fear and harvest,
joy that was difficult,
but was, at least, his own.

The snake? It would not rust
on its forked tree.
The snake admired labour,
it would not leave him alone.

And both would watch the leaves
silver the alder,
oaks yellowing October,
everything turning money.

So when Adam was exiled
to our New Eden, in the Ark's gut,
the coined snake coiled there for good
fellowship also; that was willed.

Adam had an idea.
He and the snake would share
the loss of Eden for a profit.
So both made the New World. And it looked good.

SAINT LUCIA'S FIRST COMMUNION

Derek Walcott

At dusk, on the edge of the asphalt's worn-out-ribbon,
in white cotton frock, cotton stockings, a black child stands.
First her, then a small field of her. Ah, it's First Communion!
They hold pink ribboned missals in their hands,

the stiff plaits pinned with their white satin moths.
The caterpillar's accordion, still pumping out the myth
along twigs of cotton from whose parted mouths
the wafer pods in belief without an "if"!

So, all across Saint Lucia thousands of innocents
were arranged on church steps, facing the sun's lens,
erect as candles between squinting parents,
before darkness came on like their blinded saint's.

But if it were possible to pull up on the verge
of the dimming asphalt, before its headlights lance
their eyes, to house each child in my hands,
to lower the window a crack, and delicately urge

the last moth delicately in, I'd let the dark car
enclose their blizzard, and on some black hill,
their pulsing wings undusted, loose them in thousands to
stagger
heavenward before it came on: the prejudice, the evil!

Poetics: Caribbean bard Derek Walcott and East St. Louis poet Eugene B. Redmond exchange notes during a winter 1991 party for Walcott in St. Louis.

GROS-ILET

Derek Walcott

From this village, soaked like a grey rag in salt water,
a language came, garnished with conch shells,
with a suspicion of berries in its armpits
and elbows like flexible oars. Every ceremony commenced
in the troughs, in the middens, at the daybreak and the daydark
funerals
attended by crabs. The odours were fortified
by the sea. The anchor of the islands went deep
but was always clear in the sand. Many a shark,
and often the ray, whose wings are as wide as sails,
rose with insomniac stare from the wavering corals,
and a fisherman held up a catfish like a tendrilled head.
And the night with its certain, inextinguishable candles
was like All Souls' Night upside down, the way a bat keeps
its own view of the world. So their eyes looked down, amused,
on us, and found we were walking strangely,
and wondered about our sense of balance, how we slept
as if we were dead, how we confused
dreams with ordinary things like nails, or roses,
how rocks aged quickly with moss,
the sea made furrows that had nothing to do with time,
and the sand started whirlwinds with nothing to do at all,
and the shadows answered to the sun alone.
And sometimes, like the top of an old tire,
the black rim of a porpoise. Elpenor, you
who broke your arse, drunk, tumbling down the bulkhead,
and the steersman who sails, like the ray under the breathing
waves,
keep moving, there is nothing here for you.
There are different candles and customs here, the dead
are different. Different shells guard their graves.
There are distinctions beyond the paradise
of our horizon. This is not the grape-purple Aegean.
There is no wine here, no cheese, the almonds are green,
the sea grapes bitter, the language is that of slaves.

FOR ADRIAN

APRIL 14, 1986

(To *Grace, Ben, Judy, Junior, Norline, Katryn, Gem, Stanley, and Diana*)

Derek Walcott

Look, and you will see that the furniture is fading,
that a wardrobe is as insubstantial as a sunset,

that I can see through you, the tissue of your leaves,
the light behind your veins; why do you keep sobbing?

The days run through the light's fingers like dust
or a child's in a sandpit. When you see the stars

do you burst into tears? When you look at the sea
isn't your heart full? Do you think your shadow

can be as long as the desert? I am a child, listen,
I did not invite or invent angels. It is easy

to be an angel, to speak now beyond my eight years,
to have more vestal authority, and to know,

because I have now entered a wisdom, not a silence.
Why do you miss me? I am not missing you, sisters,

neither Judith, whose hair will banner like the leopard's
in the pride of her young bearing, nor Katryn, not gem

sitting in a corner of her pain, nor my aunt, the one
with the soft eyes that have soothed the one who writes this,

I would not break your heart, and you should know it;
I would not make you suffer, and you should know it;

and I am not suffering, but it is hard to know it.
I am wiser, I share the secret that is only a silence,

with the tyrants of the earth, with the man who piles rags
in a creaking cart, and goes around a corner

of a square at dusk. You measure my age wrongly,
I am not young now, nor old, not a child, nor a bud

snipped before it flowered, I am part of the muscle
of a galloping lion, or a bird keeping low over

dark canes; and what, in your sorrow, in our faces
howling like statues, you call a goodbye

is – I wish you would listen to me – a different welcome,

which you will share with me, and see that it is true.

All this the child spoke inside me, so I wrote it down.
As if his closing grave were the smile of the earth.

Nobel Laureate Derek Walcott signs autographs for Adelia Parker, left, and Dagmar Von Tress at a 1991 St. Louis reception in his honor.

Scholars, novelists and poets gathered following a fall 1992 Cultural Plurality conference at University of Illinois at Urbana-Champaign. From left: Laurence Lieberman, Ray A. Young Bear, Zohreh T. Sullivan (conference coodinator), Richard Powers (McArthur fellowship recipient), Elizabeth Alexander, Phillip Graham, and Eugene B. Redmond.

THE YOUNG WIFE

(For Nigel)

Derek Walcott

Make all your sorrow neat.
Plump pillows, soothe the corners
of her favourite coverlet.
Write to her mourners.

At dusk, after the office,
travel an armchair's ridge,
the valley of the shadow in the sofas,
the drapes' dead foliage.

Ah, but the mirror – the mirror
which you believe has seen
the traitor you feel you are –
clouds, though you wipe it clean!

The buds on the wallpaper
do not shake at the muffled sobbing
the children must not hear,
or the drawers you dare not open.

She has gone with that visitor
that sat beside her, like wind
clicking shut the bedroom door;
arm in arm they went,

leaving her wedding photograph in
its lace frame, a face smiling at
itself. And the telephone
without a voice. The weight

we bear on this heavier side
of the grave brings no comfort.
But the vow that was said
in white lace has brought

you now to the very edge
of that promise; now, for some,
the hooks in the hawthorn hedge
break happily into blossom

and the heart into grief.
The sun slants on a kitchen floor.
You keep setting a fork and knife
at her place for supper.

The children close in the space
made by a chair removed,
and nothing takes her place,
loved and now deeper loved.

The children accept your answer.
They startle you when they laugh.
She sits there smiling that cancer
kills everything but Love.

MENELAUS

Derek Walcott

Wood smoke smudges the sea.
A bonfire lowers its gaze.
Soon the sand is circled with ugly
ash. Well, there were days

when, through her smoke-grey
eyes, I saw the white trash that was
Helen: too worn-out to argue
with her Romany ways.

That gypsy constancy,
wiry and hot, is gone;
firm hill and wavering sea
resettle in the sun.

I would not wish her curse
on any: that necks should spurt,
limbs hacked to driftwood, because
a wave hoists its frilled skirt.

I wade clear, chuckling shallows
without armour now, or cause,
and bend, letting the hollows
of cupped palms salt my scars.

Ten years. Wasted in quarrel
for sea-grey eyes. A whore's.
Under me, crusted in coral,
towers pass, and a small sea-horse.

Excerpts from *Omeros*

Derek Walcott

Chapter II, Section III, pp.14-15

"O-meros," she laughed. "That's what we call him in Greek,"
stroking the small bust with its boxer's broken nose,
and I thought of Seven Seas sitting near the reek

of drying fishnets, listening to the shallows' noise.
I said: "Homer and Virg are New England farmers,
and the winged horse guards their gas-station, you're right."

I felt the foam head watching as I stroked an arm, as
cold as its marble, then the shoulders in winter light
in the studio attic. I said, "Omeros,"

and *O* was the conch-shell's invocation, *mer* was
both mother and sea in our Antillean patois,
os, a grey bone, and the white surf as it crashes

and spreads its sibilant collar on a lace shore.
Omeros was the crunch of dry leaves, and the washes
that echoed from a cave-mouth when the tide has ebbed.

The name stayed in my mouth. I saw how light was webbed
on her Asian cheeks, defined her eyes with a black
almond's outline, as Antigone turned and said:

"I'm tired of America, it's time for me to go back
to Greece. I miss my islands." I write, it returns –
the way she turned and shook out the black gust of hair.

I saw how the surf printed its lace in patterns
on the shore of her neck, then the lowering shallows
of silk swirled at her ankles, like surf without noise,

and felt that another cold bust, not hers, but yours
saw this with stone almonds for eyes, its broken nose
turning away, as the rustling silk agrees.

But if it could read between the lines of her floor
like a white-hot deck uncaulked by Antillean heat,
to the shadows in its hold, it nostrils might flare

at the stench from manacled ankles, the coffled feet
scraping like leaves, and perhaps the inculpable marble
would have turned its white seeds away, to widen

the bow of its mouth at the horror under her table,
from the lyre of her armchair draped with its white chiton,
to do what the past always does: suffer, and stare.

She lay calm as a port, and a cloud covered her
with my shadow; then a prow with painted eyes
slowly emerged from the fragrant rain of black hair.

And I heard a hollow moan exhaled from a vase,
not for kings floundering in lances of rain; the prose
of abrupt fishermen cursing over canoes.

Chapter LIV, Section III, pp.271-272

All that Greek manure under the green bananas,
under the indigo hills, the rain-rutted road,
the galvanized village, the myth of rustic manners,

glazed by the transparent page of what I had read.
What I had read and rewritten till literature
was guilty as History. When would the sails drop

from my eyes, when would I not hear the Trojan War
in two fishermen cursing in Ma Kilman's shop?
When would my head shake off its echoes like a horse

shaking off a wreath of flies? When would it stop,
the echo in the throat, insisting, "Omeros";
when would I enter that light beyond metaphor?

But it was mine to make what I wanted of it, or
what I thought was wanted. A cool wood off the road,
a hut closed like a wound, and the sound of a river

coming through the trees on a country Saturday,
with no one in the dry front yard, the still leaves,
the yard, the shade of a breadfruit tree on the door,

then the track from which a man's figure emerges,
then a girl carrying laundry, the road-smell like loaves,
the yellow-dressed butterflies in the grass marges.

Novelist Maxine Hong Kingston (facing camera), author of Return to Manzanar, *speaks to St. Louis literati during a reception for her and Derek Walcott at Washington University in 1991. Facing camera, left, is poet Shirley LeFlore. At right is Kingston's husband, Earll.*

UNIVERSITE DE LA SORBONNE NOUVELLE
PARIS III

AFRICAN AMERICANS AND EUROPE
LES NOIRS AMERICAINS ET L'EUROPE

CONFERENCE BOOKLET

LIVRET DU COLLOQUE

ORGANIZED BY — ORGANISE PAR

CENTRE D'ETUDES AFRO-AMERICAINES (SORBONNE NOUVELLE)

W.E.B DU BOIS INSTITUTE FOR AFRO-AMERICAN RESEARCH (HARVARD UNIVERSITY)

CENTER FOR AMERICAN CULTURE STUDIES (COLUMBIA UNIVERSITY)

CENTER FOR THE STUDY OF SOUTHERN CULTURE (UNIVERSITY OF MISSISSIPPI)

FEBRUARY, 5-9, 1992 — 5-9 FEVRIER 1992

Rite #2

Conferences, Symposiums, Festivals, Palavers

KWANZAA '91: GWENDOLYN BROOKS IN EAST ST. LOUIS

Kofi L. Dunbar

Black America's First Lady of poetry packed the East St. Louis City Hall Rotunda to the rafters during her soul-quaking presentation on Dec. 17, 1991. The featured speaker for Pre-Kwanzaa Festival '91, Illinois Poet Laureate Gwendolyn Brooks brought maturity, eloquence, cultural wisdom and a demure dynamism to an appreciative audience.

Her reading anchored the program – aimed at celebrating African-American struggle and self-reliance – which also featured readings by local poets, a dazzling performance by the ESL Lincoln Sr. High School Jazz Band (with Ronald Carter directing), a Kwanzaa ritual by students from Southern Illinois University at Edwardsville, and a presentation by 14-year-old rapper Victor Mosley.

Poets who read in tribute to Brooks included Sherman Fowler, Darlene Roy, Evon Udoh, and Andrea Wren. SIUE students participating in the Kwanzaa ritual were Anthony Beasley, Marcus Atkins, Jamie Skinner, Sherry Tolson, Jamal Isaac, Marcia Hunt, and Richard Agnew.

Against background responses of oohs, aahhs, amens, tell it Sister, go on, that's right, and I hear ya, Brooks delivered a brilliant sampling of her poetry. Her reading included such classics as "Satin-Legs Smith," "We Real Cool," "The Mother," "Beverly Hills, Chicago," and "of De Witt Williams on his way to Lincoln Cemetery." She also read, to the audience's delight, later works like "To Those of My Sisters Who Kept Their Naturals," "The Near-Johannesburg Boy," and selections from a forthcoming book, *Children Coming Home* – a painfully comic and blunt work about hope and abuse of children.

A highlight of the Dec. 17 event was a presentation to Brooks of the Distinguished Native Daughter Award by Darlene Roy, president of the Eugene Redmond Writers Club, which co-sponsored the program along with the SIUE Department of English and *Drumvoices Revue.*

Following her reading, Brooks responded graciously to a cry for "encore," afterwards autographing books for more than an hour. And, to top it all off, she conducted a wonderful workshop with local authors the next morning in the board room of ESL State Community College.

GWENDOLYN BROOKS: AN APPRECIATION

Jabari Asim

Henry Taylor writes of Gwendolyn Brooks: "[Her] activities in behalf of younger writers have demonstrated her generosity and largeness of spirit, and wide recognition of these qualities has led some critics away from the controlled but genuine anger in many of the poems."[1]

Notwithstanding the bumblings of the nearsighted but well-meaning critics to whom Taylor refers, it's quite easy for this writer to appreciate the legendary status of Brooks' generosity.

I'm reminded of a crowded parlor, a room filled with students, scholars and doddering pseudo-intellectuals. The atmosphere is stuffy, stale and not at all untypical of such gatherings sponsored by the English department of a certain midwestern university. The wine-and-brie stiffness of the scene is gradually melted by the charming warmth of the honored guest, Gwendolyn Brooks. She has just regaled me and perhaps a hundred others with a reading of a few selections from her impressive repertoire. After skipping classes to catch every minute of a three-day Brooks residency filled with workshops, readings and fireside chats, I am now less than five feet from her. I'm dressed in my usual uniform of battered, faded jeans and carrying a sheaf of rough scribblings that I boldly refer to as "fiction."

Pressed into action by Jean Brown, a fellow student, I humbly approach Mrs. Brooks, shake her hand, mumble a few pleasantries, and leave my work with her. Despite her friendly graciousness, I am uneasy and eager to leave the scene. I depart soon after.

Less than a week later, I'm stunned to receive a handwritten note from Brooks thanking me for sharing my work, which she found rich with "heavy drama." The note was brief, tactful and encouraging. The fact that she'd taken time from her undoubtedly hectic schedule to acknowledge my budding ambitions inspired me to a degree that cannot be overestimated.

Brooks' generosity is legendary not only because it is apparently boundless, but also, sadly, because it is relatively rare. African-American writers of my generation have learned to expect little from our predecessors; so many of them have made it painfully clear that approaching them for a bit of wisdom and encouragement is an unreasonable act.

Although nearly ten years have passed since my initial face-to-face encounter with our Mrs. Brooks, time has afforded me ample opportunity to see that her warmth and compassion remain constant. I last saw her on December 17, 1991, when she read from her works in the rotunda of the East St. Louis City Hall, at a Kwanzaa celebration sponsored by the Eugene B. Redmond Writers Club. The blend of humility and genuine joy inherent in her reading style provided a distinctive and often ironic counterpoint to the stark severity of her material. The latter included a series of poems (from a new volume titled *Children Coming Home*) named after imaginary children; the most poignant and disturbing selection was "Uncle Seagram," which detailed the damaging life of a drunken child molester.

---

[1] Taylor, Henry. "Gwendolyn Brooks: An Essential Sanity." *The Kenyon Review* Volume XIII, No. 4 (1991): 115-131.

The empathy Brooks expressed toward the young subjects described in the poems in no way diluted the unflinching frankness of her language, which was indeed infused with the "controlled but genuine anger" to which Taylor refers.

After brilliantly elevating her grateful audience on a frosty E. St. Louis evening, Brooks patiently signed autographs for the better part of an hour. She remained patient, gracious and queenly, a picture of subtlety and strength. Her value to younger writers as a master of her craft is perhaps exceeded only by the exemplary manner in which she conducts her life.

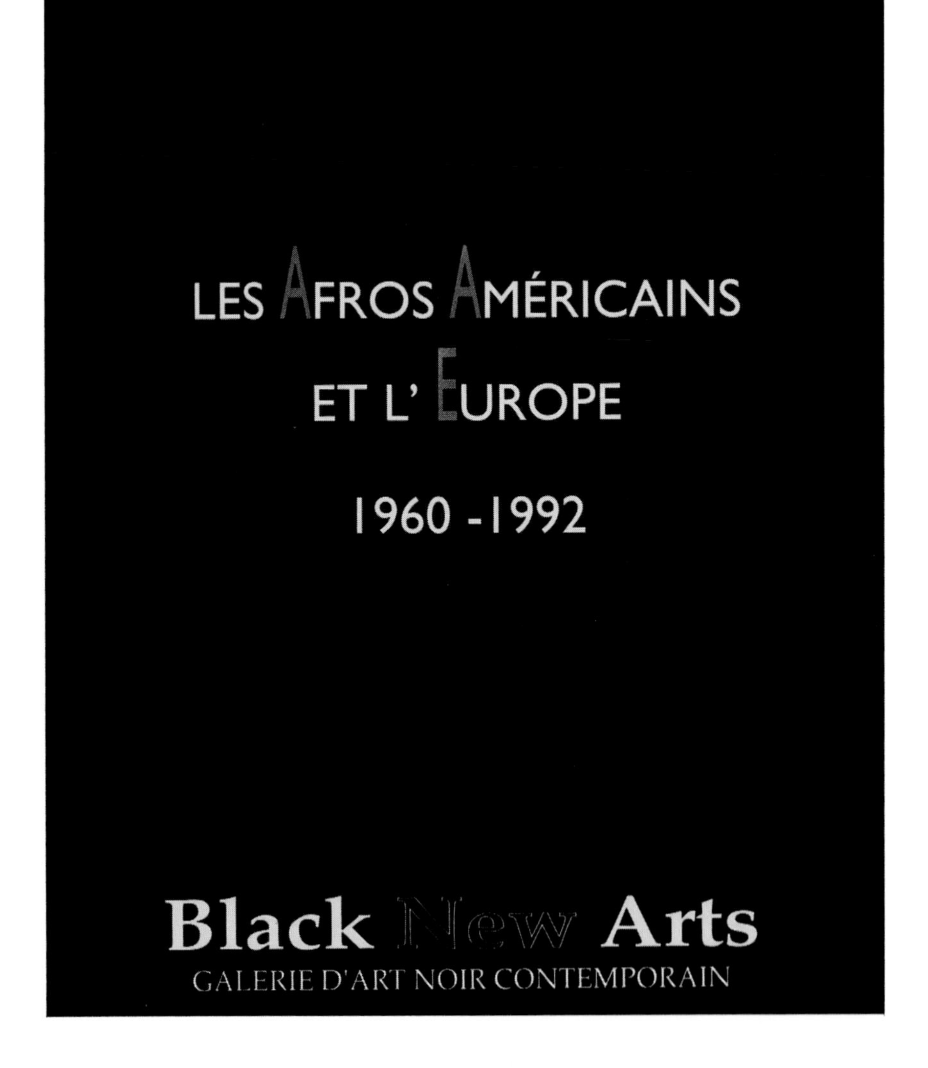

MULTI VIEWS ON MULTI-CULTURALISM

(Journal Notes: Modern Language Association Convention, San Francisco, December 1991)

Michael Castro

I
Issue of Authenticity

Saturday morning: The convention yesterday was, as expected, a madhouse. Long lines of academics waiting to register in the vast lobby of the Hilton. Crowds milling through the narrow hallways en route to conference sessions. Tension & energy & cigarette smoke in the air with snatches of conversation: academics swapping notes, renewing acquaintances. I BART* in & arrive early, before the first day's opening sessions. I acclimate to the layout of the Hilton & go into the conference room for the Native American session on "American Indian Literatures: Authenticity & the Canon." I sit reading a newspaper, half expecting someone I know to appear – but no one does. The session instead fills with a whole new generation of scholars interested in the field. No Carter Revard, Jim Ruppert, Ken Roemer, Kay Sands, Larry Evers, Joy Harjo, Andy Wiget, Paula Gunn Allen, etc. But the room is overflowing – evidence of there being more interest than ever in this now academic field of which I'm proud to have been among the founders. The "multicultural thing" has blossomed in academia & the attendance at this session reflects it. Rodney Simard of Cal State San Bernardino presents a paper broadly overviewing the issue of authenticity in Native American literature and the wide range of viewpoints contained therein. His conclusions are somewhat opaque, but he makes a plea for inclusivity – which I assume means not over-limiting what can be considered authentic. *Black Elk Speaks* is, for instance, by some standards an unauthentic text because of Neihardt's editing of the original interviews. Works by Welch, Silko, Momaday are considered unauthentic by some because the bloodline & upbringing of the writers and the forms of their writings are not "pure Indian" enough.

Ruth Lindeman of the University of Illinois offers a study of *Blackhawk's Autobiography*, taking the position that the book's two anglo editors embellished & imposed in such a way as to justify their subject's demise *and* victimization. Ellanne Brown of Montana State University takes a similar tact with her paper on "The Editorialization of Morning Dove," demonstrating how the input of the editor McWorter tended to impose his own concerns & self-image as a castigated "good Samaritan" onto the resulting book. She cites letters from McWorter to

---

*Editor's Note: Bay Area Rapid Transit

publishers that make a convincing case. Jennifer Seighi, a beautiful young woman from University of Rhode Island, does a presentation on "Storytelling: Tradition & Preservation in Erdrich's *Tracks* – All this is followed by a lively if inconclusive debate/discussion on the issue of authenticity. People talk on all sides of the issue. Clearly there is something to be said for bloodline or upbringing in connection to the culture you write about – but also, a case can be made for the outsider's ability to bring a useful perspective. Clearly intent, accuracy & sensitivity – areas that must be examined on a case by case basis – are among the most telling criteria. Perhaps scholars should be establishing a list of criteria points – blood connection, sensitivity, accuracy, universality, commercialism, etc., by which to evaluate individual works rather than groping for some magical unilateral formula. The session ends on the note, that seems to contain the sentiments in the room, of "Perhaps instead of searching for the answer, we should be reformulating the question." When I discuss this session with Rebecca, she recounts a meeting with Martin Buber in which, regarding a non-literary topic, the issue of authenticity comes up & he gives her virtually the same answer. We need questions that enable us to get beyond the limits of our assumptions. I forgot to mention the personal high point of yesterday's session. After the Native American session a woman came up to me as I was talking to Susan Scarberry-Garcia & noticing my name tag, said – "I'm happy to meet you. I've read your book [*Interpreting the Indian*] at least eight times. It's opened up whole new areas of interest for me. Thank you."

II
Highlights; Hindsights

The MLA conference was over for me. A good, rich two days. Some highlights: a session on Ginsberg's great poem "Kaddish." This year marks its 25th anniversary. A pall over the proceedings as the lights dim inadvertently in the overcrowded room (someone leaning on the rheostat). Kush, the Berkeley poetry archivist & activist who's setting up recording equipment, announces, comically: "We can now reveal the secret message of this session." As people chuckle and after a pregnant pause, he announces, "Allen Ginsberg won't be reading 'Kaddish' tomorrow as scheduled. He's hospitalized in Cooperstown, New York recovering from congestive heart failure." A little buzz of disappointment goes through the assemblage, though not the sense of grief and personal concern you'd hope for. I feel for Allen. Say some OM's for his recovery. Later Gordon Ball assures us he's on the mend so, I guess, not to worry. Ball introduces the proceedings, citing some of the early reactions to "Kaddish" – Robert Lowell: "a terrible masterpiece;" Louis Simpson: "Before 'Kaddish,' no one thought such things could be said in a poem." Then he introduces Helen Vendler, the first speaker. She speaks of the poem as an invention of a 20th century elegy rich with satire & pathos, an instance of "ethnic modernism" which reverses the cultural icon of the Pieta & has the son holding the broken body of the mother. The poem is about Naomi Ginsberg, Allen's mother, "from whose pained head I first took vision." The most powerful parts of Vendler's presentation are her readings of actual passages from this great poem. The mocking "caw, caw, caw" refrain of the crows echoing the "Lord, Lord, Lord" of Hebraic prayer, all the more telling, she points out, when the "Lawd" of New York accent is realized. Vendler sees "Kaddish" as a Jewish poem in three major ways – 1) a highly historically conscious poem: just as Judaism is historically conscious & places God within human history & is concerned for it, "Kaddish" is historically conscious & presents a historical vision of Naomi's life & the historical vision & analysis of thirties Jewish urban socialists; 2) "Kaddish" is also a form of prayer, its rhythmic base the *yisgadol v'yisgadash sh'mey raboh* of the death liturgy, the caw, caw, caw/Lord, Lord, Lord mentioned above; and 3) "Kaddish" is Jewish in its being a poem of the body – its sometimes brutal accounts of the physical history & decay of Naomi's body reflecting the absence of imagery of the afterlife in the Jewish tradition, its inventory of the body recalling the ritual viewing of the dead's body one final time in the funeral home. It's Jewish in its tragicomic vision, and traditionally elegiac in its transcendent ending, Naomi's last words – "Get married Allen. Don't take drugs. The key is in the sunlight in the window. I have the key." This final message transcends the scene of tragic non-recognition, when Allen visits her in the hospital, & Naomi's words are "You're not Allen." The poem, like historical elegies, comes to an acceptance of death & the beyond.

Barry Miles, the English scholar and cultural historian, then discusses how "Kaddish" got written. Its germination he relates to the fact that Ginsberg did not attend Naomi's funeral (he was in Berkeley) and that only seven people did attend, thus there were not enough men present to form a minion so that she could get a final and proper Kaddish. Shortly thereafter, while walking with Kerouac in San Francisco, Allen passed a synagogue & spontaneously went inside and asked if they could say a prayer for his mother. Again, there were not enough men present for a minion and no Kaddish could be offered. Naomi died in 1956 and Allen wrote fragmentary notes about her and toward a Kaddish in the months following. Then in 1956, after an all night session with Raymond Fetterman, getting high on heroin and speed and reading poems, he went home and wrote a draft of the poem he had discussed with Fetterman in a non-stop 36-hour binge, aided by Peter Orlovsky bringing him coffee, and only occasional breaks to go to the bathroom. The draft was sent to Ferlinghetti, with the note "You figure out what to do with it." Ferlinghetti praised it, but said it needed cutting. Allen, almost immediately, set to the task, & cut five pages that digressed from the focus of Naomi. In all, according to Miles (though the particulars are a little sketchy), the poem was written over eighteen months, and three years in the editing.

III
"Speechless Shame"

Lewis Hyde of Kenyon College then speaks of "Speechless Shame, Shameless Speech." He recounts an incident in a classroom in which a student innocently asks Ginsberg, "How do you become a prophet?" His reply, "You tell your secrets." As any reader of Allen's work knows, that concept has been at the heart of his poetry and poetics and it dates back to Whitman's notions of the poem. Hyde brings out how this decision represents a major break with Louis, his poet father, who actually wrote him that "a man must resign himself to established values, even if he recognizes their absurdity – or kill himself." Hyde called the first page of "Kaddish," "55 lines of stalling," because Allen feared what would be uncovered if he actually wrote the poem he had in mind. He asserts that Allen's objective is to "change the landscape of shame" with a poem written in the "shameless prophetic mode." In "Kaddish," the shameful is associated with the sacred: "Blessed the homosexual"... among a catalogue of blessed shame-attached concepts. Again Whitman is echoed & extended (Song of Myself's "through me, forbidden voices . . ."). Ginsberg's overall aesthetic & ideology, Hyde says, involves a refusal to enter any ordered world because ordered worlds inevitably include concepts of shame & thus exclude some element of the sacred. Instead Ginsberg's resonates to a Buddhist "openness" & a Keatsian "uncertainty principle."

Czeslaw Milosz is the fourth speaker. The great Nobel Prize-winning poet (1980) offers a poem dedicated to Allen in which he confesses his own weakness in submitting to customs even though he knew they were absurd, "united with others in a blessed normalcy" while "I envy your courage of absolute desire." The poem concludes, "Walt Whitman listens & says 'Yes, that's the way to talk.'" Milosz adds a few more comments on his theme of Ginsberg & Whitman & poetry. The art of poetry, he says, is essentially about "describing reality," and a poem's value lies in "how much reality it describes." His final words are: "The America of Walt Whitman is real. The America of Allen Ginsberg is real. But its things are only props, & cannot ruin genuine poets."

IV
River Styx

After the talks I introduce myself to Kush, who is very gracious, accepting a *River Styx*, and telling me he does a lot of traveling these days & may pass through St. Louis; he is interested in doing a program on the poet Lew Welch. "I'm spending almost all my time on archivist work," he says. "Allen has kind of hired me." A guy named Jeff Zable recognizes my name as the editor of *River Styx*, & says hello. He's the author of *Zable's Fables* & in turn introduces me to short fat Harold Norse. Norse's response to "River Styx, St. Louis," is "My, St. Louis, that really is in the sticks." (Sticks, Styx – get it: this guy is really a wit/twit). I feel my anger rise & hold it in. A minute too late, as usual, I realize I should have replied, "Paradise is where you make it, Mr. Norse."

This scene is followed by a reading by Fannie Howe, which I go over to catch a bit of & meet Fannie & give her a copy of (*US*). We've published her in *River Styx*. She is a friend of Quincy, Jerry Rothenberg, etc. Jan Castro introduces her to the audience. As I enter the room I overhear a guy mentioning to someone he's a poet and recently lived in India. I introduce myself. His name is Tom Jones; he taught at Shantiniketan University (Tagore's old ashram) & published a book there which he flashes. I recognize the cover style. "P. Lal!" I say, amazed to see the familiar sari woven cover of one of Lal's books from Calcutta. I give him a copy of (*US*) and then split for the University of Oklahoma Press reception. There I renew acquaintance with Paula Gunn Allen, Andy Wiget, Kay Sands, Jerry Vizenor, Carter Revard, Larry Evers, Jim Purdy, Laura Coltelli, LaVonne Ruoff – the talk among the old Native American crowd is the stir caused by the rising generation of "young Pomos," actually one Greg Sarris, half Jewish & half Pomo, who's come out against the anglo scholars in the field. Kay says "I won't write on Native American stuff again. I won't participate in it." She's in a good position to say that, as she's moved into another area of scholarship, the Charro tradition, among a Mexican cowboy community in Arizona. She's gotten their confidence because she's a skilled rider, she says. "What else could I want, great horses, handsome men ..." U of Arizona is doing a book of hers on the subject. I let myself be cornered by Ruth Rosenberg, my admirer. It turns out her husband's a rabbi who's written books on Jewish history and Kabbalah which, after I press on her (*US*) and *River Styx*, she promises to send me. She's also a Blake freak. We talk about Blake – how did he know about American Indians, & how did he have such a grasp of the sacred clown tradition? Could he have come across descriptions of the "north American savages rolling in the dirt & eating dung" somewhere in the eighteenth century? & somehow known the purpose of such bizarre activities was to "raise men to a perception of the infinite." She lauds me as being the originator of far more than I can claim, asks me what it would take for me to come back to New York to teach – "a lot of money," I reply. "How much?" she persists. I name $60,000 as my price. "I'll see what I can do," she says. Sure. Sweet lady.

I ride home on BART & eat a late dinner at the Indian Pavillion with with my wife Adelia who's excited about some museum stops she's made with Seymour & Rebecca.

V
"Jews and Other Differences"

That night I realize I didn't get Tom Jones's address & phone as I thought I had (I'd given him mine) & hope to run into him again to talk in a more extended fashion.

I go in early on Sunday the 29th to catch a 10:15 program on "Jews and Other Differences" at the Marriott. The guy who made the closing remark on "changing the nature of the question" regarding authenticity on the first day shows up and sits next to me. We introduce ourselves. He's Arnold Krupat of Sarah Lawrence College, a well known Native American Literature scholar. We listen to Daniel Boyarin of Berkeley, Elaine Marks of the University of Wisconsin, and Jonathan Boyarin of the New School of Social Research discuss various aspects of perceived Jewish difference. The younger Boyarin (Jonathan) does a joint presentation with the ubiquitous upstart Greg Sarris – a self described "announcing the sound" a la Eric Dolphy's compositional technique in "Epistrophy – on the theme of how critics & scholars giving voice to silenced others often continue the policies they set out to reverse." Boyarin picks up on some remarks by Elaine Marks on "allegorization of the Jews" by European cultures, who "don't know what to do with the Jews." Marks had described some of the historical and current forms of antisemitism in her native France – how current neo-nazis publish lists of Jewish names and Jews in prominent positions as if laying the chilling groundwork for some imminent roundup. Sarris picks up the theme from an Indian perspective, attacking Paula Gunn Allen specifically for her technique of building large generalizations to fit a feminist agenda upon scant direct quoting of her Indian informants. Krupat calls Sarris dangerous – "half Jewish & half Indian & all academic." "You can't resolve the authenticity issue," he says. "Lots of people took cheap shots at your book (*Interpreting the Indian*) when it came out, but if you didn't write it nothing would have gotten done."

Daniel Boyarin speaks on diasporan consciousness, rather than monotheism, as representing Judaism's most significant potential contribution to the world. "The chief genius and chief danger of Christianity lies in its concern for other peoples of the world," he says. "The chief genius and chief danger of Judaism lies in its ability to leave other peoples alone." The diaspora & the effect of the Jews dominated status, Boyarin suggests, allow Judaism to realize the Biblical concern for social and historical justice. The diasporan tolerance for others (not the current dangerous aspect of it – cold indifference), he proposes as a more useful model, than the failed Zionism in Israel, for a new and lasting local and global peace. His views are attacked by several Israelis in the audience as "unkind" and "inappropriate," but he refuses to back down, further specifying the implications as leading to a truly open multi-cultural society in Israel with no one group having more rights than any other.

VI
Defining Multiculturalism

From this talk I go to a rather dull session on "The Stanza" but its worth it as I run into Tom Jones there & we proceed together to a subsequent session on multi-culturalism. A deadly statistical presentation by Benita Huber of the MLA is followed by three wonderful papers by Marie Louise Pratt of Stanford, Shawn Wong of the University of Washington, and Dan Runnels, a Salish grad student also from the University of Washington. Pratt's talk is a kind of defining of the term. "Who's in the room?" she proposes as a key question to ask in looking at how issues are decided. She recounts eye-opening experiments in her own classroom: surveying how many generations of students' families have spoken English inevitably reveals that relatively disenfranchised Blacks are the dominant group who have been speaking English longest. Multi-culturalism she posits as a "decolonization of consciousness" as "Eurocentric consciousness is what stands behind American politics." Conversely, in America, white students see themselves without culture, and when probed harder a discernible rage about this that frequently translates as hostility toward other groups who hold onto their own cultural richness. She proposes a four-pronged definition of what multi-culturalism is: 1) a struggle against ethnocentrism, racism, sexism, that is rooted in the history of the American rights struggles; 2) it is not a "stopping off place;" 3) it does not have a referent, but depends on the particular possibilities of particular situations – thus compromises can be seen as accomplishments not defeats; 4) it is not a substitute for economic justice – rather it is concerned with institutions and consciousness. Shawn Wong also offers a generalized definition, perhaps the most simple yet most profound one I've encountered: "Multi-culturalism is an accurate definition of who we are and how we live." He is a Chinese American, born in Taiwan, and the author of the novel *Home Base*. Dan Runnels offers with incredible dignity a beautifully sensitive story about Coyote, the ancient Trickster, who "did a lot of good things and a lot of bad things – the way of the world," and who "is always coming and going but never here" yet "always there grinning behind the mask of words."

Poets/St. Louis/Duff's Restaurant/River Styx Reading/fall 1992: Michael Castro, Maria Guadaloupe Massey, John Brandi.

XMAS, 1991

Michael Castro

75,000 workers to be laid off by General Motors
Merry Christmas America
I don't want to leave my house
to shop, to work, to party, to make
appearances – i skipped the Christmas Party
at the St. Charles Country Club, wherever that is,
missed out on my gift of cheese & an oily handshake,
now I worry over being laid off
& glower with a bad attitude –
also missed the Pre-Kwanza Celebration
at the E. St. Louis City Hall,
a time to be with my friends & the poet Gwendolyn Brooks,
but also a scene "in public" & "in poetry"
& I don't even seem to want to be in my body
these days, my daze, extended to
the page, the bank balance sheet & credit card
debt column – Juan Felipe Herera writes
in *Tornado Alley* of his Iowa Writer's Workshop
experience with a mixture of awe & defiance
I marvel at his passion: for language, for himself,
for "the people" – I remember them
sometimes, its like this thing gestating inside me
how many years now, my mother's wound
turned inside out, alone in the universe & cursed
with a reflective nature, emerged full blown
like a Buddhist demon dominating the tanka of my consciousness
& devouring it from the inside out

Winter begins in two days – I will huddle in the cold
& watch the sunrise over the Cahokia Mounds
Maybe I will climb to the top of Monk's Mound
& look out over the bleak landscape abandoned long ago

Russia, the "evil empire," collapses upon itself
in countless fragments, of an inner corruption,
neo-Nazis beat up foreigners & smash Jewish storefronts
in Germany, i cold shoulder my wife, puff out my lip
like a blowfish – I am no longer a young man –
nor am I a butterfly dreaming – the whole system is corrupt –
you can hear the trees screaming in the middle of the night

dragged in chains from the hillsides of the planet,
You have to talk to "the right guy" at the Fulton Fishmarket
if you want a shipment unloaded, the politicians
sit on the knees of Corporate ventriloquists –
the bus stations of every major city cities unto themselves
filled with those in flight & those with no where else to go –

Can I sit & follow my breath & realize the transiency
the mental constructions & not be attached
Do I want to? Is there something permanent
in our makeup, between the in hale & ex? the ground
for all these figures? A pregnant emptiness
to look forward to look forward to look forward

Poet Quincy Troupe (seated, center) joins bi-state (Illinois-Missouri) writers, musicians, actors, and students after a standing room only reading in November 1992 at Duff's Restaurant in St. Louis. Seated (l-to-r): Jan Garden Castro, Darlene Roy, Troupe, Andrea M. Wren, Marcus Atkins. Standing: Ron Himes, Dwight Bosman, Dwayne Bosman, Michael Castro, Robin Mack, Charles Wartts, Jr., Percy Wells, Chris Hayden, Marsha Cann, and Ira B. Jones.

FEBRUARY IN PARIS: "AFRICAN AMERICANS IN EUROPE"

A Journal by Darlene Roy

Dans ma vie
Like Langston Hughes
Who too

Liberateur (aussi!)
Dans ma formation sensible
Et intellectuelle

Tedjoans

"Because we are a creative people,
as everyone knows, and if we lend
ourselves to the creation of literature
like we did to the creation of Jazz
and dancing and so forth, there's
no telling what the impact will be."

Chester Himes

Superlatives flow whenever I convey my emotions, ruminations or reactions to the first African Americans In Europe Conference held at the University of Paris, the Sorbonne, in France from February 5 through 9, 1992. I was thrilled to find myself seated at a heavily laden table of Afrocentric creativity, a virtual Black-feast of dance, drama, literature, architecture, music and visual arts, with more than six hundred participants. Our multicultural, cross-gender gathering hailed from seventeen countries or provinces and had converged on Paris to celebrate, recollect and pay homage to those notable African Americans who had lived and worked in Europe. Appropriately, the official conference poster depicted an African American woman as Miss Liberty holding her torch high to light our way.

The event was sponsored by the Centre d'Etudes Afro-americicaines de la Sorbonne Nouvelle; W.E.B. DuBois Institute for Afro-American Research, Harvard University; Center for American Cultural Studies, Columbia University; and the Center for the Study of Southern Culture, University of Mississippi. At least one hundred and forty-five papers were delivered on forty-five panels with a dozen poetry/fiction readings and two roundtable discussions interspersing each day. Three activities were slotted concurrently for each time period. Events were located at seven sites scattered all over Paris. This made it difficult to attend a lot of the sessions; but it also allowed me the chance to see more of the city. I walked a lot, which brought me closer to the people and the feel of Paris. Throughout the conference there were special window displays of African American culture at many of the bookstores. And a film festival featured titles such as, "A Duke Named Ellington," "The Many Faces of Billie Holliday," "Afrique sur Seine," and "Native Son." A guided tour was available, by request, of African American historical sites in Paris.

As an emerging writer from a small, Midwestern, predominantly African American city, I relished the opportunity to move from a vicarious view of Paris to an experiential one. What follows are journal entries of my personal experiences, remembrances and reflections of the conference from the time I boarded the flight to Paris until my return home.

4 February, 1992 (Tuesday), Lambert International Airport, St. Louis
5:24 pm

The anticipation of attending the African Americans In Europe Conference was warring with my anxiety over the fact that mechanics worked intently on the left engine of TWA flight 818. To counter this battle of emotions, I began to reconnoiter my surroundings aboard the plane. My preoccupation was interrupted when Kenneth Kinnamon, from the University of Arkansas, Fayetteville, hailed Eugene Redmond who was seated next to me. He told us that he had been on the flight the evening before and that it had been cancelled because of problems with that same engine. TWA had put the passengers up at Henry VIII hotel. Kinnamon was trying to get to Paris early because he would be presenting a paper on the Richard Wright panel that Friday. Indeed, we were all anxious to embark on our literary/cultural romp through Paris.

8:30 pm

At last, we were soaring through the cloud-filled, star-flung night towards Paris, the City of Lights, that was only eight hours and fourteen minutes, or two movies, two meals and several snacks, away. During the flight, we celebrated Redmond's literary delivery of twins, *Eye In The Ceiling* (selected poetry) and *Drumvoices Revue* (his new literary journal published under the auspices of Southern Illinois University at Edwardsville). *Drumvoices* also served as the first anthology of writings by members of a writers club named in Redmond's honor.

12:00 Noon

We deplaned at the ultramodern DeGaulle Airport with its glass tube people transporters. It was the portal to haute couture fashions, delicate pastries, antique book stores, ancient buildings, fabulous restaurants, vanilla ice cream and many, many seeds of the African diaspora. We took a taxi into the city and checked into the quaint Hotel Notre Dame on the left bank of the River Seine.

I began to learn about accomodations in some French hotels while checking into my room. I had reserved a room with a shower and was shocked to find that it did not have a commode. Redmond had reserved a room with a bathtub therefore he had a commode and a bidet. I thought that was overkill. I could not change my room for one with a bath because they were already filled. The cost of your accomodations depended on whether you reserved a room with a face bowl (the least expensive), a room with a shower (moderately priced), or a room with a bathtub (the most expensive). For those of us who did not have a commode in the room, there was a common one on each floor. This was a culture shock for me because every decent hotel room in America has a commode.

The view from my room somehow made up for the cold and inconvenience. I could see La Cathedral Notre Dame to the north, La Conciergerie (main police department) directly across from me, the famous River Seine flowed tamely within its concrete banks just below street level, and on the sidewalk across the street there were vendors (*les bouquinistes*) selling post cards, magazines and posters.

3:00 pm (15.00 h)

The French use the maritime system; instead of being 3:00 pm it was 15.00 hours. I had to learn to tell time all over. We got directions from the desk clerk and with a map of Paris in hand, Redmond and I started out for the opening session of the conference. It was very cold and the dampness wrapped itself about me and would not let go. As we walked to the main campus of the Sorbonne, I noticed numerous shops and restaurants on side streets that looked like alleys. There were more restaurants and bookstores per square block than in any place I had ever been. The sites, sounds and smells of the city had a foreign yet familiar air about them. There were times when a building, word or face would revive a scene from one of the many novels that I had read about Paris. Upon arriving at the Sorbonne, we discovered that the opening session had been moved to the Sorbonne Nouvelle in the Amphitheatre.

We tried to take a taxi, but the driver did not want a short trip when he could wait for a bigger fare. We had to ask directions every few blocks as we walked and even then we were not sure of the directions. Eventually we met Amritjit Singh, of Rhode Island College in Providence, whom Redmond already knew. He would deliver a paper on "Europe and Afro-Asia: Perspectives for the Final Phase of Richard Wright's Career." Singh introduced us to the gentleman walking with him, E. Raja Rao from Berhampur University, Orissa, India, who would deliver a paper on "Clarence Major and the French Tradition of *nouveau roman*."

5:00 pm (17.00 h)

Because I had not been able to preregister for the conference, I was apprehensive when we entered the opening session; however, no one questioned or restrained me. Redmond introduced me to Cecil Brown, of the University of California at Berkley (*The Life and Loves of Mr. Jive Ass Nigger*), who stood just inside the door. We could not do more than exchange acknowledgements because the session had started. As I looked down upon the stage, a face leaped to recognition – Henry L. Gates Jr., director of the W.E.B. DuBois Institute of Afro-American Research, Harvard University. I had met him in New York at the National Black Writers Conference in March, 1991.

A young man to my left told me that his name was Ron Ramdin and that he worked at the Library of London. He showed me a copy of his recent book, *The Making of a Labor Class in Britain*, and offered to sell it to me for $12.50 which was half-price. Since the book had over 600 pages, I figured it was not a bad deal. He said that his first book about Paul Robeson was no longer in print and that he was looking for a publisher. His paper on "The Black Experience in Britain: Ethnic Minorities in Europe" was to be presented on Saturday. He said that he had come to the conference to network because there weren't that many African American writers in England. I told him that I wanted to introduce him to Redmond, a master at literary networking.

Other dais guests included the female president of the Sorbonne, a female representative from the Ambassade des Etats Unis (United States); Paule Marshall, writer, Virginia Commonwealth University, Richmond (*Praisesong for the Widow*; *Brown Girl, Brownstone*; *Daughters*); Michel Fabre, directeur, Centre d'Etudes Afro-americaines de la Sorbonne Nouvelle (*The Unfinished Quest of Richard Wright*); Maria Diedrich, Professor Universitat, Hannover, Germany ("Black Antiphrasis: *Uncle Tom's Cabin* and the Sweet Home Episode in Toni Morrison's *Beloved*"); Gwendoline Roget, writer from Bala Cynyth, Pennsylvania; Genevieve Fabre, professor, University of Paris VII ("Toni Morrison: figures et frontieres du recit"); and James Emanuel, writer from Paris (*The Broken Bowl*; *Treehouse and Other Poems*; *Langston Hughes*). They welcomed us in French and/or English and gave the rationale for the conference, traced the origins and growth of African American arts in Europe and/or gave praise to the works of Richard Wright (*Native Son*; *Black Boy*), Langston Hughes (*Montage of a Dream Deferred*; *Not Without Laughter*), Jean Wagner (*Black Poets of the United States: From Paul Laurence Dunbar to Langston Hughes*), Nathan Huggins (*Slaves and Citizens: The Life of Frederick Douglas*), James Baldwin (*Another Country*; *The Fire Next Time*; *The Amen Corner*), Chester Himes (*If He Hollers, Let Him Go*; *Fields of Wonder*; *The Third Generation*) and other deceased writers and artists who had lived and worked in Europe.

At the end of the opening session, I went up to Paule Marshall and introduced myself. She had given a deeply moving and authoritative tribute to Langston Hughes, who had brought her to Europe to work as a young writer, and a memoir of the 1965 Royaumont Afro-American Conference. It was wonderful to see novelist Elizabeth Nunez Harrell, director of the National Black Writers Conference (*When Rocks Dance*) who was in East St. Louis (IL) with the writers club for our Black Writers and Thinkers Conference in November, 1991. I renewed aquaintances with writers I had met before, including Clyde Taylor, of Tufts University, who is associate editor of *Drumvoices Revue*; Kevin Powell, a young poet from New York and editor of *In the Tradition*, and poet Jayne Cortez (*Pissstained Stairs and the Monkey Man's Wares*; *Coagulations*). Redmond introduced me to Bernard Bell (of Pennsylvania State University) and his wife. And I finally got Redmond together with Ron Ramdin for a lively exchange.

In the lobby Elizabeth introduced me to her sister, Mary Nunez, Lydia Lindsay of North Carolina Central University at Durham, and Carlton Wilson of University of North Carolina at Chapel Hill. I introduced them to Ron Ramdin. In fact Elizabeth, Mary and Ron found that they shared a common homeland: Trinidad. When Redmond returned from getting registered we decided that we would attend the reception at the Palais DeVille. The seven of us took the Metro (subway). According to rumor, the originally scheduled reception at the United States Embassy was cancelled due to financial (and political) constraints. As we entered the Metro turnstile, we bumped into Amina Dickerson, the former director of the Chicago DuSable Museum of African American History.

7:30 pm (19.30 h)

Under a canopy of exquisite paintings reminiscent of the Sistine Chapel in the Vatican, surrounded by heirloom furniture, gold leaf detailing, gigantic crystal chandeliers and mirror polished parquet floors, I felt like I was on the movie set of the rich and famous French royals. I met and mingled with the Parisian dignitaries and some of the African American creative elite of the world. The reception was hosted by M. le Conseiller de Paris (Mayor) Jean-Jose Clement, professor Henry Louis Gates, Jr., professor Jack Salzman and professor William Ferris. Michel Fabre was also on hand to bring greetings on behalf of the Sorbonne. I chatted briefly with Arnold Rampersad, of Princeton University (*The Life of Langston Hughes*), and later with Gates. Through Redmond, I met Ernest Gaines, of the University of Southwestern Louisiana, (*Bloodlines*; *A Gathering of Old Men*; *The Autobiography of Miss Jane Pittman*) and Lorenzo Thomas, Writer in Residence, University of Houston-Downtown.

As I moved through the gathering, I ran into Pinkie Gordon Lane, Poet Laureate of Louisiana (*Wind Thoughts*; *Poems By Blacks, Vol III*; *Girl at the Window*). She had also participated in the Writers and Thinkers Conference hosted by the EBR Writers Club in 1991. She was with Virginia Tiger, dean of Faculty of Arts and Sciences, Rutgers University.

10:00 pm (22.00 h)

We walked several blocks before settling on a little restaurant around the corner from the Hotel Notre Dame on Rue St. Jacques. Writers for the most part are great conversationalists, as was the case that evening. I was surprised to see that Eugene and Carlton did not hesitate to tear into their hamburgers that were topped by sunny side up fried eggs instead of the usual bun or toast. My meal cost 9OFF (French Francs) or $18.00. Each cup of coffee was priced individually. Redmond bought four bottles of mineral water and two Cokes and paid 6OFF, or $2.00 for each item. He explained that he had been warned about drinking the water from the faucet in his room. It seems that others in our party had received the same warning. The restaurants in Paris even served bottled water to their patrons upon request.

6 February, 1992 Thursday
11:45 am (11.45 h)

Mary and I played hooky from the conference after making plans to attend the Fiction Writer's reading moderated by Elizabeth at the Palais du Luxembourg. I thought that it would be a travesty to be in Paris and not visit the Louvre. Mary had been to Paris several times but this was her first trip to the Louvre. She could speak a little French. I had studied French in high school, could read it a little but could not converse in it. On the walk to the Louvre, we frequently asked for directions. It was not too long before we were able to use the correct phrasing. The French are demonstrative in their conversation, therefore it was easy to understand. Mary and I were pleasantly surprised by the obvious glances of appreciation from Frenchmen we encountered along the way and a couple of times they engaged us in conversation.

From a distance, I saw a structure that resembled a telephone booth. As we got near, I read, "toilettes." It was a pay toilet. Mary said that they were all over Paris and cost from 2FF to 3FF or 40c to 60c to use. I never got the nerve to try one out. Maybe next time.

12:30 pm (12.30 h)

A walk that would have taken 15 minutes from the hotel if we had known where we were going took us almost an hour. We finally arrived at the Louvre. I was impressed by those aged but well kept buildings that hugged modern structures obviously influenced by Egyptian architecture. A large glass pyramid dominated the center of the stone courtyard and gave entrance to the recently renovated museum. Flanked by a smaller pyramid on either side and two spraying fountains, it was gorgeous. The central lobby was underground and boasted of an information center, a restaurant, gift shops, a post office and the entrance to the Denon, Sully and Rechelieu galleries. After we paid 31FF or $6.20 to enter, we had access to all the galleries. Because it would have taken at least two or three weeks to see everything in all the galleries, we settled on seeing some Egyptain art and the Venus de Milo in the Sully and the Mona Lisa (formally known as the Joconde) in the Denon. Anything we discovered in our search for those works was considered a bonus.

The marbled, art deco beauty within the temperature-controlled galleries caused us automatically to speak in subdued tones and to strain our ears in hopes of overhearing any secret those ancient walls might disclose. No matter how much famous art I have seen in galleries throughout America, many of the pieces that I saw here were the oldest. I was deeply moved by the experience and knew then that Africa would be moved to the top of my travel agenda. We bought post cards, filled them out and posted them because there was a post office.

As we left the Louvre, we saw a fully dressed pantomime artist performing in the Marcel Marceau tradition as a small crowd looked on. We did not stop because we were to meet one of Mary's friends for a late lunch.

4:30 PM (16.30 h)

Mary and I took the bus from the corner near the small restaurant where we had lunch (we did not find her friend) to the intersection of Rue de Vaugirard and Rue St. Michel, which was near the Palais du Luxembourg. It took us four walkbys before we found the correct entrance. We were subjected to intense scrutiny and security checks before we were premitted to enter the institution where the French Senate meets. Our permits had to be secured to our clothing in plain view for check by the numerous security guards we passed to get to the auditorium where we thought the reading was being held. As soon as we entered the door, we knew that we were in the wrong place. Instead of the Conference fiction writers reading, we found ourselves the only African Americans at a French seminar on William Shakespeare. We captured some attention briefly but the participants accepted our presence and continued their proceedings in French. Even though we received a poster for attending the seminar, we bemoaned the fact that we had missed hearing authors such as Ernest Gaines, Paule Marshall, Ishmael Reed (*Mumbo Jumbo*; *The Terrible Twos*; *The Last Days of Louisiana Red*), John A. Williams of Rutgers University (*Click Song*; *Mothersill and the Foxes*; *The Man Who Cried I Am*), Sherley Ann Williams of the University of California at San Diego (*Give Birth to Brightness*), Barbara Chase-Riboud, writer and sculptor, Paris (*Echo of Lions*), Melvin Dixon of Queens College, New York (*Change of Territory*), and Divida Kilgore, writer, St. Paul, Minnesota (*The Myth Makers*). Redmond told us later that the reading was excellent, being frequently punctuated with applause.

6:00 pm (18.00 h)

It was dusk when we exited the Palais du Luxembourg. During our walk to Mary's hotel, Les Familia, on Rue des Ecole, I noticed a sidewalk painting of a dog with an arrow pointing toward the street. Mary informed me that Parisians take their dogs everywhere with them and they are permitted to relieve themselves on the streets at designated spots. We stopped at McDonald's to buy something to drink.

9:00 pm (21.00 h)

Mary's hotel was more modern than the one where I was staying. The French really know how to maximize space. The room had a television, refrigerator and a bathroom with a commode. Very nice. ... While we waited for our food, we had a drink. We talked about our respective careers as we watched the music videos on the television mounted high in the corner. I was somewhat surprised to see a video of Barry White singing "In The Mix." This was the most current African American music I had heard since my arrival. Most of the music (a mixture of French, rap and raggae) I had heard on the radio in my room was several years old. They played a lot of Michael Jackson songs ... Later, I learned from Redmond that he and Elizabeth had attended a fabulous party hosted by Barbara Chase-Riboud at her luxurious two story Paris studio with the cream-de-la-cream of African American literati.

7 February, 1992 (Friday)
9:00 am (9.00 h)

The jazz panel that we planned to attend was scheduled for yet another location. Since we did not know how to get there, we took a taxi only to find that the driver did not really know where he was going. He put us out in the vicinity of the place and we had to walk to find it. We found the Images d' Ailleurs about three blocks away on the upper tier of a street. During our search we met William Ferris, director, Center for the Study of Southern Culture, University of Mississippi, one of the conference sponsors. Remond introduced us. He knew about the writers club in East St. Louis and was interested in what we were doing.

10:30 am (10.30 h)

The panel, Jazz People, addressed the trials and triumphs of African American jazz musicians who had lived and carved out careers in Europe. Panelists included Austin Lawrence, Watertown, Massachusetts, "Duke Ellington in London: 'Black, Brown and Beige'"; Lorenzo Thomas, "Eric Dolphy's Migrant Muse;" and Nathan Davis, University of Pittsburgh, and Ursula Davis, writer, "Black Musicians in Paris after World War II." Francis Hofstein, jazz critic, served as moderator and Nicolas Gerren, Professor Emeritus, Xenia, Ohio was the respondent. Each panelist discussed their experiences, and their research or observations on the European jazz scene. For a long period after World War II, Black bands had to have one or more European musicians in them to get bookings. Many of these musicians did not have the musical abilities of their Black counterparts. However, this did not inhibit or diminish Blacks' style or creative juices. A lively question and answer session concluded the panel.

Redmond introduced me to Thadious Davis, of Brown University in Rhode Island, who was on her way to another panel. I met Donald Petesch, of the

University of Pittsburgh and his wife, Natalie, who was also a writer. The Peteschs, the Davises, the Davises' eighteen-year-old daughter, a Parisian friend of Ursula's, Lorenzo Thomas and his cousin, a Mr. Washington, Redmond, and I went to lunch at the Croissant Cafe.

4:30 pm (16.30 h)

We walked from the Images d'Ailleurs to the FNAC at #71 Boulevard St. Germain, one store in the largest chain of bookstores in Europe. It was the location of the poetry and fiction reading. Those slated to read included Al Young, of Stanford University (*Sitting Pretty*; *Who is Angelina*); Colleen McElroy, writer, Seattle, Washington; Divida Kilgore, Cecil Brown, Lorenzo Thomas, Eugene Redmond and a couple of other writers. The moderator was a female, African American student from the Sorbonne who spoke impeccable French. The audience, composed of the local community, students, conference participants and visitors, was very quiet during each presentation, but exploded with plaudits and praise at the conclusion. The authors had come to share their spirited, witty, terse, contemplative or rhythmlaced verses. Kevin Powell and his friends, Tony Medina and Willie Perdomo, were out to cheer their older cohorts. This was another opportunity for me to take some photographs.

8:00 pm (20.00 h)

Al Young, Lorenzo Thomas, Redmond and I had dinner at the famous Polidor Restaurant, which is known for having been Richard Wright's favorite eating place. It is located on Rue Monsieur le Prince and is just one block from Wright's former home. Thomas and Young had eaten there the previous evening and said that the food was delectable. We had to wait a short while for a table. I had my usual steak and fries and the guys had baked chicken and vegetables. The food was excellent. We topped the meal off with exquisite French vanilla ice cream. I was even tempted to accept the seconds offered by Young but fell back on my reserve will power. As we were leaving, the waitress teased Redmond about the jaunty tam that is so much a part of his personality and said that he could stay because he belonged to France.

A stroll down one block found us standing in front of #14 Rue Monsieur le Prince, which housed the former fourth floor apartment where Wright had lived with his wife, Ellen, and daughter, Julia. When I read Margaret Walker Alexander's book, *Richard Wright: Daemonic Genius*, I did not think that one day I would touch the building that had contained and comforted that prolific writer and his mind-reeling philosophies and works. I quickly pinched my arm as a reality check. Yes, I was indeed on the very doorstep of literary history.

10:00 pm (22.00 h)

Redmond turned on his tape recorder to capture the interview he was conducting with Al Young, Lorenzo Thomas and myself. He delved into the significance of the conference being held in Paris, the ramifications of Black artists coming to Europe to work and the impact on their creativity. There was some discussion on the "been too" phenomenon that attends one's trips to Europe. Because we were in one of the local hamburger restaurants, much on the order of McDonald's, we did not have enough time to complete the interview because it closed at 11:00 pm. We said that we would try to complete the interview some other time during the conference but the opportunity did not arise.

8 February, 1992 (Saturday)
9:00 am (9:00 h)

I thought I would slow my pace some. Instead of rushing out of the hotel, I decided to have breakfast. The diminutive dining room held three tables somewhat larger than checker boards and each had two chairs. A black and white TV was playing in the corner. Breakfast was part of the room fee and I had had breakfast a couple of times since I had been at the hotel. It consisted of half a loaf of French bread sliced down the middle, a croissant, and individually wrapped servings of jam and butter. I had a choice of coffee, tea or milk. I could not eat everything but it was tasty and very filling. A breakfast like this everyday eliminated concern about high cholesterol.

Redmond had gone over to the Institute du Monde Anglophone to carry books for display and sale from 9:00 am until 6:00 pm that evening.

10:30 am (10.30 h)

Feeling secure about getting to where I wanted to go, I walked over to the Institute du Monde Anglophone from the hotel. I went to the book display area to browse and to purchase a few books. There was a wide range of free literature to collect as well.

12:30 pm (12:30 h)

I went down to the courtyard to meet Mary and Elizabeth for lunch. Redmond joined us at a popular eating place, The Select Latin. It was close to the Sorbonne and was crowded but we waited until space was available.

Other than the Cheese Quiche for lunch on Thursday and the Tuna/Vegetable Salad on Friday, my meals were pretty much like movie reruns. I always had steak and fries. Lunch was spiced by recaps of what we had seen, heard or done while in Paris. Eugene left early to get ready for his reading at the Sorbonne.

2:00 pm (14.00 h) to 5:30 pm (17:30 h)

A reading Fest was held at the Salle Liard in the Sorbonne. I was particularly enthusiastic because of the large number of well known authors who would be reading and because Danny Glover, one of my favorite actors, sat in the audience. Wording Afrocentric rites, ritual and rhyme were Anne Bailey, African American Studies, University of Pennsylvania, Philadelphia; Hart Leroy Bibbs, writer, Paris (*Double Trouble*); Pinkie Gordon Lane; Colleen McElroy; Louise Meriwether (*Fragments of the Ark*); Eugene Redmond (*Eye In The Ceiling*); Mona Lisa Saloy, writer, New Orleans; Charlotte Watson Sherman, writer, Seattle, (*Killing Color*); and Al Young. Other writers not scheduled to read were also given the opportunity to share their works: Steve Cannon (*Groove Bang and Jive Around*); Ishmael Reed, Sherley Ann Williams (*The Peacock Poems*), and Sam Allen, aka Paul Vesey, an international negritude poet and guest lecturer (*Ivory Tusks*). I had to pass on the chance to read because I was still suffering from the laryngitis I had caught on Thursday.

7:00 pm (21.00 h)

Redmond, Sherley Ann Williams and I received an unexpected tour of Paris when the taxi driver had problems finding the Amphiteatre de UNESCO where a special jazz concert by the Chansse Evanns Quartet was to be held. The driver found the complex but let us out at the wrong building. Through the grace of the Muses, we met Jayne Cortez and her husband Mel Edwards. They had just obtained directions from someone in one of the buildings. We walked and exchaged anecdotes until we found the Amphiteatre.

As we were removing our coats, Danny Glover, his wife and another couple entered the lobby. Redmond and Glover hugged, laughed and slapped each other's backs while I quickly snapped a photo. Jayne and Mel already knew the Glovers. Eugene introduced them to Sherley and me. Danny had a warm, friendly, outgoing personality much like many of the characters that he has played in the movies.

Needless to say, there was a major stir when we entered the main hall where the concert was to be held. It was already filled with about five or six hundred people and there weren't any tables left. The group had to split up to find somewhere to sit. Soon after getting situated, I could see Danny towering over his admirers, signing autographs and taking pictures with them. I grabbed Mary by the hand and went over to where he was standing so that we could have our pictures taken with him before the concert got started. I gave my camera to Cecil Brown who took the photo of Danny and me and then I took one of Mary with Danny. He was full of smiles and humorous quips.

A buffet dinner preceded the concert. It was true to the French tradition in its beauty, distinctiveness of taste and the artfulness of arrangement. There was a large variety of food and it was plentiful. The dessert torts were certainly the perfect touch. Several varieties of French wines and other beverages were provided. We grabbed some chairs and arranged our food on our laps to eat.

The concert opened with a spiritual song that was the first one written in Europe. It was played on piano by the gentleman who wrote it. He was in his eighties. He looked in good health and was fairly agile.

In addition to the Evanns Quartet, there were two female African American singers; one of them was Annette Lowman. They sang a few songs individually and then sang "I Love Paris" as a duet. At the end of the piece, they called for anyone from the United States to come up, give their reactions to Paris and sing something. Ron Ramdin, who had been practising his Nat King Cole imitation on us, was up there in a flash. He sang one of Cole's songs very well and the audience cheered him on. Because Ramdin was not from the U. S., they again asked for someone to come up. In the spirit of the occasion, I went up, brought greetings from East St. Louis, Illinois, introduced myself as President of the Eugene B. Redmond Writers Club, and told them about *Drumvoices Revue*. I mentioned the the Lincoln High School Jazz Band, of which my son, Troy, is a member. I thanked Michel Fabre and the Sorbonne for inviting us to Paris in such grand style. Annette reminded me that I was supposed to sing too. I replied by saying that I could not sing but I could dance r-e-a-l good. On a more serious note, I reminded the audience of the importance of creative writers, thinkers and artists. For without them, just what would the world be?

During the intermission I met Femi Euba, playwright from Louisiana State University at Baton Rouge, through Redmond. Euba is a good friend of Tess Omwueme, a young Nigerian playwright. Euba presented a paper entitled "An Evaluation of Ira Aldridge's Adaptation of Anicet-Bourgois's *The Black Doctor*. I also met Lamont Steptoe, writer and photographer.

After the second or third song into the second set, one of the singers called for the young lady who said that she could dance r-e-a-l good. I love to dance and had won a few dance contests in my time. I hit a few swerves, shakes and sassy sweeps to the drum solo and then danced my way off the stage to amens and hoops of glee. Pinkie Gordon Lane told me that my comment about writers, thinkers and artists was so timely and true.

As we put on our coats in preparation to leave, Redmond introduced me to Melba Joyce Boyd, director of African American Studies, University of Michigan at Flint and the official biographer of poet-publisher Dudley Randall.

9 February, 1991 (Sunday)
9:00 am (9.00 h)

I met the artist Clifford Jackson of Stockholm, Sweden on the stairs at the Hotel Notre Dame. I had seen him at Conference activities and had noticed his name on some of the paintings on display. He said that he had come to Paris from New York many years ago on an art scholarship. After he met and married his wife, they moved to Sweden. He said that I would be surprised by the number of African

Americans living there. He stated that the only reason he visits America now is to see his mother who still lives in New York. Redmond joined us on the stairs and I introduced him to Jackson. The painter had heard of East St. Louis, but mainly the negative stuff in the press. Amazed that there was a strong writers club in existence, he congratulated us on our vision and tenacity.

9:30 am (9.30 h)

A closing plenary session was scheduled for the Amphiteatre d'Institut du Monde Anglophone. During the walk over there, we stopped by a Currency Exchange to exchange more dollars for francs. The rate of exchange was about 5.45 francs for every dollar; but we only got 5 francs per dollar because the Currency Exchange had to make a profit. We would have gotten the exact amount at a bank. However, the Currency Exchange had better rates than a restaurant or store. After the closing session, we walked three or four blocks to Richard Wright's home.

10:00 am (10:00 h) to 12:00 noon (12.00 h.)

In spite of efforts by the Paris police to keep the street open to traffic, it was entirely filled in front of #14 Rue Monsieur le Prince: hundreds had come to pay homage to Richard Wright under a gray and weeping sky. A prominent banker spoke on financiers' investment in the restoration of the building where Wright had lived and worked some fifteen years. On the second story there was placed an impressive marble plaque whose gold lettering read, "Richard Wright, African American man of letters," along with the dates he had lived in the building. One after another, Wright's family members, friends, colleagues, literary heirs, and well wishers shared their remembrances, anecdotes and impressions of him. Ellen, his widow, Julia, his daughter, and Malcolm, his grandson were present. Ellen Wright christened the building with champagne as onlookers smiled their approval and lifted their voices to cheer. Many times, the festivities were blocked from my view by the umbrellas. Despite the spasmodic drizzle, most people stayed until the dedication service was finished. Many lingered even longer to talk with the Wright family, get autographs, take photographs, and share goodbyes.

Redmond and I went to the Select Latin for lunch because we had not made reservations for Leroy Haynes' historical soul food restaurant. We met a young French woman who said that she was Ellen Wright's cousin. She was having lunch in the booth next to us, along with her boyfriend who was from Mexico. There was also a couple who had four very active young sons in tow. The man, who was physically impaired and walked with the aid of a cane, told us that his name was Arnoldo Palacios (*Les mamelles du Choco*, 1989) and that he was a writer and lecturer and would be at the University of Missouri in Columbia in April. [Messr. Palacios did not actually arrive in the midwest until spring of '93, at which time he addressed an East St. Louis gathering on March 16.] Ellen's cousin told us a bit about Richard and Ellen Wright as a young couple in Paris.

4:00 pm (16.00 h)

Dusting the hemline of lateness, we rushed to the poetry reading at Shakespeare & Company, one of the oldest and most famous book stores in Paris. As I opened the quaint wood and glass door, I was greeted by angry, screwed up faces, grunts, shouts and the flailing fists of two young African American male writers. Underneath the combatants and on the verge of being trampled was the disabled African-Latin writer we had met earlier at the Select Latin. His face was grimaced in pain. Instinctively, I began to push on the back of the closest combatant to keep him from stepping or falling on the man. Redmond leaped over the downed man and began to separate the combatants. Redmond then took the gladiators out of the bookstore to calm them down and to find out why they had locked horns. I was able to get the man up with the assistance of the bookstore owner. He was shaken but not injured. He used his cane to walk into the store and find a seat. Two of his young sons were with him. After the tension abated, the reading began. Later, I realized how upset I had gotten over this unexpected scene from The Boyz N The Hood.

The reading started late, therefore less time was allowed each participant. The first reader was Colleen McElroy; then came a witty and interesting prose reading by Sherley Ann Williams. Ifa Bayeza, writer from Lawrenceville, New Jersey, acted out a one woman, mini comedy/mystery in costume. Redmond mesmerized the standing room only crowd with a reading from *Eye In The Ceiling* and *Drumvoices Revue*. The owner of Shakespeare told Redmond that he had not been that excited by a reading in years. He offered Redmond free living quarters if he wanted to return to Paris to write that summer. He purchased copies of the books for the bookstore and asked Redmond to autograph them. He also placed an official Shakespeare Bookstore seal in a copy of *Drumvoices Revue* for each of us.

After a brief reunion with Ifa Bayeza, Redmond introduced her to me and said that she was Ntozake Shange's sister. Bayeza was co-producing a television project for ATT on the African American male in the United States. She planned to focus on positive and reaffirming images instead of negative, destructive ones. Planning to be in St. Louis in another couple of weeks, she wanted Redmond's input and assistance. He agreed to help. Annette Lowman, the jazz singer who had performed the night before, was at the reading. She gave me her card and asked me to look her up the next time I was in Paris.

Hart Leroy Bibb was also at the Shakespeare reading. I had read his works but had never met him. He was full of stories about life in Paris. I loved his Africanized delivery of the French language and his great sense of humor. Bibb, Redmond, and I attended a reception upstairs in the owner's private quarters and looked at the many photographs of famous writers who had visited the bookstore. A young man followed us around trying to get us to come to hear him sing at a little cafe a block away. He approached me first and I referred him to Bibb and Redmond. We discussed the offer and decided that we would go for a short while. He said that he wanted to come to America and perform with us.

When we arrived at the cafe, it was closed and in the process of being cleaned for later that evening. The pianist, excited to have us there to hear him play, gave us a mini concert and bought us a round of drinks. He was good but the singer could not carry a tune. We walked back to the corner of Rue St. Jacques and Quia St. Michel where Bibb left us.

On our walk to a restaurant, Redmond and I noted the posters on the clear plastic bus shelters, posts and doors. One advertised a magazine entitled *Black Sex*. Its cover featured a nude black woman crouched in the sand and boasting an article on black and white love. We also saw an ad for a reggae concert, one for Printemps (a large department store), and another for the latest movies playing. After dinner, we shopped for souvenirs.

10 February, 1992 (Monday)
8:00 am (8.00 h)

Up and packed. It was time to leave the picturesque city on the Seine. We took a taxi to De Gaulle Airport and paid 242 FF ($48.40). The porters attended to unloading the trunk while we were paying the driver. Somehow Redmond's camera bag was left in the trunk of the taxi. We did not realize it until our baggage was being checked. By then it was too late to catch the taxi and we did not know the name of the company or the taxi number. Redmond called the Hotel Notre Dame to find out if they knew the company's name or number but they did not. He told the desk clerk that he would pay a reward if the camera bag or, more importantly, the twenty-two rolls of exposed film were returned. He was concerned about losing the irreplaceable film that documented the many writers, sites, and events he had experienced during the conference. This was the BLUE NOTE in an otherwise beautiful score.

Thankfully, poet Sam Allen (Paul Vesey) was at the airport waiting for his flight. This helped Redmond to focus on something else for a while until Sam boarded his plane for Boston.

11:15 am (11.00 h)

Without delay or further incident, we boarded TWA Flight 819, which departed on schedule for the 9 hour and 30 minute flight to St. Louis, the Gateway City. When I have had a really great time, the return trip is always somber because part of me wants to continue the great time, yet the other part knows that I have to get back to work. We met a lot of nice people on the return trip. We were also saddened to learn, on the flight back home, of the death of Alex Haley, The Roots Man.

Travel provides a valuable education. Because of my broadening experiences on this trip, I felt as though I had earned a baccalaureate in intercontinental travel and advance memoir writing. When the plane landed at Lambert International Airport, I cleared customs, adjusted my watch for the six hour time difference and headed home to East St. Louis, Illinois, armed with my new degree.

DRUM-AESTHETICS CALL LITERATI TO ATLANTA

Literary Celebration 1992

Georgene Bess

> *As the drum stands at the crossroads of traditional African and Afro-American culture, so the poet should stand at the center of the drum . . . Both the metaphysical and the metaphorical word stem from and return to the drum: life, love, birth, and death labored out in measured rumble or anxious cacophony. Between the lines are the rattle of choruses, the whine (hum) of guitars, and the shriek of tambourines, framed by rivers that will not run away. And the drumvoices urging us to cross them, cross them.*
>
> (Eugene B. Redmond, *Drumvoices*)

Drums. Drums telling stories. Drums celebrating our African heritage, our *neo*-African selves. Sacred Drums. Drumvoices. Although the drums were taken from us when we were captured in Africa and enslaved, we continued to beat the drums of our heart, our memory, and our experiences. The Third Biennial National Black Arts Festival, held in Atlanta, August 3-11, 1992, was a gathering of the sacred drums calling all – from near and far – together to remember and celebrate our legacy of hardships and triumphs.

The Festival's Literary Celebration appropriately opened with a powerful, riveting performance/sermon by preacher/teacher, storyteller/griot, singer/dancer, poet/writer and phenomenal woman Maya Angelou. Speaking to capacity-filled King Auditorium at Morehouse College, Angelou stirred the audience to a higher appreciation of the literary arts. Her sermon was laced with names like Nikki Giovanni, Langston Hughes, Georgia Douglass Johnson, Paul Laurence Dunbar, and Mari Evans, and her testimony echoed her spiritual debt to the great body of African American poetry: "[It] saved my life many times. The black poets spoke for me and kept me alive." Knowing the true healing power of the Black Word, Angelou urged us to expose our children to the creative arts – poetry, dance, drama, prose – so that they might understand and profit from our beautiful and rich heritage.

Full of panel discussions [held at Clark-Atlanta University], poetry readings, and storytelling, the Literary Celebration '92 was sponsored by the Atlanta Writers' Posse in conjunction with the NBAF. It was "literarily" a poetic excursion into the Black Aesthetic.

The first panel, "The Black Aesthetic: Examining Ideology in Black Literature," was held Thursday, August 8. Like the African drum, the panel provided a polyrhythmic, polymetric, multi-layered, and multi-faceted exchange of ideas. It featured Eugene B. Redmond (*Eye in the Ceiling*), Georgene Bess, and moderator

Askia M. Toure (*From the Pyramids to the Projects*). This panel explored myriad issues, but focused primarily on the Black Aesthetic, what it is, what it isn't, and its impact on black America. According to Redmond, the Black Aesthetic takes place everyday in the black experience. It is "part mythology, part folklore, part folktale, part church, part passed on word (in the kitchen, on the front porch, and in the barbershop), and music in general." Redmond expounded on the Six Ancient African Organizing Principles of Music and Social Behavior; thus he demonstrated just how the Black Aesthetic is readily evidenced in the collective behavior of people of African descent.

Examining the impact of the Black Aesthetic on black writers – yesterday and today – Bess focused on inherent connections between Zora Neale Hurston and Terry McMillan. Noting the similarities between Hurston's *Their Eyes Were Watching God* and McMillan's *Disappearing Acts*, in terms of plot, theme and character, Bess' analysis illustrated Hurston's profound impact on the present generation of black women writers. Comments on the Black Aesthetic, and the need for it, were then given by respondents Valerie Boyd and Donald Stone (*Fallen Prince*) who led a lively hour and a half exchange of ideas with the audience.

Continuing the call of the drum, the Celebration's second panel, "Multi-Dimensions of the Writer's Task," was held Friday, August 9. It featured many new poets and writers – moderator Tamara Jeffries (*Essence* fiction writer), Darlene Roy (*Drumvoices Revue*), Catherine Smith-Jones (*Songs for My Sister*), Kevin Powell (*In the Tradition*), Jabari Asim (*Eyeball*), Tony Crooms (1991 NEH Fellow), and playwright Shirlene Holmes (*The Cotsville Stories*). The panel explored the nuts and bolts of writing. Although the participants' literary experience and expertise varied, each panelist emphasized diligence and workshopping. Eugene B. Redmond Writers Club president Roy stressed this point: "These workshops allow the writer to hear honest criticism and provide an opportunity for improvement." The panelists also encouraged self-publishing: "Self-publication is not a dirty word. It is time for a revolution; it is time to put out a contract on the literary mafia," Smith-Jones noted. Asim focused on the need for the development of our own literary critics: "We're going about the documentation and institutionalization of our history. We don't want to have to respond to criticism by outsiders." Stressing self-promotion, Catharine Smith-Jones commented, "I read my book in the beauty salons, on the Marta bus. I even read it to the passengers on an airplane. Because of this self-promotion, my book was sold before it was printed."

Commenting on the reluctance of some "established" black writers to assist the newer and less established ones – "No one helped me. Why should I help you." – Powell discussed the development of *In the Tradition*, a literary anthology published by Harlem River Press. "We [younger writers] decided to do our own thing. That's how *In the Tradition* was started."

Crooms listed the various tasks of the writer – to entertain; to promote social change; to exult the spirit; to pass on the culture; to explore the world of his/her time, with reflections from the past and speculations about the future. Crooms noted the most important task: "The writer has no obligation to any of these things.

S/he needs only to write." Holmes further explained her obligation to write about the African American female experience. She said the highest task for a writer is to preserve the people. Because of this, "I have an obligation to preserve black women, to preserve their culture, their beautiful language, feelings." Respondents Robert Earl Price (*Blood Elegy*) and editor/literary agent Marie Brown led the audience and panel participants in an intense dialogue about the writer's tasks, responsibilities, and roles. Like Thursday's panel, this one proved to be intellectually stimulating and challenging.

After satiating our minds with food for thought, the Celebration then roused our souls with the rhythmic drumvoices of poetry and storytelling. There were Twilight and Around Midnight Poetry Readings held at the Penta Hotel and Just Jazz. Poets Melanie Rawls, Pamela Plummer, Harriet Harris, Tu-read-ah, Sam L. Gresham, Kenneth Zakee, Lenard D. Moore, Valerie Kemp, John Trammel, Danny Bellinger, Debra Medows, Anthony Grooms, Jacqui-Marie Gordon, Gwen Russell-Green, Barbara Eklof, Kimberly Collins, Eugene B. Redmond (and East St. Louis poets and writers: Sandra English, Darlene Roy, Evon Udoh, Andrea M. Wren.), WordSong (poetry and jazz), Alice Lovelace, Dennis McCluster, Dorothy Perry Thompson, Janice Liddell, Gil Hines, Tarik Nia, Kalamu ya Salaam (*Word Up!!!*) eased tensions, soothed troubled minds, stirred up complacent ones, lifted burdens, and R(h)apsodized us with their visionary insights, foresights, and hindsights.

Highlighting the Celebration was "In the Tradition," a poetry reading which featured young poets – ages 19-35 – from around the country, including Sonya Brooks, John Keene, Joette-Harland Watts, Lisa Teasley. St. Louis poet Ira Jones' poem "For Josephine Baker" was a moving tribute to a woman who gave so much and died with almost nothing. Boston poet Sharan Strange's poem "Barbershop Ritual" told the story of a little brother's rite of passage. Poet Kevin Powell's poem "Aunt Cathy" demonstrated a powerful sensitivity to and understanding of his aunt's pain. Poet Kimberly Collins of Atlanta recognized the contradiction in her concern about a lover's infidelity when there's so much "serious shit going on." Boston poet Thomas Sayers Ellis wrote of watching his parents' shadows on the wall in "Kissing in the Dark." Georgian Tamara Jeffries read a stirring and thought-provoking story "Orphan," which explored the psyche of a successful black draftsman searching for happiness while he has to "wear the mask." East St. Louis' Andrea Wren (a past winner of the Zora Neale Hurston-Langston Hughes Literary Award) imagined the long-awaited reunion of Winnie and Nelson Mandela. Yolanda Joe of Chicago, author of *Fallen Leaves of Ivy*, a murder mystery, read her touching poem "Kiss and Be Kissed." In the tradition of the African griot, Stagger Lee, and today's rappers, poet Jabari Asim of St. Louis funked the audience with rhythmic, hip-hop poetry. Noted Chicago poet G'ra dedicated his poem "Contagious" to the young writers.

Drums beating. Drums carrying messages. Drums telling stories. Drum voices passing down the legacy. Although Literary Celebration '92 didn't literally feature drummers, it did employ a storyteller – Akbar Imhotep – who used his voice as a drummers, it did employ a storyteller – Akbar Imhotep – who used his voice as a drum to tell stories of Africa's past, of our ancestors, of the living, and the unborn. Drumvoice Imhotep regaled his audience at the Wren's Nest with stories of flying Africans, Brer Rabbit, the buzzard, the eagle, and the tortoise, to list only a few.

Although the Celebration is over, reverberations of the poetry, panel discussions, and storytelling will continue in our hearts and our minds. We take back home with us the message about the drum that is so pivotal to our existence. Angelou testified of the life-saving ability of black poetry. Those of us who experienced the Celebration can also testify. Like black poetry redeemed Angelou, the Literary Celebration saves us. It renews our spirits, and inspires us to write in praise of our blackness.

What is remarkable about this Literary Celebration is that it was sponsored almost solely by the Atlanta Writers' Posse. Despite a lack of funding and full support from NBAF, Literary Celebration '92 was a beautiful drumscripting of our heritage. But we have always been able to make a way out of no way and hit a straight lick with a crooked stick.

NBAF Literary Celebration '92 served up the drums of our ancestors, encouraging us to follow the rhythm of their messages. The Celebration a la sacred drum, carrier of poetic inspiration, was rich in cultural affirmation – and sheer

Young literati gather following In the Tradition *reading at Atlanta's Penta Hotel. Participant-readers included (front row, l-to-r): Yolanda Joe, Kupenda Auset (Joette Harland-Watts), Lisa Teasley, Sonya Brooks, Jabari Asim, Tamara Jeffries, Andrea M. Wren. Back row: John Keene, Thomas Sayers Ellis, Sharan Strange, Kevin Powell, Kimberly Ann Collins, Ira B. Jones. The August 1992 literary spectacular was in conjunction with the National Black Arts Festival.* In the Tradition: An Anthology of Young Black Writers *came out from Harlem River Press (1992) under the editorship of Powell and Ras Baraka. Asim, Jones and Wren are publishers/editors of* Eyeball, *a new St. Louis-based literary magazine.*

'MAGIC REALISM' BRINGS MEN AND WOMEN TOGETHER *

Earnest McBride

Ed Bullins came to Jackson State University, in Mississippi, for the first time Monday [October 19, 1992]. Ossie Davis came the day before. Bill Cook, Ronald Freeman and Eugene Redmond had arrived Friday.

So why had this group of world-famous Black men – a playwright, an actor/orator, a critic, a photographer and an editor/poet – come to Jackson? Mainly, most people suspected, to meet up with some Black women.

And women were there to be met in droves. Special women. Great women. Loving and lovable women. Easily accessible, smooth-talking, mind-blowing, awe-inspiring women. Women, man, women! There for everybody to talk to, to touch, to lean one's head upon, to laugh with, to whisper to and to fuss with, if that was what turned you on.

Naturally, at an event billing itself as the "International Conference on Black Women Writers of Magic Realism," a man could dream and have that dream come true. Never a dull moment, never a bitter dispute between opposing factions. Five days of busy, busy mind-boggling speeches, music, poetry and general boosting of spirits in the name of magic realism took place at Jackson State.

"Magic realism is the reality that Black writers have to involve themselves with to attain any kind of true validity in the contemporary literary marketplace," said Bill Cook, professor of Oratory and Belles Letters at Dartmouth College, who spoke at the opening general session. He shared the podium with Violet Harrington of Dillard University, who is now in semi-retirement.

Cook laid the groundwork for the conference theme that continued to weave its way throughout the five-day event, despite some vast digressions from the announced main purpose, which was the examination of Magic Realism, the device now attributed especially to Black women writers in Africa and the Americas. Though men also fall within the scope of the magic realist domain – Gabriel Garcia Marquez won the Nobel Prize on the basis of his use of such techniques – Black women writers have been the ones to lay the groundwork for the final apotheosis of magic realism into either a new genre or an ongoing movement.

Duality – of meaning, purpose, interpretation – being one of the hallmarks of magic realism, such was the magnitude and amorphous character of the conference that a dual set of activities paralleled those connected to the magic realism celebration.

The second set of events celebrated the 50th anniversary of the publication of Margaret Walker Alexander's *For My People*, a classic set of poems, which had

---

*Editor's Note: This article originally appeared in the weekly newspaper, *Jackson Advocate*, October 22-28, 1992.

the distinction of being one of only two books written by a woman and published in 1942.

Although many people had come that first day to hear Maya Angelou, who was unable to attend, hardly anyone expressed disappointment once the program gained momentum the following day, Saturday, a day devoted to poets and poetry. Eugene B. Redmond of Southern Illinois University at Edwardsville, poet laureate of East St. Louis, and editor of *Drumvoices*, a revue of Black literary and cultural arts, moderated the program, which included a book fair and autograph forum. [Participating poets were William W. Cook, Ja A. Jahannes, Roy Hill, Virgie Brocks-Shedd, Tess Onwueme, Jerry Ward, Billy Jean Young.]

The greatest event by far scheduled for Sunday was the Ossie Davis-Ruby Dee dramatic presentation of a sizeable hunk of Margaret Walker Alexander's oeuvre, her body of literary works. Just as Esther Rolle had delighted the many attendees the night before, so did Davis-Dee sweep away most hardened skeptics there to flush out this mysterious creature called "magic realism."

Though Ossie and Ruby didn't exactly convert the most severe critic of the purported new ticket to the literary valhalla, meaning magic realism, they at least forced the hard-hearted skeptics to lower their guards. Then they socked them between the eyes with some powerful imagery and pathos from the works of Margaret Walker Alexander.

By the onset of the third stage of the conference Monday, at least half of those determined to see the whole thing through began to complain of fatigue. But being tired did not seem to diminish their enthusiasm for the swirl of events going on around them.

Many visitors looking around and not seeing Walker Alexander in her favorite seat near the rear of the auditorium, began to take a perverse delight in thinking this thing was too much even for her, a body known to have endured the most bone-wearying of leftist and idealistic conferences and harangues in the Chicago of the 1930s and 1940s.

But just when they took joy in thinking their perversity had won its rightful place, Walker Alexander would come strolling in, either on her cane or on the arm of some other literary stalwart, whose will and body were attuned to maybe five or six days of pleasurable torture.

Mari Evans and Sonia Sanchez, two of the nation's best-loved poets – Black or white – shared a panel discussion with Joanne Gabbin, also a poet, of James Madison University in Virginia. They read from their works, in effect, living upto the title of the session, "Magic Realism: A Poetic Perspective."

A few male sexist pigs apparently found their way into the conference at different stages of development. Apparently, the magic aspect of "magic realism" was designed to attract all disparate elements of our lowly species under the same tent.

Even the few MSPs walked away smiling after viewing the lower anatomy and posteriors of two young dancers from a closeup vantage point. The two young ladies are members of the Prancing J-Settes, who were on stage before Davis and Dee Sunday.

At the luncheon with Haki R. Madhubuti, formerly known as Don Lee, owner/publisher of the Third World Press, the conference learned of the perils of waiting. He delighted the audience with his piece that told of how waiters waiting on things to change will go on waiting forever.

Bullins, the Obie-winning playwright who returned to California after nearly 30 years of East Coast productivity, read many samples of the kind of stuff that he became known for during the time of the Revolutionary Black Playwrights, both on and off Broadway.

It was he and Amiri Baraka (Leroi Jones) who set the standards for nearly all Black theater productions of the late '60s and early 70s. Today, Bullins teaches at San Francisco State University, back finally to one of the cities he had embraced as a young, struggling playwright-poet more than 30 years ago.

The conference learned a new approach to reading the literature of slavery as proposed by Eleanor Traylor, chair of the Humanities Division at Howard University. She urged listeners to abandon labels like "Slave Narratives" when dealing with the tracts that came out of the oppression of the pre-Civil War South. She urged the adoption of the term "Emancipatory Narratives" instead.

Morgan State University's Ruth Sheffey followed Traylor and joined her in calling for the retention of a healthy disbelief vis-a-vis the white literary establishment. White critics insist that "magic realism" began in Latin America, she said. "But here the word is that magic realism began with Margaret Walker when she wrote her delightful poem, 'Mollie Means.'"

Dilla Buckner, head of Tougaloo's Department of English, said she too had had some difficulty with the concept of magic realism, particularly as it has figured into a literary movement. Her problem, however, stemmed from ignorance of the topic rather than any particular dislike for it. The more she learned, she said, the more she liked it.

More severe, however, were the skeptical comments of writer-critic Acklyn Lynch of the University of Maryland. He cited examples of many cases of violence against the innocent – plagues, starvation, war and abject economic exploitation throughout the Black world. That was the reality that Black writers were faced with, he said. But where is the magic? he asked. How does one account for the great sacrifices in Haiti? he wondered.

While his topic was that of male writers of magic realism, Lynch kept pounding away at the question of whether magic was real, whether reality consisted of an entirely different set of constructs than did the magic of magic realism.

"Either I am a nobody, or I am a nation," Lynch declared. "If you are not a reality, then whose myth are you? Where is the magic in magic?"

The following day when questioned about whether he was a devotee of the magic realism under discussion at Jackson State, Lynch demurred and joined the ranks of those involved in its development. This approach was also the one taken by Aime Cesaire, whose famous work legitimized the concept of returning to one's native roots for both inspiration and to bring justice to one's own native ground.

Some of the most powerful drama of the conference was saved for the very last day, drama both on the stage and in the audience. Tommie Stewart, former speech and drama professor at Jackson State, now a professor at Alabama A&M and a member of the cast of the popular television series, "In the Heat of the Night," did an extensive dramatic interpretation of Walker Alexander's poetry on video-cassette.

Following that on-stage performance, the audience then turned its attention to the apparent conflict between science and their beloved magic realism. A few bold members of the audience held out for literary excursion founded on hard-core, street corner realism–stuff that's scientifically based, objective, tangible and credible. Magic realism, one critic said, appeared to be nothing more than warmed-over Christianity served to separate the "saved" from the "lost," just as the original version did over so many centuries of pain and suffering by Black people around the world. But no one was going to allow such impertinence to corrupt the spirit of magic realism at Jackson State, not at this year's conference, they wouldn't. Walker Alexander finally took the floor and ended the dispute.

"I know where you're coming from," she said.

"I'm coming from Vicksburg, Miss.," said the skeptic.

"You're trying to address magic realism from the point of view of materialism," Walker Alexander said. "And that just won't work. There is magic in everything. Even the scientists will tell you that there is a moment in their discovery that just can't be explained in a rational way. The whole birth process. That's magic. Magic is the key to the creative process."

With that, the conference wound its way down to the final two sessions, summing up everything that everybody thought they already knew. And for some, it was a delight to be able to get back to a bed that one could claim as one's own for a minimum of eight hours.

Making A Point: Septuagenarian author-educator Margaret Walker (Alexander) speaks on October 16, 1992, at the opening of the International Conference on Black Women Writers and Magic Realism at Jackson State University, Jackson Mississippi.

CULTURAL PLURALITY: THE COMMUNITY AND ITS INSTITUTIONS

Zohreh T. Sullivan

From October 29 to November 1, the campus of the University of Illinois at Urbana-Champaign was temporarily transformed by the presence of a diversity of cultures clustered around Levis Faculty Center: by community organizers, representatives from labor unions, school teachers, high school students from East St. Louis, Urbana, Champaign and Park Ridge, ethnomusicologists, composers, corporate executives, poets, professors and writers. The occasion was a conference hosted by The Program for the Study of Cultural Values and Ethics at the UIUC: "Living and Working with Cultural Plurality: The Community and Its Institutions."

The overwhelming consensus was that the conference was a valuable and useful forum for its varied participants. In the words of our outside evaluator, Bruce Michelson: "There are reasons to count the 'Cultural Plurality' conference as the most complex and ambitious cross-disciplinary, cross-*everything* meeting that University of Illinois academic units have sponsored on this campus in the past ten years, and to regard it as an unparalleled and almost miraculous success. The conference sought to bring together campus theory and street-wisdom, Grey Eminences and high school students, professional critics working in relative sequestration, and sometimes-touchy practitioners in volatile, dangerous venues – and to do so in a time when discourse about the reality or the promise of a multicultural United States is liable to posturing, to reductive thinking and orating, and to paralyzing hostility."

The aim of this conference was to enter the debate provoked in part by the issues raised about 1492 in 1992: the construction of American identity and multiculturalism by moving it away from abstract theorizing and media simplification to dialogue between groups who write about and live with cultural pluralism. We tried temporarily to collapse the boundaries between discrete disciplines and cultures within our society, opening a new space for dialogue, by constructing the debate as a healthy and belated response to Culture as finalized monolith, and by affirming a society which is about becoming, always in process, and freed from the anxiety of resolutions about identity.

The speakers and panels worked at several questions and issues in the three and a half days of the conference. As the sessions began to formulate themselves, the conference seemed to ask what multiculturalism meant in terms of (1) the translation of cultures as they hyphenate themselves in America, and in the constitution of identity and ideal nationhood, (2) rethinking possibilities for the disempowered in our streets, in public housing and in our neighborhoods, (3) in popular culture and the media, (4) in labor unions, in the work place, and in corporations, (5) in music and ethnomusicology, (6) in class rooms, alternative school systems, and in education, and (7) in arts: poetry, literary anthologies and music.

The conference had fourteen key sessions in addition to workshops on writing, high schools and business; and working luncheons on popular culture and media, housing, the university, secondary education, and the community college.

The keynote session on Thursday night had Catherine Stimpson (Rutgers University) and Michael M.J. Fischer (Rice University) approaching the problems of multiculture from appropriately different perspectives. In "O Brave New World: A Vision of Cultural Diversity," Stimpson was, for the night at least, the feminist-humanist celebrating cultural-pluralist-democracy and the five principles of what she called a "creative multiculturalism." In his "The Orientalizing of America," Fischer was the cultural anthropologist who tried (through literature and film) to move the concept of multiculture away from the "identity politics" of essentialized ethnic cultures, with their own values, towards a new understanding of the concept as the creation of hybridities and of an acceptance of multiple overlapping identities for individuals and groups.

On Friday, Zohreh Sullivan, the conference director, started the day with a brief introduction that explained the current debate over multiculturalism, the history of the concept of "culture" as it seesaws between the elite and the popular, between the modern and the postmodern, between Matthew Arnold, Adorno and Andreas Huyssens, and the problem of what it means to live in "a nation of nations."

Session #2, moderated by James Barrett (professor of history, UIUC), was a panel on "Building Culturally Plural Neighborhoods" with Abdul el-Jamal, the Director of the Champaign-Urbana Area Project, discussing how his group tries to empower families through developing community based support systems. Salim Muwakkil, senior editor of *In These Times*, in a talk titled "McJobs and Tribalism," connected the global to the local by considering the impact of consumer capitalism and the fall of Communism on African-American cultures – an impact he saw in the rise of defensive tribalism and Afrocentricism. Eugene Redmond (Professor of English at Southern Illinois University at Edwardsville, Poet Laureate of East St. Louis, editor and community activist) presented a narrative of his moves away from the academy, into streets and communities and back again into the academy – but this time with a difference. Dominic Pacyga (professor of sociology at Columbia College, Chicago) offered yet another narrative of his work called "Maintaining Diversity in the Inner City: Chicago's South West Catholic Cluster Project." With slides and lecture he described first the problems, and then the dynamics and the historic evolution of what was once a white racist community into a bi-racial and diverse neighborhood.

Session #3, because of the titles chosen by its hip panelists, drew more students from freshmen rhetoric classes looking for trendy paper topics (and graduate students from cultural studies) than any other session at the conference. Herman Grey (professor of African-American studies at the Center for Cultural Studies at the University of California at Santa Cruz) delivered a paper on "Jazz as Cultural Practice and the Politics of Diversity" that addressed the making of Wynton Marsalis into a cultural icon. Carol Stabile (Unit for Criticism, UIUC), in a talk titled "Erasing Racism: Murphy Brown, Dan Quayle and the L.A. Riots," considered the ideological, racial and economic implications of the logic that linked the L.A. riots, Dan Quayle's speech and *Murphy Brown*. And Keya Ganguly (professor of Literary and Cultural Theory at Carnegie Mellon), in her paper "At the End of History We are all in Ancient Egypt," discussed the ideological implications of the erasure of time and space in two Michael Jackson videos.

On Friday afternoon, session #4 was an ethnomusicology lecture by Bruno Nettl (professor of music and anthropology, UIUC). Armed with a boom box and some powerful musical tapes, Nettl began with an essay on the culture of music, moved to Native American expression and the specific example of the Ghost Dance, and finally, in his tale of two cities, to the modernizing and hybridizing of classical musics from Madras to Tehran.

Session #5, Corporate Views of the Workplace, consisted of representatives from various corporations discussing how they responded to population changes in their ranks. The panelists included Isaac Hawkins, a manager in Sears Workforce Diversity Department, Brenda Lane, a manager at Ameritech, Chicago and Guadalupe Quintanilla, assistant vice-president for Academic Affairs at the University of Houston, Texas.

The rest of Friday afternoon and evening was occupied with music, music teachers, music composers. Session #6 explored how music was used by ethnic groups and other subdivisions of American culture to symbolize ethnic identity and intercultural relations, and how issues and problems of cultural pluralism can be and have been addressed in educational and other institutions. Louis Ballard, a Quapaw-Cherokee composer, educator and writer, in a paper titled "Multi-Perceptual Consciousness and Native Americans," demonstrated some of the ways in which his music adapted, transformed and realized the central values of his culture. Dominic Rene de Lerma (director of the Center for Black Music Research, Columbia College Chicago), in "Lessons from the Harlem Renaissance," discussed the racial tensions that currently and historically inform the politics of music. Barbara Lundquist, retired professor of music education at the University of Washington, who long supervised music in public schools, demonstrated actual classroom techniques in her talk on "Cultural Pluralism and Music Education." And Isabel Wong (UIUC) ended the session by considering the mainstreaming of music in Asian-American ethnic communities in the U.S.

That night the audience was invited to a Louis Ballard concert at Smith Music Hall (coordinated by Laura Stanfield,UIUC).There we heard what was in some ways a metaphor for the conference: the repertoire ranged from raw Native American material to a westernized cantata, demonstrating how Ballard uses his Native American heritage to create hybridized forms of westem music. By defying western concert conventions and inviting the participation of the audience (in its dance and choral music), by inserting a brief lecture within the concert format, by shifting roles from performer to conductor to participant, Louis Ballard was a reminder of the possibilities available to the artist with a foot in both worlds.

Saturday's sessions ranged from Local Schools to Labor Unions, from literary anthologists to poets in performance. The morning started with session #8 on "Cultural Plurality in the Local Schools" in which Violet Harris (professor of Education, UIUC) moderated a panel of teachers who discussed the effects of the Illinois requirement that teachers include units on the Holocaust, African-American history and women's history. The panelists were Sherry McClellan (Unit 116 School District), Henry Meares (Principal, University High School, Urbana), Mike Woods (Central High School, Champaign) and Stan Yanches (Centennial High School, Champaign).

"Cultural Plurality in Labor and the Work Place" (session #9), organized by Belden Fields (professor of Political Science, UIUC), was read by some of the audience as the most unexpected and therefore special session because of the powerful narratives presented by its contrasting panelists. Stan Rosen (professor of Labor and Industrial Relations, UIC) started the audience with the labor union anthem and a paper on the possibility of rewriting an American History that included the role of organized labor. Maria Rosales (Plumbers and Pipefitters Union, Chicago) gave us a strong and moving narrative of her pre-and post-union life – the experiences of an impoverished high school dropout from a hispanic immigrant family on welfare, to training as a mechanic in the Army, to her current rewarding fulltime membership in a Chicago labor union. Clarene Roystin (Shop Steward of the American Federation of Government Employees Local, St. Louis, Mo.) concluded the session with a very different and powerful tale of the evolution of her life as a labor activist.

"The Cultural Work of Anthologies" (session #12) began with Cary Nelson (professor of English, UIUC) whose paper used Lynn Cheney's "happy family multiculturalism" as a point of contention and an idea that both transcended and concealed the unhappier historical conflicts which, he suggested, should be the real work of responsible anthologies. Nina Baym (professor of English, UIUC) looked at the differences between the teacher's illusions about literature and student responses to how texts and anthologies actually "work." Paul Lauter (professor of English, Trinity College, Hartford, Conn.) discussed the problems of putting together his monumental and revisionist Heath Anthology of American Literature. Raymond Parades, one of the other editors of the Heath Anthology and currently Vice Chancellor of Academic Affairs, UCLA, emphasized the importance of how we teach rather than what we teach.

On Saturday evening, Ray Young Bear, Eugene Redmond and Elizabeth Alexander presented a poetry reading that reflected the differences in their positions, their subjects and their lives.

Ray and Stella Young Bear sang and played some Mesquakie songs, and Ray read some old and some new poems from *Black Eagle Child: The Facepaint Narratives*, poems celebrating the clan, the woodlands, and the rituals at the heart of his culture.

Eugene Redmond's reading, from *The Eye in the Ceiling* and other poems, was a stunning demonstration of his inventiveness with language and sound, of how he could evoke a sense of place (of the physicality of East St.Louis), a sense of music, particularly in his subtle and supple use of jazz rhythms. Elizabeth Alexander's poems from her *Venus Hottentot* and her more recent poems on Muhammad Ali were striking for their visual, historical and cultural allusiveness.

Sunday was devoted to public and alternative school education from the point of view of educators and students. "Education in a Multicultural Society" (session #14) included Alan Peshkin (professor of Education, UIUC) who described some of the issues raised by his experiences at a school in a Native American Reservation; Ramon Cruz (Latino Youth High School) who recounted the need for alternative education as a response to the hopelessness and anger of inner city hispanic youth; Shalewa Crowe who described the pan-African idea behind Haki and Safisha Madhubuti's founding of The New Concept Development School, Chicago; and Elaine Mosely, who concluded by telling us of the combined Christian and African ideals that informed the ethics of the inner city Corporate School in Chicago.

"Views from High School" (session #15) was set up as a final drama, moderated and organized by Robert D. Parker (professor of English, UIUC), consisting of a large group of energetic, articulate, and disarmingly honest high school students from East St. Louis High School, Urbana High School, Champaign Central, and East Maine High School. They began the session with an audience participation game intended to reveal the insidiousness of stereotype: "Who am I" was their invented game designed to trap the audience in their own construction of stereotypes. The game provided a concrete counterpart to the academic question of identity construction with which the conference had been concerned. They talked about the effect of cultural plurality on their daily lives with anecdotes about problems with teachers and texts, the color line in a Champaign lunch room which reconstituted itself in economic and familial lines in East St. Louis, about prejudice within African American groups displayed in dining room dynamics by students from single parent families towards those from dual parent families; about reactions to overt and covert racism in school corridors; about the problems a Korean student and her parents faced when their south side Chicago grocery store was repeatedly robbed by yet another disenfranchised minority.

The final session, "Poets on Plurality," provided, for some of the audience, a fitting and cathartic conclusion to the conference. Eugene Redmond and Elizabeth Alexander addressed some of the problems raised by the high school students – but with a difference. Redmond provided a personal narrative of the four revolutions during his encounters with American history inflected with his particular grace and generosity; Alexander also presented a personal narrative – one informed by the poetry that influenced her current stance. She started with a Lucille Clifton poem on negotiating the troubled past and ended with Gwendolyn Brooks in whose words she urged the high school students to "conduct" their "blooming in the noise and whips of the whirlwind." One member of the audience told me that although the entire conference had increased his awareness of diversity and its problems, the last poem provided him with what he had hoped for – that such problems need not be resolved into formulaic resolutions, that the fact of overwhelming cultural problems can be answered with the miracle of continuing and endless possibility. Or as Brooks would say, in spite of history, we must know that the "whirlwind is our commonwealth," that we must salvage, endorse, and find a way to "nevertheless live."

Smiling after their panel on Mass Media and Popular Culture are Keya Ganguly of Carnegie Mellon University, Herman Gray of the University of California at Santa Cruz, and Carol Stabile, a postdoctoral fellow at the Unit for Criticism and Interpretive Theory at the University of Illinois at Urbana-Champaign. Scene: Fall 1992 Cultural Plurality conference at U. of I.

Rite #3

Chants, Blues, Visions, Poems

Jeanette Adams
Raymond R. Patterson
Ishmael Reed
Francy Stoller
Tyrone Williams

COMMANDMENTS

Jeanette Adams

coloring calms me
I stay within the lines
on my way to your wedding
restless in my seat
I blink back memories

suddenly I am four
abused behind my door
afraid to yell
unable to tell

commandments haunt me:

Thou shall not steal trust
Thou shall not kill innocence
Thou shall not commit adult acts with children
Thou shall not bear false witness to family

I watch your wedding
sticky in my seat
the colors are too hot
the gowns too heavy
I shut out shame

now I am twenty
I have lived with this too long
shocked out of secrecy
I have sought counsel

I am telling my mother, your aunt
her sister, your mother
my father
our grandfather
the aunts
the uncles
your wife

This is about my life
This is about my loss
This is about my fear
This is about my pain

I have a new box of colors
eight old ones hard to find
I can not stay within the lines
I must break boundaries
I must make peace

GIRLFRIEND'S GOT IT GOIN' ON

for Terry McMillan

Jeanette Adams

girlfriend's got it goin' on
all over the place
we have turned off the TV
and picked up the book

Ms. Terry Mac
well versed in black
has come right back
struttin'
strokin'
shamin'
namin'
every Ron Rick and Larry
we know

girlfriend's got us
laughin' out loud
stompin' the floor
beatin' the bed
callin' our mommas
waitin' in the rain
to inhale
her righteous tale

Ms. Terry Mac
who cuts no slack
will take you back
to blue lights in the basement
and all nights on the phone
girlfriend is a story tellin'
ginger melon who's been
listening to our lives

her folks are
throwin' down
gainin' ground
short sheetin' dicksters
stir fryin' tricksters
hip hoppin'
be boppin'
double dutchin'
triple clutchin'
us in a blues sweet
world beat

July 12, 1992

Sisters: Essence ***Magazine editor Susan Taylor and Temple University poet Sonia Sanchez share smiles during 20th Anniversary of Third World Press Conference at Chicago State University, Fall 1987.***

BENT BLUES (Captain Lomax Wants to Know)

Raymond R. Patterson

Midwife bend me bad to get me born.
Grandma claimed she used an old shoehorn.

Grandpa swore he'd die before he'd break.
The Bank stole what Boll Weevil didn't take.

Cropping broke my Pa and kept us poor.
Mama never got straight with the company store.
(Preacher kept us bent a little more.)

Schoolhouse left my backbone in a crick.
Chopping cotton nearabout did the trick.
(I vowed I wouldn't hit another lick!)

Sheriff caught me, north on Forty-nine.
He said this guitar wouldn't pay my fine.

The Judge said, Boy, you're gonna like the Farm.
Just serve your time, it won't do you no harm.

First thing they did was put me on a rack
And stretched me till the crick popped from my back.

Next thing they did was lock me in a box,
Then let me out to cool off in the stocks.
(By then I was most glad to break some rocks.)

They fed me coffee that was pretty rotten.
I begged the cook to let me pick some cotton.

Six months out here, and Lord, if I don't die,
I'll kiss this lowdown crooked place goodbye
(And give ole Forty-nine another try).

Now here's a blues that you ain't heard before.
How they come to me? You know, I sure ain't sure.

LAST MILE BLUES

Raymond R. Patterson

Jailer, help me put my bowtie on!
A little while and I'll be gone.
A little while, and I'll be up and gone.

The Devil's gonna see me looking nice
When I come to pay my price –
When I pay my price.

The Warden don't care if I look well,
So long as he sends my soul to hell –
Just so he sends my soul to hell.

I ate last night, now I'm hungry again.
Hanging around here, a poor boy could get thin.
Hanging around here, a poor boy could get thin.

A whole lot of crying, and a little use for tears –
Trustee's doing life plus ninety-nine years,
Trustee's doing life, plus ninety-nine years.

Walk it steady – ha! – move on down the line.
A few more yards and I'll be doing fine.
A few more yards, and I'll be doing fine.

Poets Raymond Patterson, left, and Barry Wallenstein (with son Daniel) at the 20th Annual Spring Poetry Festival, held in May of 1992 on the campus of the City University of New York in Manhattan. Poets of all ages read at the festival in honor of Donald Hall. Among participating poets: Ann Lauterbach, Jeanette Adams, William Mathews, Aileen Rivera, Ira Cohen, Paul Oppenheimer, and Albert Depas.

OHUN PATAKI

Ishmael Reed

I

Ole
Ku -u' lé o
Eru mi ni yii
Wahala mi ni yen
Abuku mi ni yii
Ìpayà mi ni yen
Mo fún ọ ni gbogbo' è

2

Ole
Ku-u' lé o
Ìdààmú mi ni yii
Ẹ̀ṣẹ̀ mi ni yen
Àìbalè-ọkan mi ni yii
Egọ̀ mi ni yen
Aìmọkan mi ni yii
Mo fún ọ ni gbogbo

3

Ole
Ku-u' lé o
Ohun-ini mini yii
Olá mi ni yen
Ìfẹ́, mi ni yii
Èrò mi ni yen
Otito-inu mi ni yii
Èmi m ni yen

N ó bá ọ jà feyii

MISCHA/MISCHA LANGDON/THE LATE SIXTIES/ NEW YORK TOWN

Francy Stoller

Curved like a sickle
one eye
told all

Named
from the cellophane
in the back of a taxi-cab
and an English teacher
I once loved

Switchboardin'/eavesdroppin'
actress/puppeteer
one facade/a career

Even kids
thought she's a fake
dragging those marionettes
'cross the stage/ not caring
if Jack's feet were missing
the beanstalk

Her accent was Israeli
with a French twist
Vue/Vue/ Vue
did you want her
mannequin eyes
like rhinestones in moss
some dolls can't be bought

Paisley dreams pass at night
too young to be an ingenue
she ace-bandaged her breasts
played a young girl
skipping out opening night
before the second act

Smelling Revlon/ hopsteppin'
the disco cage/ collecting
dues for walking in and outta
places

Mischa/ Mischa Langdon
shot vitamins/ nouveau drugs
curved like a sickle
one eye told all
a trumpet
flat
and disgraced.

Homeless Brother, Minneapolis, July 1991.

YOU KNOW WHAT I'M SAYING?

Tyrone Williams

Something old, something new, multiculturalism is the symbol and embodiment of a marriage that may never take place but is always about to take place. It is a symbol and incarnation of brides and grooms standing before the altar of a church – America – that awaits its own marriage with that which it worships – the United States of America. In brief, multiculturalism is the legal, which is to say political, cultural, economic, and social, validation of miscegenation.

But these multiple marriages can only take place when the priest arrives. Meanwhile, these couples, who have always lived together, who have always lived in sin, wait impatiently. Perhaps it does not occur to them that the priest is always about to arrive, that the marriage ceremonies will never take place, that they are already, after all these years, common law spouses.

Something gold, something blue, multiculturalism is the symbol and embodiment of a divorce that cannot take place because a marriage has never taken place. It is a symbol and incarnation of the sun and sky, wedded, it seems, from the perspective of that which is neither sun nor sky – earth. Yet we know that the sun is not "in" the sky, that it is, in fact, 93 million miles away. Nevertheless, innumerable couples, who have remained living together, who are common law spouses in the same houses, await the finalization of their divorces. Perhaps it does not occur to them that the lawyers, who must argue before a judge, himself a lawyer kicked upstairs, are always about to arrive, that these divorces will never take place, that they are, after all these years, already separate already together, already divorced, already married, thanks to common law.

Novelist Xam Cartier (seated), author of Muse-Echo Blues, visits with faculty and students following her February 1991 reading on the campus of Southern Illinois University at Edwardsville. Standing (l-to-r): graduate student Nancy Avdoian, music instructor Alfred Duckett, student Nancy Alexander, and poet-English teacher Allison Funk. Cartier also read at State Community College in East St. Louis.

SLEEPING SICKNESS

for Lee and Steven

Tyrone Williams

When I was a little John the Baptist,
I always slept in the middle of my bed –
I always made room for Santa Claus and Christ.

Then I slept with a little Herodias –
spoons that never reached your lips,
bookends that never held your litany.

Now I'm a lazy Lazarus--
You no more will suffer me
to come to ....

EARTHBOUND

Tyrone Williams

A man in the middle of an ocean.
The man is not in a craft.
He is not dead.

Is he floating on his stomach?
Is he floating on his back?
The authorities cannot decide.

I can say this for certain.
Dreaming of land, of walking,
He treads water in his sleep.

Poets Janice Mirikitani and Maya Angelou flash victory smiles during Angelou's 65th birthday party in Winston-Salem, NC, April 4, 1993. Oprah Winfrey hosted the bash.

Rite #4

Writers Talking, Words Walking

Maya Angelou Interview

Leon Forrest Interview

Luis Rodriguez Interview

'TOUGH AND TENDER'

Maya Angelou Interview
by Eugene B. Redmond

Maya Angelou's home
Winston-Salem. North Carolina
Saturday, April 27, 1991

Eugene B. Redmond: I'm honored, Maya, to know you, to continue to know you, my sister, my friend, my colleague. I quote you a lot, all over the place. It's amazing. I have benefitted so much from the Maya Angelou wit-book. There's so much in my mind from you, although I've almost never written anything down. To begin the interview, would you briefly recall the last twenty years? [laughs] We were together in California in the early '70s, and into the early '80s, in Oakland, Berkeley, San Francisco, Sacramento, Sonoma, Davis. How do you feel about that time and what's happened since then?

Maya Angelou : Let me tell you what I really feel. My gratitude to you is boundless. In truth, a very strong woman of any race, but particularly a Black woman, needs romance and must have a brother. Lovers as such – that is, just people who care for you, just physically holding you, just being with a person, just available as husband – might be found, might then be discarded. But a brother for a Black American woman is essential because by his very talking he describes a responsibility to a person which is unending. You don't fall out of brotherhood. You don't fall out of sisterhood. The Black woman who has achieved in her life a level of profound understanding has paid for it dearly. Almost too dearly to be accounted. And what she always needs is someone who loves her enough to say, "Hey, baby, that isn't the hippest thing you ever did," and to really be able to criticize her actions without criticizing her. And at the same time to be able to say, "That's the most brilliant thing I've ever seen. You're the most brilliant thinker I've ever seen in my entire life." So you come to me as pure brother now and you came to me as such back then. And I love the blues that keeps you cool. Over twenty-one years you've seen me through love affairs, some wonderful, some disastrous. You've seen me try great ideas in books and sometimes achieve them. Yes, I did. And sometimes I fell flat on my face. You're a brother. I don't have many, but each is as precious to me as the last raw egg in the world. This is why it's been so long for us to do this, and especially now. In 1976, when it was found that I had cancer and I was so reluctant to get any treatment – I was really ditsy – because I had students. And my then husband, who was also your friend, said, "Maya, you will go in the hospital." And you said, "Not only will you go in the hospital, but you're not going to worry about your students because I'll take over your classes for the rest of the year with no financial recompense." Do you realize that?

EBR: No. That wasn't something we thought a lot about.

MA: That wasn't in it. I don't think I've ever really thought about it. Have we ever talked about that? We had a few drinks, a few dinners. I slept on the sofa. [at EBR's Sacramento home] Sometimes you got out of your bed and gave it to me and my husband. Remember that? Eugene, if you want I can make this pay, [gesturing as in check writing] how do they say, post-dated. There was nothing so reassuring to me as overcoming, recovering from such a drastic, drastic operation, ... from surgery on to therapy. You were my brother. You were there. You came into the house and said, "It's all good."

EBR: There are certain concerns at the back and front of all of us. And I think now of what it (cancer) meant at different times when as a very young man, I used it, essentially metaphorically, as a stand in for some kind of problem or plague I couldn't put my hand on. It (cancer) wasn't around as much, or if it was we didn't know it. So I think your idea of having a *brother* and having a *sister* is correct. I need a sister and you in my life in the same ways you've been describing your need for me and other brothers. I think that we come to this in many ways, by way of many different experiences and needs. I think you talked about James Baldwin figuring into this. In fact, we've had many discussions of your relationship with Jimmy; and my witnessing of that relationship at a very crucial junction (mid '70s California years) is one of a number of things that have helped me be a better brother, a better father, a better uncle, a better son . . . .

MA: A better friend.

EBR: Could you talk about how Jimmy figured into your view of brotherhood and friendship and artistry?

MA: You know, I spoke at his funeral. Toni Morrison spoke for the writer. You see, the three of us spoke the eulogy.

EBR: The three of you being...?

MA: Myself, Toni Morrison and Amiri Baraka. Toni spoke for the writers, which was the voice of the author. And Amiri Baraka spoke for the Black man, the Black American man, the Black American artist and preacher. And the Baldwins asked me to speak for the family. When the others spoke, everyone seemed to be just listening. But when I said the first words, Mother Baldwin, sitting in Cathedral St. John the Divine, screamed. People were *really* listening. So I asked, "Mother?" You know, she was sitting there crying, and so I said, "Mother, Mother." And then I quoted what Jimmy said about Mother Baldwin.

There were thirteen or fourteen Baldwins. But in the late '50s/early '60s, we met in Paris. Jimmy and I. Jimmy brought me to his mother and father and he said to them, "I'm bringing you something you really don't need, another daughter." All his brothers and sisters took me. And Mother Baldwin did too. I just had a letter from her, just three days ago. She says every time she sees me on television, she can almost hear Jimmy whispering in my ear and telling me what to say. In fact, he has been so influential in my life, that when I was in love with Paul (who wanted to get married) and I really didn't want to get married – I've never wanted to get married. I don't like the idea. It seemed insulting to *me. I'm* a responsible adult. And an honorable one. And to think that some stranger could come up to me, a responsible adult and an honorable woman, to say, "Maya, it's OK for you to love this person who is also a responsible adult and an honorable man." To me, that's an intrusion of my privacy. And I have always hated it (marriage) for myself. I would live with someone. If we shake hands, there's no bonds stronger. For me, this is it. I give you my word and you give me your word. I can't imagine that some stranger with a Bible and a Law can make me more loyal to you than my word – So, we had been together, Paul and I, for about two years. And he kept insisting, because he was British. He kept insisting, saying that if I had been American white, Australian white, or if he was American Black, then he wouldn't insist. But crossing cultures, he wanted to make a public statement of his commitment. And he was getting more and more furious.

So we went to New York, he and I. We stayed at Dollie McPherson's house. And I called Jimmy, about '72, and I said, "I have to see you." And he said, "Baby, I can't see you right now. I've got Ray Charles and Quincy Jones and we're talking." (And you know he did that Mass with Ray Charles.) He said he couldn't talk to me. So I said, "Jim, I'm sorry. I hate to do this, but I have to." He said, "Baby, look, I'll see you at . . . ." I said, "I have to see you now." He said "OK, I'll meet you at the Russian Tea Room." So I went to the Russian Tea Room and he came in, and you know, we must have made a picture. I'm six foot and I love those shoes with three or four inch heels. That was *his* joint, so he just walked in and said, "Come on," beckoning me to his table at the back. People were fawning over him. "Oh, Mister Baldwin . . . " You know. He asked. "OK, what is it?" So I said, "Paul wants to get married." He said, "Yeah, so?" I said, "I don't want to get married because I don't believe in it." And I gave him this long spiel. "You're in love with him?" I said, "Yes." "He's in love with you?" I answered,"Yes." He said, "If he had been Black, would you have all this bullshit?" And I said, "Yes." "But would you have felt it as strongly?" I said, "I don't know." He said, "Are you a little afraid?" I said, "Yes." "Well look here girl, everything you do, every piece you write, is about courage, and the courage to love. So what the shit are you? A hypocrite? You're afraid Black people are going to be angry with you for marrying a white man. The very people who will be angry with you are the very people who will die if you don't do it. They expect courage from you, the courage to love. They expect it from you, Maya Angelou. And the courage to stand by your love." So I said, "I thank you." "Come on," he laughed, "we'll have another drink." I went back to Paul after that talk and said to Paul, "I'll marry you. And I'm sorry, I'm really sorry." So in many ways, he helped me in my personal life, and you can't get any more personal than marriage. And in my personal life as a writer, Jimmy would read my work. He would say, "Maya, I want you to come to the South of France, and if you don't come, I'm bringing my ass to California. I'm coming, because I don't understand this, that, whatnot." You knew his language. Or he would call me, "Baby, I'm sending you a first class ticket. I want you to meet me in London. You have written your ass off, and it's the best thing I ever saw in my life and I love it."

EBR: You know, speaking of Jimmy, I've often heard you talk about him and John O. Killens in the same breath – when you discuss yourself as a writer. It seems each of them gave you very important assistance and support, but in vastly different ways. At least, that's what I've gotten from the tone of your voice when you talk about them.

MA: Oh yes. And I must include Julien Mayfield. That's why when you came down, when you came to support me as my brother, after Jimmy died, John Killens, Julien Mayfield and my Papa ... do you realize that when you came here for that one week (1987) to brother me, that all those Black men who had been like hands around me had all gone? So when you came and Derek Brook (a friend from England) came, I mean, that meant so much to me. I can't even write a poem about it. It's so close, I can't get it out of me and out of my heart enough to write about it. John Killens encouraged me and advised me, and his real gift, besides his love, and you know, he loved me, and I needed that. But besides his love for me, he gave me encouragement to be truthful. I would say something was greenish, or had a greenishness to it. And he would say, "Either it's green or it's not green." So, he helped me to define my own voice. And I know that my voice is a Maya Angelou voice. I read other people who are imitating me and who have not yet found their voice. But my voice is distinct.

EBR: Did John O help you gain precision and focus within your own voice?

MA: Yes. And clarity.

EBR: And could you say Baldwin helped with the passion?

MA: Yes. He helped with the passion and the enthusiasm. Jimmy constantly said, "Dare it. Fuck 'em." Excuse me, but it's true. I don't mean to be crude, but that's what he said. "Get on out there. Say it. If you want to say it, say it." And of course, there was my husband at the same time who loved Jimmy. Paul Dufeu told me, "If they hate you, I'll take you to London and build houses." So, Jimmy encouraged me to dare anything, to say it. And John Killens encouraged me to say it absolutely, strictly, to say exactly what you mean, and say it in my voice, which is always a poetic voice, a voice with a particular Southern Black female religious imagery. This is my voice. So it seems very strange when I read people who are imitating my voice who don't have this particular Southern or religious history, and I can hear it and it sounds a little jangling on the ear. But you know, they're in search of their own voices, and I understand that.

EBR: You certainly write about the imitations and the emulations. As far as I can determine, based upon my own recall, and my own reading, this is the first time in history that African-American literary figures have moved to such a popular level, celebrity status, heroes; or, to use a word you love, sheroes. In fact, I've been talking about this across the country; about the new audiences, especially for Black women writers. I sat in an audience (Detroit, 1990) of 1500, mostly Black women, although there were some white women and a few men, but 1500 mostly women, listening to Gloria Naylor. What was stunning there was the nervousness. It was like waiting for Baldwin in the early '60s. We were just waiting for him to come out. And now I sit in audiences, and Maya, they're waiting. You should be out there among the young females. The anxiousness, the anticipation! It's like theater. It's like movies. It's like sports, a concert. But I want to ask you something. It seems to me that most of your literary influences, the literary artists who have influenced you, who have been on a socially intimate basis with you, have been men, although I know you talk about women. It just seems you read the women, but you knew the men. Is this because of the history?

MA: It's the history. Of course Paule Marshall was my friend in the late '60s, but Paule had already published *Brown Girl, Brown Stones,* which became an American classic. And *Soul Clap Hands and Sing* came later. And Ossie Davis optioned it and did it like he did. Miss Anne Petrie had done *The Street,* 10, 15 years earlier. Rosa Guy published *Bird At My Window* in 1966. And I had returned from Africa and gave her a book party in '67. So we had relationships. First, I had an apartment across from Paule Marshall when I did *The Blacks,* which was in 1960. I had done *The Blacks* in 1959 in New York with Roscoe Lee Brown, Raymond St. Jacques, Cicely Tyson, Lou Gossett, Godfrey Cambridge, and so on.

EBR: I have a program from that show. I was in south-east Asia. But someone gave me one late. I was in the Marines.

MA: So I had rented an apartment across the hall from Paule Marshall and that's where I really started meeting the Harlem Writer's Guild, in the late '50s. John, Julian and Jimmy and all that group. And Jimmy and I made our real friendship then in my apartment and in Paule Marshall's apartment. Then, when I went off to Africa, which was really more than a passing interest . . . .

EBR: You mean the trip to Africa?

MA: Well, the marrying of that particular African with the brothers, my brothers, who again I could not live without. But John Killens, Max Roach, and Jimmy said, "Who is this dude?" and so forth and took him out. When I came back (from Africa), Paule Marshall and I resumed our friendship, in the late '60s. I went back to California and had that book party for Rosa Guy. So, my relationships with the lady writers and the sisterhood – we began a sisterhood – influenced writing for me right then. I admired them so.

EBR: Your work is quite different from these other women writers.

MA: My work is different, yes. But I have an admiration for them that is boundless; for the quality and quantity of their work. Last night, Friday night, in New York City, there was a big fete for Rosa Guy, for the twenty-fifth year after the publishing of *Bird At My Window*. I sent flowers and this and lace and balloons and whatever. I've been supportive of her all along. And her play, *Once On This Island*, which is now on Broadway, is dedicated to me. But I have relationships with the women, with Miss Margaret Walker and Miss Gwendolyn Brooks. Those ladies influenced me a lot. Their work influenced me a lot. But they were beyond me in time. They were older and not within my circle. And again, because of Bailey, he was so great as a brother that his love trained me to be a great sister to a Black man.

EBR: When you speak of Bailey as a brother ...

MA: As a young man.

EBR: But the foundation was ...?

MA: The foundation was laid with Bailey during the years when I couldn't speak, when I was strange looking. You know, he was so little, and pretty and Black, and everybody adored him. And he was so glib. My family came closest to making a genius when they made Bailey. We have not come that close again. Not again, not in all the generations since. Maybe Colin, my grandson, with his mathematical stuff, maybe. I don't know. but we haven't come that close. So Bailey loved me and because I was so tall and gangly and because I didn't look like anybody, Bailey told me, "Cool it. I'll take care of it." And he told me height had nothing to do with being female. Nor did it have anything to do with being male. I believed everything he said. So, that kept me from ever becoming rough. He said, "You're a female and I'm supposed to open up the door for you." He was five-foot-four! And I'm six foot and he would do that. So, I had always this yearning for a brother, not so much for a sister.

EBR: Could you speak about this fusion or culmination of strength and vulnerability. I'm kind of reminded of the image of the hardflower that Gwendolyn Brooks used in a little book *A Capsule Course on Black Poetry Writing* that she coauthored with Haki R. Madhubuti and William Keorepetse Kgositsile. Much of the way in which I deal with women, and have been dealing with them over the last twenty years or so, is very, very deeply influenced by my relationship with you. And much of the approach I take to men regarding women is very, very much influenced by our friendship. I've heard you say on several occasions that you maintain a kind of vulnerability or fragility, while at the same time you are obviously very much in control of what's going on. You're a professional woman. You're in charge of a number of different systems. You're an educator. You're a director. I'm just amazed and have a great deal of admiration for this ability that you continue to show. On the one hand, managing like a field marshal or a commander a whole number of different kinds of systems and operations, while at the same time being as you say a lady, being willing to accept, and even as a lady, to demand the kind of respect and protocol and decorum that's proper for a Southern lady. This just fascinates me. I've heard you talk about it at different occasions in bits and pieces, here and there. It's a great model as far as I'm concerned, and I always share some of the things you say, and if not what you say, then the image of what you project to other women. I said to some young women one day, "I would like to see in you a woman of 50,000 years or so." And they asked me to give an example. "Maya Angelou," was my reply. I tell my students this. I don't want to see somebody coming out of some shadowy situation, bowed down and broken. I want to see five, ten, 50,000 years of regalness. And they ask, "Who?" And I say, "Maya Angelou."

MA: I think that somebody decided that things must be either/or, so a woman must be either, as you say, a mover and shaker and doer and controller, or else she must be downleveled. But I don't see that. I think that it is both/and. You can be both this and that. For roundness, for balance, a woman, like a man, is comprised of these complementary hormones and if she or he is intact, then the person should be tough and tender. So, that means that one is capable, as Southern Blacks used to say, of "sittin' in mid-ocean and spyin' dry land." You should be able to do that. At the same time, you should be as accessible as a hand on the gate.

EBR: Then gender does not necessarily preclude or include one or the other or any combination?

MA: Indeed not. No, I just don't trust a man who is all macho and all that stuff and holds his genitalia as if somebody's out there. You know, please, please. That's Black? Or a white man who only has power to rule. I don't trust any of that. It doesn't even make sense to me. Nor do I trust the woman who is fainting all the time. There's something wrong with that. There's no balance. And the one thing about Nature, the only thing in Nature – I see no mercy in Nature. She says, "You're in your bikini in Buenos Aires, but I'm going to snow." Mercy--What I do see is balance. The tides go in and the tides go out.

EBR: And synthesis?

MA: Absolute. Constant. The overflowing of it. It's in rhythm. And that seems to me to be the greatest lesson any sentient, conscious being can learn. All nature says, "There's balance, idiots. Don't you see me? Then I'm spring, then I'm summer. Then I'm fall, then I'm winter, then I'm spring! And so on." Balance. And then you die. And out of the death blue irises grow, out of the dead eye sockets. So, balance. If the sex itself was only one, then that would be different. But in the sexuality, not just the sex itself, there is longing. One is fortunate if the person has the good luck not to be overly attracted to one's own sex. Overly! But a person lies if she or he says, "I have not seen anyone of my own sex that I find attractive."

EBR: Yes, yes. I agree.

MA: You lie. But you're lucky if for your own ease through life, the majority of your interest is in the opposite sex. You're lucky. But there is this: there is balance in nature. That's great, I think.

EBR: Order out of chaos. But I was thinking of asking, "What if you were unlucky?"

MA: People I have loved, I think, were unlucky. I have loved one man who was bisexual. And I think, truly, only a bisexual **with** me. I think he would normally be a homosexual. But Sam Floyd. I loved Sam. We had what we had for a long time.

EBR: Were you aware of Sam's homosexuality before you connected?

MA: Oh, yeah, darling. I knew, and he knew it. And knew that I knew. There was nothing hidden. But we loved each other, and it was wonderful when it was wonderful. And we kept our stuff long after I met someone else. He wouldn't die until I got to New York. [April, 1986] Rosa Guy and Louise Merriwether and all were waiting; and I got to New York and had a limousine fly me straight to the hospital. And I walked in, and I said, "Sam." And he said hello in a low, hoarse voice. So I kissed him. I said, "Are you going to leave, man? Really, please . . ." He said, "I'm trying," again in a raspy voice. Sounding just like B.B. And three minutes later, I was standing outside having a cigarette in the lobby, when a nurse came out, and said, "He's had a respiratory collapse." . . . I hope that I would have the compunction, the courage to support my love, I mean sexually in love. It's been my fortune, and I thank God, that (homosexuality) has not happened to me, because that would just complicate my life. I'm grateful that it hasn't been my fortune, but I would hope that I would be woman enough to support my love. If I didn't, I would be disappointed in myself.

EBR: Pulling order out of chaos at the level of integrating various interests and faces of the personality, of course, is one huge chore which you've tackled quite successfully. You've also done it in the disciplines. Here too, you are a first in history, to my knowledge. I know of no other instance in which a woman writer – and in very few instances with a male writer – has been simultaneously acclaimed in so many fields. The word "multi-talented" is often used before or after your name. I wonder how you feel about that. As far as I'm concerned, you've done a fantastic job developing a symbiosis, a sense of harmony and balance among your *selves*. Do you see yourself primarily as a writer or primarily as something else?

MA: I think that talent is like electricity. We don't know what the hell electricity is. We just don't know. We use it, and we probably use one-millionth of one-percent of it. We only know that if we can plug in a hole in the wall then we can light up a cathedral, a church, a synagogue, we can light up an operating room, or we can electrocute a person strapped in a chair. Electricity makes no demands. It just says, "I'm here. If you're a fool, you'll misuse me. If you are smart, you will use me constructively." Talent is just like that. I am sure of that. It is an energy and everybody born is born with it. Now, to decide that I am only this and somebody writes that into my ledger, bullcorn! I can be that, and that, and some of that, and some of that. Now, that doesn't mean I'm going to be great. But I can be competent in any of them. If I study the craft of painting, I will be competent. Absolutely. If I can see. You see? My physiognomy will control some of what I can do. If I'm color blind, obviously . . . If I'm tone deaf, I will not compose quite as well. You see? But, if I am reasonably OK in these areas, I should be able to do it; if I study the craft and put that energy into it. Now, you can only be great at the thing you love. Because it means you're willing to sacrifice time, people, your own self. Then you have a chance of being great in that field. I direct well, and I'm grateful. I am a good composer. I'm good. I'm not great. I would never be great. I don't love it. But I have a chance at being great as a writer. I love it. I will give up sixty hours to try to work one paragraph so that it seems that it fell right out of my mouth. So that critics say, "Oh, Maya Angelou has a new book. And it's good. But then she's a natural writer." That's like being a natural open heart surgeon. I work so hard. Ernest Hemingway said, "It's easy reading. It's damn hard writing." I've written so well that it just flowed. But that's what I do; to write it so that the reader reads thirty pages and doesn't even know he's reading. That's it. That's it!

EBR: And writing is the thing you love.

MA: That's it. I love that. I am committed to it. And it gives itself to me. It does. We work together, that muse and I.

EBR: How are you feeling about the general reception to you and your work?

MA: I'm grateful.

EBR: I'm in awe. And so are other people. I was just talking by phone to a friend named Addie, and she said, "I know that Maya's your friend and you've known her many, many years, but it's still hard for me to believe that you're calling me from her house."

I saw you on Arsenio, by the way, reading that Hayden piece and that Baraka piece.

MA: It was nice, wasn't it?

EBR: Ooooooooo! I wanted to call you at home right after that, but I called later, after you'd gone.

MA: You see, I wanted to use two Black men to talk about a Black man.

EBR: I saw that, I saw that! Ooooooooo! I saw it, and I *saw* it.

MA: You saw what I was doing.

EBR: People were asking me, "I wonder why she didn't use anything by a Black woman?" You see, it was women!

MA: There aren't enough platforms for Black male voices. So when I was going on, I said, "Oh, Lord, help me. Let some Black men speak through my voice and pull us together again." So to speak of one great dead poet and one great live poet, . . . Baraka says, "The end of man is his beauty." Go on honey!

EBR: Ooooooooo!

MA: So. Anyway, I'll tell you why I'm grateful . . .

EBR: For the reception to your work?

MA: Yes, I can't stay with it too much, because then I start to take myself too seriously.

EBR: The reception, that is?

MA: Yes. But, I know there are colleges, white male colleges, which have used books of poems of mine for senior classes of young white men. They use *And Still I Rise* as their senior class theme. These big white guys walk around with T-shirts on with "And Still I Rise" and on the back "Maya Angelou" or something. It's very interesting. I'm grateful. I'm owed nothing. I'm grateful. Two years ago, I was the most popular writer in Britain. When a writer sells 10,000 books he or she is considered a bestseller and Virago has sold over a quarter of a million of my books in Britain. So it's a blessing. And in Japan and around the world, Spain and Italy. In Finland and the Scandinavian countries, tops, 100,000 books. So, that's amazing. What it says to me is the theme of this class I am teaching. "I'm a human being. Nothing human can be alien to me." That somehow, if you tell the truth about a human experience, it's the truth about all human experience. And one sees that when one reads Charles Dickens or Tolstoy. One sees that when one reads Richard Wright. One sees that if you tell the truth. Pearl Buck, a white American, told the truth about China, a China she knew, and it was a truth. So, if you tell a truth, it is translatable through the human veins, like Langston Hughes. Langston Hughes never lied.

EBR: About?

MA: Anything! Langston never lied. That's why these young white men and women can do him on the stage today. And that young white man who came out, the red hair, in my company. . . . (literature/drama class she teaches at Wake Forest University.)

EBR: In shorts?

MA: He hadn't been able to speak. He came to my class and I thought, "He hadn't been able to speak." And I gave him all the work. And I said, "You'll do it." So now he says, "Look like what drive me crazy,/don't have no effect on you. But I'm gonna keep on at it/'til they drive you crazy, too." He's got Langston all between his teeth. Amazing, because Langston did not lie.

EBR: Yes, yes. Sounds like ageless, boundless . . .

MA: Truth. Boundless human truth.

EBR: Bottomless, heightless human truth. Even a different race can handle it.

MA: That's right. That's why the theme is, "In the quarter, in the quarter of the Negro, where the doors are made of paper." And I have these young white and young Black men and all these young white women saying that. And saying, "I, I am Black." Let them say it. Yes. That's the truth. That's what they are. They're White. And they're Black. They're Asian. They're Hispanic. Native American. That's who they are. And unfortunately, their teachers and their parents and their preachers and their leaders haven't had insight to tell them who they are. So I try to tell them who they are.

EBR: I wanted to ask you something about the social/racial microcosm. It's something that's troubling me, something I'm trying to work with and that I'm trying to get a grip or handle on. This has especially to do with my home town, East Saint Louis, Illinois, which is about 98-percent African-American. What's happening to East Saint Louis has happened to a lot of places, obviously, inside the U.S. and outside the U.S. We have just got a new administration, a new mayor, Gordon Bush there, and we hope at least to get some sensible, sane expression of commitment and some clear language coming out. People are finally being referred to as "citizens."

MA: Good Lord!

EBR: I have been wrestling with a number of ideas and issues stemming from and going back to this huge issue of the inner city, the urban hub, Black America. Black people, which way Black America, which way East Saint Louis, in particular, is going. You do best with what you know, and I want to use art in general, and literature in particular, to help lift people, to help lift the community, to the extent that I can. We have a writers group, for example, of which you are a Trustee. What are your thoughts? You've been observing these communities firsthand and through the media. You know what's happening in D.C., Philadelphia, Los Angeles, Houston, Chicago, Detroit, and Atlanta. What are your thoughts as an artist, as an activist, a cultural organizer, a parent, a Sister sojourner in this struggle.

MA: Sister sojourner! Sister sojourner!

EBR: Yes. And as a model, of course, highly emulated.

MA: I don't know about that. I don't know how to respond "as a model."

EBR: Sure. I understand that. But that's what the people are saying. I agree with you, Maya, because I don't accept it either (over emphasis on "model").

MA: Eugene, the truth is a lot of people say they want change. But what they really want is "exchange." They don't want to change the system where somebody has had their foot on their throats. What they really want is exchange where they have their feet on somebody else's throat. So the decision has to be made: Do the people really want change? Do they want an open field? Do they want a chance for all the people to be better? or just those in power, to change the power, just to have a chance to keep other people down? Black Americans, especially in our inner cities, must examine if we really want to make a change. If so, then we have to go back, we must examine our past, and I know there are a number of people who say "I don't want to hear about history." But the truth is we examine our past to see how we came so late and lonely to this place. What did we do wrong? Where did we go wrong? Where did we get off the track? We must do so. And so, I would suggest going back to David Walker, in 1830. I would. And reading and teaching the children everything from Walker's appeal through Frederick Douglass. I would let them see how Black men and Black women have tried to trudge up this mountain. I would not let anybody go. I would let them hear Miss Sojourner Truth. I would let them hear Miss Harriet Tubman. I would let them hear Mr. Martin Delaney. I would let them hear everyone of the men and women in this particular climbing of the mountain. I would not put down Mr. Booker T. Washington. I would let them hear everybody. Just see how people have tried to climb this face of the mountain and that face of the mountain. If they get enough of that, they would find out how we came to this place where we find ourselves today. This is what I would do. You talk about literary rehabilitation? I would do just so.

Women's Corner: ***Maya Angelou, left, captivates sister-artists and scholars during a July 1992 reception for Atty. Kathleen Cleaver (also on couch) at Richard Long's Atlanta home. Clockwise from Angelou are playwright Pearl Cleage, Atlanta Olympics '96 administrator Stephanie Hughley, filmmaker Cheryl Chisolm, and Natsu Jenga. Cleaver recently joined the law faculty of Emory University.***

DIVINE DAYS: AN INTERVIEW WITH LEON FORREST

by Eugene B. Redmond

On the road in Southern Illinois and St. Louis, MO
Monday April 20, 1992

Eugene B. Redmond: Leon, I'm so happy to have you in East Saint Louis, St. Louis, Edwardsville, Fairview Heights, Belleville, Alton. I wanted to start out with a general question. How are you feeling right now about your life, your work as a writer and as an academician? How do you feel about Northwestern, Evanston, Chicago? What's happening right now for you in those arenas?

Leon Forrest: Well, hell, I'm waiting on publication of my new novel, *Divine Days*. I hope that it will be well received. That's my main concern right now. And I guess because of the great length of the book, it's 1,135 pages, I'm hoping that reviewers will read some of it before they say this book is too long. But I guess the better reviews will be in the quarterlies where they have time to read. If you write a book this long, if you've got a right mind, then you're really asking whether there are people willing to see how well you sustain character development and so on. It's a lot to ask. Particularly in an age where people don't have that much time for reading. People who do read don't read that much. And then I have a collection of essays. It's coming out next year. And one of them is new. One I recently wrote about Billie Holiday. It's kind of impressionistic. I don't think that it adds anything to the Billie Holiday canon, but it was a lot of fun to write. There are about twenty in there that run a range from Billie Holiday to some literary essays. So that will be out next year.

EBR: Do you find the Evanston-Northwestern-Chicago environment a good place to work? Apparently you've produced quite a bit of work there. Are there hindrances of any sort, such as teaching or administration?

LF: Well, yeah, there is. And I would predict another generation will probably not go into the university, that writers will do other things. I don't know what shape that will take. But there are a lot of problems in the general M.F.A. programs where you get people who are talking the same talk, and it means that young writers get snapped off from getting out into the field, from doing things like waiting tables, bartending, running with gangs and so on. So sometimes you get people going from M.F.A. to teaching who've never had any life experiences. That's one thing that bothers me about a lot of the writing cadres that you see now. So they talk to each other, but also it drives away experimental fiction, which is really my interest. You have all this predicted path of what you must do. I came to Northwestern primarily because the writers I admired most were back in the university, different from many years ago. Writers weren't working on newspapers when I was coming along.

So, I had worked as a journalist for about ten years, and I thought that the university would be a place where I could grow intellectually, which would force me to do some close rereading of books to which I had already been exposed. I was not around long enough to take a degree, so I thought this would be a way to complete my education. So it's been good in that sense. It tends to isolate you, but to a degree that's the fault of the writer. They don't force you to do that. Writing is so lonely, and the hours you aren't writing you sort of hunger for some immediate kind of conversation about books. You can't get it in bars. You can get a lot of other things in bars, but you can't get discussions about books in bars. That's one of the attractive things about the university. Here's a place where you can talk about books seriously. And there aren't many other places where you can do that in this society. And that wasn't always true.

EBR: This is all very filling. It helps for me personally to flesh out some of my own views and questions about university life, university work versus writing, if you want to bring in that kind of contention. I think that we're all facing it, those of us who work in the university and who also write and do other things related to writing. You were first established as a journalist. Could you trace or outline your life up to that point and mention a few of the things that got you into journalism. Did you work for other publications besides *Muhammad Speaks*?

LF: I had thought that the best way to support myself as I was trying to write – at first it was poetry, then I got interested in play writing and finally fiction – was through journalism. I had an interest early on in journalism. Actually my first job as a journalist was in the army. I was a public information specialist from 1960 to 1962. I was drafted into the army. I dropped out of college. That was a nice deal. I used to follow troop training and write pieces on G.I.s with unusual stories. So I did that for about 18 months of my two-year stint. And then when I came back from the army I continued to work in the family's liquor store. I stopped that after about two years and made a kind of commitment to myself that I was going to go for broke in my writing. Meanwhile, I'd also secured a job with a small community newspaper, about '65. So I worked there for three years. I was also editor of the Woodlawn Organization's newspaper. *T. W. O.* is a popular organization in Chicago. And then I left there and went to work for *Muhammad Speaks* as an associate editor. Meanwhile, I was still writing my fiction in the evening. And I was there at *Muhammad Speaks* from early 1969 through 1973, June of '73. My first book, *There is a Tree More Ancient than Eden*, was published in May of '73. So I was working on writing fiction while I was working at *Muhammad Speaks*. One of the nice things about working there and also at the community papers was that it allowed me a source to get out certain protests or anger. And to look at fiction in a different way when I came home to write. So that was very healthy. The other thing was that for a long time on these community papers I was really working about 30 hours a week. It wasn't a long 48-hour week. So that gave me time too. I wasn't married. I made enough to support myself minimally. And it allowed me time to write. But all that's part of the dues paying you have to do. After the novel was published in '73, the appointment at Northwestern came the same year.

EBR: Here's a multi-part question for you. You have now authored, including this new one, *Divine Days*, four novels, and you speak of some essays. Is there any way by any stretch of the imagination, that the novels can be seen in a thematic sequence, possibly a tetralogy? And how much non-fiction have you written? How much do you plan to write?

LF: The non-fiction is more or less occasional pieces put together in this forthcoming collection of essays. I don't know if I'll write more. But there seems to be a relationship between a sort of clearing house for essays that opens you up to possibilities that I haven't talked about in fictional form. Also, we're dealing with protest, with anger. Also, there's the influence of the university. I've lectured on this writer and that writer. Ellison and Morrison and Faulkner. And some of those essays will be in this collection. As for the sequence of the novels, the first three are a kind of trilogy, though I didn't set out to plan to do that. It was only until I was deep into the second novel, *The Bloodworth Orphans*, that I tried to make a continual pattern out of this. The new novel is quite different. There's a lot of comedy in this novel. I hope so anyway. It does take on some of this idea of a kind of mythical area or county. It's very different. It takes place in bars and churches and barber shops. So it's quite different from the other books, even though there are some earlier scenes and characters who come back.

EBR: What is the name of your book of essays?

LF: The editor offered a title that I'm not that happy about. She wants to call it *The Furious Voice of Freedom*, which seems to me to be something nice if a critic said that, but not for the title of the book. But she likes it, so I'll argue about it. Anyway, it will be out probably in May of next year.

EBR: Your answers and observations are providing a lot of insight into writing generally and, of course, for me, the way you work and how you see things. The titles of your books are very intriguing. They're very unusual, very different, startling. In some ways provocative and in some ways, for me, they suggest depth, myth and mythos, image, cosmology, theology, philosophy. When I see the titles, obviously a lot happens for me. What connection is there between the titles and texts? And what connection is there between your various titles? And is there any influence from say, the Nation of Islam or your studies into the theology of Islam under the influence whoever you were in contact with when you were editor of *Muhammad Speaks*? I just keep seeing some connections.

LF: Well, it's a good question, because the titles are very intriguing, but I can say that because none of them were my own. That is to say that the titles I had for each of the books originally were probably not good titles. Toni Morrison, who was my editor at the time, said we'll have to get some titles different from these. And it was Toni's suggestion that the title of the first novel be *There is a Tree More Ancient Than Eden*. That comes strictly from her. And I gave her the names of about forty titles one weekend and they were all rejected. And she had another title one time too. It was called *Of Eden and Thebes*. That was a title she wanted to call it one time. Then the one I wanted to use was called *Deep Rivers of the Soul*.

EBR: Again for Eden.

LF: Yes, that's right. So I also had many others, but those two come to mind. But finally she suggested *There is a Tree More Ancient Than Eden*, which I really liked a lot. It seemed too that it was really close to the Negro spiritual "*There is a balm in Gilead*." It is evocative of so many things that you were mentioning: the crucifixion, the paradise lost kind of thing. So it was a very evocative title, and immediately when she suggested it, I liked it. The next book, I had a title for it too. And she said, "Well, listen, there may be a simpler title." Because you know this is all about the Bloodworth family. So it seemed to me to make sense. So just *The Bloodworth Orphans* was chosen because I wanted to concentrate on that. And since the book itself is long and multi-plotted and there are a lot of different entangled relationships. *Two Wings to Veil My Face*, I forget now what was the original title. I think one was *To Trouble the Waters This Morning*. Morrison didn't care for it that much and I didn't either. She said, "You know, you keep using this song in there, 'Angels got two wings to hide my face. Angels got two wings to fly me away.'" She suggested *Two Wings to Hide My Face*, one of the refrains from this song. I changed it and took the other one, *Two Wings to Veil My Face*, because the veil seemed to be much more poetic, much more elusive, much more suggestive of mask wearing and so on. Then the new book, I was originally going to call–Toni wasn't the editor for this new one–I was going to use the title *The Memoirs of Jubeart Jones*. This is his name, the main character, Jubeart. After a while that seemed to be a little, well, I tried it on people and people would sort of say, "Well, that's all right." And one of the churches in the novel is called Divine Days and there are other allusions to "Divine Days," so I said I'll try this one and everyone I've mentioned it to has said it's intriguing, this "Divine Days."

EBR: That is really informative and exciting. I don't know if I've ever been on such an odyssey before with an author concerning titles. This is one of the most enlightening experiences I've ever had. You and/or Toni came up with those titles, and they are very provocative, and very profound, really. As are your works. The use of myth is very evident, the application of folklore, the use and application of magic, and if I might say, mysticism, ancient things, ancient thoughts and so on. What do you think about myth and folklore and ancient texts? How are you feeling about those as you continue to write, since you apparently rely heavily on what are sometimes called things unknown?

LF: Well, some of it has to do with what I've found intriguing in the culture. Again, it's the culture that is the more important source that I seem to be attracted to as a writer. But the source is there and one of the sources is the idea, as you mentioned, of myth. Myth to me is the language attendant to the ritual. And my books are very much about rituals and about anti-rituals. Or about discovering rituals to sustain life, because one of the great, maybe even gifts, of Black Americans is their ability to reinvent life and make do out of nothing and then put a stamp of style or eloquence upon this reinventive mode. And the myth explains that. The myth reveals that. There's a lot of taboo breaking in Black life, but that's necessary. It's been necessary for us to survive and to put style to it. And style too has to do with myth. Then I guess too I'm attracted to it because of my own background in Catholicism, which really has a mythical quality to it with all the rituals in the Catholic Church and the grand language attended to it. I guess that the South for me has been a kind of mythical home because I don't know the South, but the South comes to me sort of secondhand the way maybe it does with Baldwin in *Go Tell It on the Mountain*. For me, the South is sort of the "Old Country" for African-Americans. So that perhaps if I knew it firsthand the way Wright knew it, it would be less awesome, less mythical. It's not mythical when you know that if you walk down that street, that white man's going to shoot you. So to me, in the sense of the lynching and what not, and I would hear a lot about this in my own family, but this was removed from the South here in the North. So it has that quality to it. It seemed to me too that there was always something larger than life in so many of the Black characters that I found I was attracted to or interested in long before I started writing. And these heroes and heroines were often times athletes, sometimes tricksters, sometimes hustlers. Often people who seemed to be larger than life with a very complex personality. I never saw enough of that in our fiction, of this complexity. So that was something that really bedeviled me when I began writing fiction, to try to get some of that complexity of Black life into my work. You know, when you talk to people and you say, "That's a complexity," and they say, "Oh, that's not complexity. That nigger's crazy." But looking at it from our perspectives as writers, we say this man is layered, he's moody, he's the thing you hear Black women talking about in bars, "I can't figure him out." That's complexity for the writer. One of the things I'm doing in this new book is a kind of mythical character who's always leaving the scene and coming back with new stories. There's always the story, "Well so-and-so won't be back," or "He's dead." Three months later, well here he appears again. Well that all is mixed up in my imagination with a kind of secular resurrection. He comes back with all these new stories, all these new travels, all these new women he's had, all these new scenes he's seen. There's so much of that, so much ingrained in the Black experience and that's what I've been so attracted to, these larger than life stories. In fact, our story itself is larger than life, if you consider it. And underneath, there's the reading of things that have influenced me like the Bible, and Ellison, and Faulkner.

EBR: Do you find any conflict at all in the multiplicity and the various uses of influences, I mean, across the racial and cultural spectrum? Some writers talk about renouncing or pulling away from influences that are not culturally amenable or culturally similar. I know you mix them in. And whether that's good or great, you accept the influence. Can you say anything at all about that?

LF: I'll steal anything I can get my hands on, man, because everything's been stolen from us. And people keep on stepping and making a lot of money off it. I think there are unconscious things that happen in the imagination because long before you start reading you've seen a lot and these things influenced you. But I'm very moved by the Russian writers and I've learned a lot from them. Wherever I can get influence, wherever I can be moved by something, maybe I can use it. To me, it's like if we were surgeons we wouldn't even be talking about this. We would be saying, "Say, you know, the Chinese have made a breakthrough over here. Africans have made a breakthrough over here. I just met this interesting Indian doctor the other day and he told me something about a certain new technique." This is what we're talking about, where I can get new techniques. So I don't have any problem with that at all, but I think a lot of younger people do. Well, it's too bad.

EBR: This is very helpful. It places a lot in perspective and helps to frame ...

LF: *I'm* at war with myself on a lot of levels, but that's not a war I'm in, about influences and hang-ups and problems.

EBR: You probably addressed this already, but not under the rubric which I am going to suggest it right now. First, do you agree that a good writer or a great writer needs a system of art? I think you outlined something like that a little earlier. And if you do, do you 1) impress this upon writers you train and 2) are you constantly and consciously working out of a system of art?

LF: Yeah, I like that term too, because one of the nice advantages I had when I was starting writing rather seriously was that I was involved with the musicians, jazz musicians, painters, academics, and also I was involved with a lot of people who had dropped out of college and were still very interested in reading; films of all kinds, and all of that was useful. So I think that the writer should be one who nourishes himself or herself in all kinds of other areas of the arts. Certainly, you will be exposed to other writers. That's understandable, but talk to other people in other disciplines. For example, I'm a good friend of Richard Hunt, the sculptor, and sometimes we talk about the process of creativity and it's very enlightening to me because here we do something so different, yet there are a lot of similarities. We believe in work in progress, of leaving something alone and coming back to it, coming back to it with new energies. But again, this goes back to the earlier question you asked about exposing yourself to all kinds of artistic creations. I think the problem for the writer is to develop a rich inner life. That's secret. That's private. What's a rich inner life for me might not be a rich inner life for you. You never know when you talk to a writer. He or she might come on with a big spiel about this or that, but they might not have a rich inner life. Maybe someone over here is rather quiet and may have found the sources to develop a rich inner life. That rich inner life can come from a vast amount of experience, travel, reading, talking to all kinds of people, learning to be a good listener, religion, having a certain stability of home life, having established a certain continuity or pattern of behavior, having a sense of cultural history. All these things you carry within yourself in a certain fragile way that nobody knows about. Learning to develop a secret inner life that's highly contemplative. So all these are sources that go into the imagination of the writer.

EBR: Again, quite strong and quite full. Stemming or flowing from this idea of an art system, what about mission? Are they one and the same? Are you often conscious of a mission when you're writing? If so, is the mission in the head more than it is in the writing? Is it in the work that's ancillary to writing? Is it in the writing itself? If indeed you see a mission, and I'm thinking of this in the broadest possible context.

LF: Yeah, yeah. Well mission isn't a bad word, because there is a sense or feeling of a kind of calling after a while. That may sound a little self-serving. But really if you survive a certain amount of time, . . . for example when I look at all the people I knew who wanted to write, but never wrote, or who stopped writing, and somehow I'm still writing, I'm still struggling. That's got to make you feel, "Well maybe there is something, maybe I do have a calling." And then I think the older you get, if you survive that long and have published a little bit, you begin like I do to have a certain responsibility: maybe I've wasted a lot of time, maybe I should even be more cautious with my talent, with my mission as you're saying. And that mission is for me first of all to try to develop my talent the best I can, and I guess a certain level of mission is to try to add to the body of literature of my people and hopefully to influence the national literature. I wouldn't have said that as a younger person, because writing was still sort of fun. I wasn't sure about it. But I do feel through some sense that I've survived this far and, as they say, as certain preachers say, "The Lord wasn't through with me yet."

EBR: When you said that you've survived this far, it seemed that there was a silent sigh there and at the same time a silent hurrah. I wonder how a statement that Toni Morrison made sits with you. She said, "The writing is very difficult and very dangerous." We know it's difficult. She said it's very dangerous. She was quoted in Ebony magazine, and she has made this statement repeatedly. "Very difficult and very dangerous." Would you concur or cosign that? And how would you embellish it?

LF: Well, I don't know concretely what she's talking about, but I would say too that writing is dangerous in the sense that it opens you up to avenues that are not predictable when you first started writing a short story or a novel. Morrison of course is an extraordinarily imaginative writer and writes out of the powers of the imagination and I certainly try to write out of the powers of the imagination. And that means that you don't know where that imagination might take you or what it might unleash within you. And what it unleashes in you might be all kinds of chaos and all kinds of unpredictable and even dangerous perceptions about life and the human condition, race relations, the relationship between men and women; and you wouldn't have predicted it in just normal conversation. The life of the artist is dangerous, and that is why I was talking about just surviving. The artist, maybe even particularly writers, is often times self-destructive. So to try to deal with developing your talent but also deal with your own vulnerabilities and your own weaknesses, that's something to overcome too. Also to have the LUCK to live. You can have the terrible tragedy that happened to your friend [Henry] Dumas. If you have the luck to live and you don't have a terrible illness like Lorraine Hansberry or Frank London Brown or so many talented people like that. If you can survive not drinking yourself to death or dope or sexual vagrancy, all the things that can trap the individual, this means that you've developed a certain kind of toughness. Artists tend to be very destructive, so that you've got to turn those engines over into your creativity, as opposed to those areas of your life that will actually destroy you. That's been a great problem for our great jazz musicians. Charlie Parker, for example, not being able to control that great furor to create. It consumed him.

EBR: We are pressing on in our effort to understand literature and the machinations of the mind and the techniques and devices of the writer. I've used the word intrigue quite a bit, but I *am* intrigued by your work and by your life. I'm interested in how you work, the manner in which you work, your use of discipline. I know it's a severe discipline, "a very stern discipline," as Ralph Ellison calls it. How do you work? What tools do you use? Do you use longhand, computer, typewriter? Do you work at night, in the mornings? Do you outline stuff and work later? Or do you just use a stream of consciousness thing and then go back and reshape?

LF: Well I try to write in the morning, and I find the older I get the better it is to write in the morning. Usually, about 6:30 or 7:00. I'll try to write as long as I can, maybe 'til 11, stop, maybe do something else, have lunch, and then write if I have the energy, but generally I don't, and I'll probably read in the evening. I find that if you can get three, three and a half, four hours of writing in a day, of intense writing, that's something, because writing takes so much energy. And that energy is not only physical. It's intellectual. And that's different from the painter. A lot of what the painter does is the stroke itself, just filling in spaces. So painters can sometimes paint all day. There's also the fun of painting. Writing is pleasurable. It's not fun to me, I don't think. So it takes a lot of energy to write. It takes a lot of concentration. I usually work from a very general, loose outline, then I'll write a scene over and over again until I get sick of it, then put it away, leave it alone for a long time and then come back to it in maybe two or three weeks or a month later, and then I come to it with a certain kind of coldness, a certain kind of tough-mindedness, I hope. So those are some of the ways I write. Endless rewriting, putting it away and coming back. And another thing for the writer to develop is a sense of living with loneliness, since writing is so lonely. You may be working on something for a long time without showing it to anyone. While if you're a painter, your natural impulse is to have people in to look at what you're doing. Certainly if you're a composer, you'll say, "Here's a tape of something. You can put it in your car and listen to it." But writing seems to be something you've got to sit down and look at, and read, and we don't have that one on one communication with your audience in the way that the other arts do. And yet, you have to be clever enough as a writer, particularly as a Black artist, to use these other arts. We've accomplished so much in the area of music, of course, and a writer would be foolish not to try to learn a lot about Black music because that's perhaps the art closest to the African-American consciousness, at least that's historically been true. Also, the dance is another area we've accomplished so much in, and it's perhaps one of the closest gauges of our consciousness as a people. So the writer needs to be able to draw on those areas of his culture, her culture, where we have accomplished on a very consequent level.

EBR: It's quite a scheme, quite a paradigm for how we work as artists generally, as we move down the scale to how the writer works in the overall sense and specifically how you work. W. H. Auden said, "No poem is ever finished. It is only abandoned." How do you know when a work by you is finished for any number of reasons, either you're not going to take it any further, you're not going to show it, or it's ready to be shown or to be published, assuming there is a publisher around? When do you know a work should be abandoned?

LF: Well, that does involve a certain amount of risk taking and there's the danger that you might just be exhausted, you as a writer. That's why it's important to put things away and come back to them, and come back with new energies. But maybe more specifically, I can tell with a character when all of the questions I have raised or should have raised about the character and his character in process have been resolved and his energies seem to be spent in the plot. I'm very interested in this novel, *Divine Days*, and I have been since my first novel, in the idea of the character not only in process but also in evolvement, so that it's necessary to put a character through many scenes to draw out all the sides of him or her. So I can usually tell if it [novel] seems to have resolved all of the questions that I can think are demanded of this character in terms of his own quest or the quest of the plot. Now that inherently demands that you put the book away, that you put the manuscript away for a while, and come back and say, "Wait a minute. There's something else demanded of him that I haven't asked and has not been resolved yet." Those are the ways in general in which I feel a sense of closure or completion. In this novel, the new novel, it's so very long and I have so many plots going on, but I have a sense, in reading the galleys anyway, that I have brought into fruition the different plots and brought them into resolution. How successful this resolution is, how eloquent it is, that I don't know. At least I feel relatively comfortable that I've brought all these strands of the plot together.

EBR: What do you see down the line? I think of that folk saying immortalized by Baldwin, "I looked down the line and I wondered." Do you look forward to retiring and then writing? And is retiring in the near future? Will you write only fiction and some non-fiction prose? Will you write plays? What's in the future for you as a writer and as a person?

LF: Well, I don't think I would think about retiring yet and I still want to teach. As far as writing goes, I want to continue writing novels and more than anything else, that's the dearest. I could see maybe one or two novels already in mind in a general way that I'd like to write. I've kind of enjoyed the two careers, but as we were talking earlier, I'd prefer to have more time to write and perhaps less time to teach.

EBR: I think that's a statement that sums up the situation for most of us who are academicians cum writers, or writers cum academicians. Is there a specific project that you are looking at, or is this question too soon behind *Divine Days?*

LF: Well, no. I've already started working on something new. And then there was a lot that didn't go into in *Divine Days.* There's at least 150 pages I cut from the manuscript. The manuscript was 18,029 pages. And with the cuts and everything, the finished novel is 1,135. But there's a lot that didn't go into it, and I hope to use that in another work. So, there's work to be done. The problem is to find the energy.

EBR: I have one last question of you, Leon. I'm most grateful to you and humbled by your great work and the good thinking that has gone in to produce you and all the good stuff around you. Would you indicate by name some of the most indelible influences on your work. Eras, periods, types of writing? Writers? And when you do that, would you also note writers today, kind of star some writers who you feel are doing some things today, whether or not they've influenced you? Who's out there now and what and who is helping to make up what we call American literature, world literature, Black literature, multi-cultural literature?

LF: I guess mainly I've been influenced by what you might call the poets of the novel: Thomas Hardy, William Faulkner and Ralph Ellison. And then to a large degree, too, I was influenced earlier by poets. Auden and Dylan Thomas are among the ones who have really influenced me a lot. And more towards the recent twenty years, I would say the Russian writers for characterization and for depth of the human agony and this whole problem of how do you create a character with these questions of spiritual and political and ideological anguish. Then, maybe even recently, the Latin American writers like Donoso and Marquez and Borges. These are writers who create these mythical worlds. They've also given me a lot of confidence in dealing with my own Catholicism, since Catholicism is really a minority strand in the Black American experience. So those are some of the writers who've influenced me generally over the years. As for contemporary writers, I might not be as good there. You tend to read certain types of writers you like over again. But the ones I still admire would be Henry Dumas. I like him. I'm still interested in so many things he published, and so many things that weren't published. Morrison of course. The problem too with teaching is that you tend to reread the books you're teaching over a period of time and you aren't as adventuresome as you might be. I think what has happened to me in the last couple of years is that I haven't been doing enough reading because I've been so consumed with trying to finish this novel. So there are a lot of new writers I want to read, like [Carl] Phillips and [Terry] McMillan and [Trey] Ellis. I have found a lot in the work of the stage plays too of the author of *Ma Rainey's Black Bottom* and *Joe Turner*, August Wilson. I really like the kind of rowdy power in those scenes of his. Those are some of the influences. I think more of the influence of individual books than I do writers. For instance, I certainly don't like all of Faulkner, but a novel like *Absalom, Absalom!* had a great deal of influence on me. I don't know all of Thomas Hardy, but I like *Return of the Native* and *Tess of D'Urbervilles;* and some of the Russian writers have been very influential. Particularly in doing long fiction, the Russians are great. Maybe it's those Russian winters; they don't have anything to do but read. The American writers have not really stretched out and tried to do big novels, in the sense of the great novels of the 19th century. I don't know quite why that is. Maybe it's just the impact of the visual age and people just don't seem to have the time. A lot of those novels [19th century] were published in newspapers, as scenarios in newspapers, and newspapers don't do that anymore, hardly. Only occasionally.

EBR: I said that last question would be the last one, but I do have one more, and it's regarding aspiring, developing and emerging writers and your advice to them. What would you, what do you say to writers who are new, not necessarily young because some writers come to the craft in middle age or even in senior age, but what do you have to say to writers aspiring, developing, professional, even mature writers seeking to expand, to probe, to extrapolate those jewels, to mine those fields of experience and other literatures? What do you say?

LF: I was laughing at what you're saying because I was in an organization and there was a wealthy woman, and she said she wanted to help young writers, she had just been talking about dancers, these were people 18, 19 years old. We were trying to convince her she wasn't going to get any young writers who publish who are 18, 19. Young writers? We would consider someone in their early 30s a young writer.

Writers do develop later than the other arts. I would say that anything to develop the imagination, that's your strongest tool. You have to treat it with tender loving care. Read a lot. Get a lot of different varied experiences. That is to say, when you're young, do all kinds of volunteer work in hospitals, in senior citizens homes. That would be a great thing, for instance to read to someone who's blind. Just to read. Try to move away from whatever is the trend. On the other hand, there's always much to be learned from being a bartender or a waiter. Try to find jobs where you aren't drained so that you have time to write when you get home and to read when you get home. If you have a job where you have to bring a lot of work home, that's going to drain you. A young writer has to be willing to make the sacrifices, and those sacrifices are obviously money; and you have to delay a certain level of natural fulfillment. A good thing would be to learn to develop a good ear for listening and to listen to all kinds of conversation. The other things would be to take a good personal assessment of yourself and to find out your weaknesses and your strengths as a person. A lot of times, I would know people who would give away some great lines in bars – they wanted to write, but ended up always writing in the bar, emptying themselves out in the bar. Or maybe someone else has got a problem of running after women. Or somebody else is a heavy drinker. Or another person just doesn't seem to have the discipline. Or maybe another person just doesn't have good health and needs to learn to try to take care of that. It's good to learn and know your strengths and your weaknesses and to learn to work around those. And to develop, if you can, sustain patterns of relationships and friendships. Those are things you borrow on over time. Also, I guess, as a Black writer, to learn the traditions of our people, as I was mentioning earlier, in the dance, in music, as well as in those areas that are strong in the race that you aren't attracted to. For instance, say you're an atheist. That's your business, but you'd better learn something about church, because that's so deep in the history of the race. Also to find the sources that haven't been written about. You were talking earlier about going around and talking with people like the Elks and so on. That's a whole area of culture that hasn't been investigated. It behooves the writer to find out about those sources that haven't been investigated that much and to write about them.

EBR: Thanks very much, Leon. That was very inclusive. Any writer with his/her wits about him listening to what you just said ought to be able to carry the bacon on in. Leon, you are, among other things, an urban writer. This is not a statement meant to type, of course, but you do work out of an urban setting? – though one would be hard pressed to lock you into any setting since the experiential and experimental, seem to work quite well, almost interchangeably, interdependently and interrelatedly in your work. What do you think about these cities, the struggle in these cities, the people in these cities, the art in these cities, the language in these cities? What are your thoughts about cities? Cities dying? Cities living? Cities coming back? Cities fading?

LF: Well, I guess I was going to say too at the end of the things to the writer, that maybe the Black writer needs to find out his or her relationship to other ethnic groups. Just as we are much concerned now with our relationship with Africa and our African past, we need to know our relationship to the growing Hispanic population. The dwindling, but still very powerful, white population, white ethnics in the city. Then how can that be translated into political authority and might. And to try to find some new techniques for survival. Because you go to these conferences, and always the theme is "Where do we go from here?" That's been going on since Malcolm died. So, nobody has any new answers. One of the things I did like about the civil rights movement was that at least people were addressing techniques for how to deal with white power. Now all we need is bright people to come along with new techniques for how to deal with our problems in the cities. I guess, from a perspective of people like ourselves, it would certainly have to do with the importance of reading, of course, because we've got to see that it is one of the tools we've got to use to help free ourselves. So massive programs to bring in reading, almost to force young people to read, and to see that this is an important part of our liberation. That's one thing. Maybe, to approach this problem with great humility and say, "Well, look, you know, best I talk about reading and writing since that's the only thing I've proven I could do. I cannot tell you about government or anything else." Try to have people to bring in their expertise in a specific way, rather than these people who get up and give you this great sermon on our problems and in the meanwhile ain't told you nothing new.

EBR: Thank you, again, for observations on the city, survival and struggle, possible innovative looks and approaches to uplift and self-reliance, multi-culturalism and so forth.

Chicago-based poet and literary activist Luis Rodriguez listens to students after his reading at Southern Illinois University at Edwardsville, April 1992.

"BEARING WITNESS UNDER SIEGE"

An Interview with Luis Rodriguez
by Eugene B. Redmond

EUGENE B.REDMOND: It is right around noon on Wednesday, April 8th, Luis, you're in East St. Louis, Illinois, and you've appeared in a variety of venues over the last twenty-four hours. You came in Monday night, and we started off early Tuesday morning with the radio interview. You were called at your hotel room at the Best Inns, and then you went on to speak at SIUE to an SRO crowd of students, faculty, staff people, and seriously aspiring writers; and you conducted a workshop in the afternoon, and later did a reading and workshop in East St. Louis at State Community College. And just this morning you spoke to–oh, I guess there must have been about 75 gifted elementary and early high school students at A.M. Jackson School in East St. Louis. How is what you're doing here similar to or different from what you've been doing in other places, Luis?

LUIS RODRIGUEZ: Well, it's been similar because I've been fortunate that I've been coming into communities like East St. Louis. These are cities that are pretty much being written off by the government, but are vibrant communities. People have a lot of creativity; they're doing a lot of important work, and they're unsung kinds of works. So in that sense it's very similar, and I am really glad that I was able to get into the schools and talk to people, off the beaten track, as they say, you know, because it's good for a poet to not just be talking to other poets, but talk to the community, and I'm looking forward to coming back here again and opening up even more areas of the community. To me, this is the key thing about having been here, that I've seen so much about East St. Louis, and cut through all of the bad rap and hype that you've got to go through all the time.

EBR: Yeah, thank you ... that's a fairly comprehensive response, and I think I speak for most of the people who've heard you, that we'll be eagerly awaiting your return to speak again to people with whom you've communed while you were here this time, and to share with an even wider and newer audience. How do you feel about the response to you as a poet, as a multicultural person? I know that you go among various people. Here, you spoke to, on the one hand, a predominantly white audience, an Anglo audience, and on the other hand, a predominantly Black audience, and there was a mixed audience last night. How do you feel about the response to you, and what does it say?

LR: I'm going to give another lengthy response. I don't know; I'm very pleased. I find that despite the differences of people there's something that's tying, linking us up as a community. And I think it's tapping into the poetry that every one of us has, that every one of us needs to express. Every community is going through some devastation, and if you can touch that like a resonant chord, and really link up with that, I think you get a good response. Somehow, when I talk about my experience and what I go through, it tends to touch some of these people, and, hopefully, it begins to open them up. So I've found all of the audiences very receptive, and I'm very pleased that all of them were very into it, ... and good questions, good engagement, good discussion.

EBR: Okay, does the East St. Louis-Edwardsville experience compare or contrast in your mind to any specific place to which you've been recently, any particular terrain or atmosphere or environment?

LR: Well, you know, it's very close to what I saw in cities like Gary, Indiana, another devastated community, where the steel mills have basically closed down most of their operations and boarded up buildings. It's similar to what you see in Michigan – Flint and Ann Arbor and Lansing – these places that were thriving communities because there was industry and people came in to live, and now they basically don't have anything hanging on, nothing productive anymore. So more and more I see a lot of communities like East St. Louis. I think East St. Louis, though, is particularly devastated and is under attack. It's one of the few communities run by Blacks, and I think that it's under siege, and it's important for people to see that, because it's terrible what's going on as far as the way people respond to East St. Louis, and I think that's important to point out. But more and more I've seen a lot of cities like this, just falling apart, and very little hope, and very little investment, but there's still a lot of spirit among the people.

EBR: Thank you again. You spoke of siege; that's a very strong word – I think a very good word – contextually speaking. What is your role, specifically, and what is the role of the artist or poet generally in a predicament of siege, when he or she – that is, the artist or poet – is speaking out of a condition of siege, speaking to people who are under siege?

LR: I think it becomes a very vital role. One is, of course, we always talk about bearing witness; we need the writers and artists to bear witness to this crisis and what's going on. But the other thing, too, is that I think we need to integrate ourselves with that community. There's too much separation between the artists and poets and what's going on day by day in people's lives, and we need to integrate with that, participate with them – not just talk to people, but talk with them and through them, and I think that we need to get artists to participate in figuring the way out of this stuff. Where are we going to go from here? What does the future hold? And through my art I think I can help, at least point the way to some ideas as to where we need to go, and just illuminate what's going on. Art can dramatize a lot of these situations.

EBR: I wonder, Luis, do you see a deepening, a widening of the poet's role – speaking now in April of 1992 – as a result of the siege of which we've been speaking?

LR: Absolutely. I think that in all crises the artist plays a role. In general, when things are pretty stable artists kind of don't seem that important for some reason, but when communities are in crisis the way that we're seeing them, all of a sudden creativity seems to burst out; writers come forward, artists come forward, musicians come forward, and I think that's very important, and I see it now, more and more. More poets, more people interested in trying to do something through the arts. So I'm really excited because I really hadn't seen this in twenty years since the '60s, you know? In the '60s we had this big explosion, right? And for about twenty years it didn't happen. Now I'm beginning to see it again.

EBR: That was cogent and I think quite poignant. What is the situation now with multicultural artists, with multicultural people, and this sudden revival of interest in the Native American or indigenous American experiences? Is it good or bad, or both, and how is it working for the artist, and how is it working for the cultures themselves, in a general sense?

LR: Well, I think the 500-year celebration for the so-called discovery of America by Columbus is doing the opposite of what the government and some people wanted it to do. They wanted to use this as a way to celebrate primarily the European contribution to America, as America coming *to be* once the Europeans came here. But I think it's turned into something else. It's turned into a debate about culture itself and about the role of the Native Americans and the Africans and the Latinos that are in this country, the Asians. It's becoming a national debate of whether there is a role for us, or whether we're going to be excluded continually, or whether we're going to be part of the stew that is America, because it's not one culture, and it's not one people; it's the amalgamation of so many different people. So I think in this sense, this is a good time. As far as what it means for us, it means that there are some opportunities beginning to open up, not many, but some, for people of color to have their place among the artistic community. But it's not enough yet. I think we're going to have to keep struggling; it's going to be a fight, because it's not going to be easy to have us be integral to the whole artistic community.

EBR: Yes, I can see where you're coming from and how you're looking at this phenomenon. Where do you think art generally is going in this country – we're talking, of course, in multicultural terms, I would say in cross-gender terms – we're talking about creative expression and struggle. Are there any new vistas or horizons for art and artists? Can you connect the literary artist's activities to the popular culture?

LR: Well, one, I think the official canon is changing. There's going to be a multiplicity of forms, I think that we're going to see, of flavors, of colors, a tapestry of varied quilts. But the key thing is that it's not going to be marginalized as much; it's not going to be the "other." We're beginning to enter into the mainstream and change it. And you're going to see the canon shifting. The center is shifting, from a European-based cultural expression to something more worldwide – which doesn't **exclude** Europeans; it means that it includes the rest of the world in the milieu of culture. This is a very important development; I think there's going to be a lot of opposition to it, a lot of scared people, people who don't want to see this happening. But that's fine. I think this is the way it's going to go; the center is shifting.

EBR: I see, I see. I'm thinking now, in line with what we've been discussing, of the question of continuity, of cultural continuities. And I know that in the African-American cultures we speak of something called the African Continuum, Afrocentricity. Do you see yourself as a writer, activist, person of Mexican extraction, but who is an American, as part of a continuum? Do you link in with a long line, and if so, can you kind of suggest how far back you go, and how that continuum – if indeed you see yourself as part of one – continues to activate, actualize, realize itself in your work and in you?

LR: Yeah, I think so. And I think it' s going way back; it's going back to the first peoples in the continent. We're in the Americas, and the Latin people represent something valuable to the Americas, in that we have this thing called *mestizo.* I don't know if it's used that much among other people, and the whole idea behind *mestizo* is that the Latin people are a mixture of ***all*** peoples.

EBR: Is that *mestizo*?

LR: Yes, that we have the native culture. It's in our blood. We have the European; it's in our blood. We have the Africans who were brought in as slaves throughout the Americas, and that's in our blood, because, unlike the northern part of the continent, in Latin America we mixed with them much more. In the northern part they kept a strict separation. Even so, there was some mixture. So the Latin people are really a great mixture; really, I think that's the future in many ways of the whole continent, and possibly the world, that we come in as brown people, but within our brownness is the mixture of all these various elements. I understand that, for example, the second largest Japanese population is in Brazil, that even the Asians have come in there and mixed very well. So we can go back to the first peoples, and we can still take in from the other peoples who have come to our continent, and we are the **new** race, the mixture of people that now come forth as Mexican and Puerto Rican, from where, you know, we've got these various elements within us. I think that this is an important thing that I see as my continuity--that I may want to touch all these cultures and still be a whole new being, a whole new person.

EBR: That again is quite comprehensive and it segues – if I can use a theatrical term – into this idea of cultural pluralism and diversity. Speaking of cultural bases and continuities again, would you hazard a comparison or contrast of the communities of Los Angeles and Chicago, based on this idea of multiculturalism, pluralism, and cultural diversity?

LR: Yeah, well, one thing is that Los Angeles is really becoming a world city. It's got one of the greatest mixtures of cultures and peoples of any part of the country, probably second to New York. The thing that I find about L.A., though, is that it's also linked to the Pacific Rim. Somebody said it's probably connected more to Asia than it is to the United States, because of the shipping and intercourse between Japan and Korea and all of these other countries and L.A.; it's becoming a much more vital Asian center. It's also a big link for Latin America; the largest Latin American population in the U.S. is in L.A., even greater than in New York, and greater than in Miami, which are the next two big ones. So L.A. has all that.

Chicago, ... what's really interesting about Chicago is that it really is the heart of America. You realize that all of the railroad tracks meet there. You got people from the South, you got people from the East, you got a lot of Latin people, you got a large native Indian population, so you're getting at the heart of America when you're in Chicago. Very industrial, but even when that industry dies, that Midwest center is there; the people still have the flavor of being hard-working people, working on the land, working in industry, and it's still there, and I think it reflects itself in the culture. Significantly, it was also the first city in which a Black mayor rose out from among the communities themselves and Mayor Washington was a very important phenomenon, I think, for the whole country. To have been there and seen it myself, I feel very privileged, because he was a hell of a man, because he wasn't just a politician; he really came from the community, and there was a power struggle, a real struggle for power, that took place, and one of the few times in our history, the community won. Unfortunately, it's been set back since his death. But it was an important taste of victory that I think other people around the country should recognize how important Chicago has been in politics.

EBR: What about the corollary and ancillary aspects of the culture and the cultural expression? I'm thinking, we talk about writing, we talk about creative expression generally. What about things like cuisine, style in the community, peer group relationships, dress, music, again popular culture – magazines people read and music they dance to. Where do they go and what do they do to have fun? Can you speak about that in L.A. and Chicago?

LR: Sure. I think it's all being infused with the communities of color's contributions. In the music, I don't care if it's a white audience primarily or whatever, they're getting a multicultural flavor. Through the music, through the clothes that they wear, the styles came from our communities in various ways. I see a lot more color, for example, in peoples' clothes; in Africa and in other native cultures it's very popular to have multi-colored clothes, and I see it now in people walking down the street. Sometimes they don't even know that it comes from these communities, but it's important to point out that we're infusing every aspect of American culture, everywhere. Even our literature is starting to infuse every aspect of the literary scene. In spite of that, we're still marginalized. That's the contradiction – that we're still put in the margins of mainstream culture – so it's kind of an ironic dichotomy that we have to deal with; but I think the fact that even white kids rap says a lot about how important the culture is from the communities of color.

EBR: Thank you. Yes, so the style of multicultural people, as you say, is very pervasive in this culture, very observable. Turning to the subject of writers and literature, can you name some of the writers who've had an influence on you in your early development and perhaps who continue to influence you, and talk about how they influenced you, what you feel you got from them, who introduced you to them, what were your reading habits, how have your reading habits evolved into writing habits, and so on?

LR: I started off actually picking up books that were the most relevant to me when I was a teenager, and those were the books from the Black experience. I remember *Man-child in the Promised Land* (Claude Brown). I remember Piri Thomas' *Down These Mean Streets*, *The Autobiography of Malcolm X*. I mean surprisingly people wouldn't know that, but there were no other books at the time; there were no Chicano books, very little Puerto Rican, so I gravitated to these books. Later on, you know, when other people were being published – Jose Montoya's one book, I remember, Pedro Pietri, and people like that – then I would pick up those books, and I learned a lot.

Over the past ten years, I think I started going back to some of the classics that are really important, but when I was growing up I didn't care for them because they seemed so irrelevant. People like Walt Whitman and Emily Dickinson, and Emerson and people that are good to read now, because I can look at them – and I can learn from what they contributed. Shakespeare even – these are important people to know; whether you like them or not, it's just good to know what the English language has done before.

Nowadays, I read a lot of Native American writers who are coming up. Joy Harjo, I picked up one of her books – very powerful; Lucy Tapahonso, a Navajo writer, I picked up her book – she's from Arizona, I think, or New Mexico. I'm also looking into international literature; I've always been a fan of Pablo Neruda and Garcia Lorca from Spain, and, of course, Garcia Marquez. I'm now reading some French writers, Artaud, Rimbaud, Baudelaire. I'm trying to internationalize my understanding of literature. I picked up Mishima from Japan. It's important, I think, that your horizons get broadened all the time. I feel that my community of writers is really international. So anything in translation I try to pick up, so I can get a better feel for what's going on. I picked up some Caribbean-based writers when I was in London – so that's important. Anyway, I think that's really where I'm at now, and again it's a mixture – it's a very big mixture – because I've learned not to be very systematic about my reading, but just pick up everything and learn as I go along, because I didn't go through school and learn anything systematic. I have so many books, and I pick up bits and pieces here and there. But I think it helps me.

EBR: Yeah, I think you need an encyclopedic or catholic command of literature, especially if you're going to teach it and suggest models and so on. I think it's very useful, the training that you have undergone and are continuing to undergo. I don't think we ever stop being students. Can you describe the literary scene in Chicago, the poetry scene in Chicago? We hear a lot about poetry slams, now, and competitive poetry readings.

LR: Well, it's a very interesting phenomenon, and I don't think that there's any city in the country that has this at the level Chicago has it. But what it is, is that almost every night in Chicago there's about four or five places in which you can go into a bar or cafe or somewhere and read poetry. It's open mikes; the slams occur every Sunday at the Green Mill –

EBR: What is a slam?

LR: What it is, is poets come in and compete with each other. They actually have judges picked from the audience; they go from one to ten. They have one poet competing against another, poem for poem, and the judges choose. And it goes on for several weeks. You can win the Mini-Slam; you can win the Grand-Slam; you can be the Chicago Slam Champion. And now it's become national. They have seven or eight cities that come once a year together to do a national slam, and then that person becomes the National Slam Champion. So it's starting to spread, and I think what's good about it is that it's not just within the white community, even though the white community plays a big part in it. We have readings in the Black community, in the Latino community; some of the key major players in the poetry community in Chicago are African American, Puerto Rican, and Chicano. So we're at the heart of it, unlike other cities where it seems there's a big separation, and you have the literary scene, and every once in a while they bring in people of color to kind of blend in. But basically it's a white scene, though I think St.Louis might be an exception. But still most cities are like that. Chicago is very much mixed in with all these various communities.

EBR: Thank you again for another very enlightening dissertation on the poetry scene, and especially the performance poetry scene in Chicago. We're still exploring this idea of literature, writing, and writers. Maybe we can get a bit more specific, and perhaps futuristic, about you and your work, Luis. Where do you see your work going now, what do you see yourself as having been, and what kind of foundation has that provided for where you're going? Are you going to do new things? I understand you'll have a memoir coming out soon – will there be any new poems? Will there be a novel? Will there be plays? Will there be more memoirs? Just where are you going with your work, and you future, your career, your life?

LR: Right now the poetry's been going very well, so I'm really going to be playing off that for a long time. I'm going to do a lot of readings, and my two books are going to help, you know I'm going to keep doing that. But I've got to branch out, because I think that a writer needs to be broad and be good at various forms. The memoir will be out hopefully next year. I've got a book of essays that I'm working on now, trying to get that published, and then I've got a screenplay that I'm working on with somebody. I'm working on some plays, you know, trying to really broaden my horizons as far as writing goes. Though I think the poetry will be the center of what I do, because it's just been very good--I've done pretty good, and I want to continue doing poetry. So my future is to do that. The other thing too is that I want to be able to do these workshops – I'm finding a lot of people who want to do the same thing. Get into these communities that are "not poetic communities," and get poetry out of them. Because I really believe that there shouldn't be a separation of poetry and literature and art from the community. The only way to do that, though, is to get the people themselves to do the poetry, to work out their own lives, and bear witness to their own times. And hopefully I might expand in some of these communities that I'm beginning to come across, in these area shelters, youth detention centers, and schools; wherever we can do it.

EBR: Again you were broad and inclusive, not only about your own writing, but where you might go. Do you see yourself staying in Chicago for an indefinite period of time? Do you ever consider relocating back to East L.A., or moving to another part of the country, or out of the country?

LR: Right now I don't have plans to leave Chicago. Chicago's been good to me, and I love it there. But there is a possibility that I might go to Mexico for a couple of years. Immerse myself in the language; get closer to the language that I need to get back to. And start writing some stuff in Spanish, because there's a whole world out there that I'm not even tapping into, by not speaking Spanish or writing in Spanish. This will probably be done in the future, and I anticipate that I am someday going to be going back to East L.A., because that really is my roots, and a lot of what I write about is still based there. But right now I got no plans. I like Chicago because it's central to everything, so that from there I can travel all over the place. Do I want to do a lot of international traveling, go to Europe again, go to Latin America, maybe Africa? I would love to go to as many places as I can.

EBR: As we continue our tour, along the scenic Lake Drive which fronts Lake Park, now Frank Holten Park, and some of the most beautiful homes in the city of East St. Louis, I wonder what reflections you have on having come through the fiery passage of writing, across the "grid," through the grist-mill required of the journeyman, of the person who would take the oath of poetry, seek the knighthood of literature and struggle. How have you seen this ordeal in personal terms, and on the strength of that, what advice do you have for writers seeking to do the same?

LR: Well, for me, being a poet has given me a great responsibility. I don't feel that I am a poet separate from my community, and every day my community gets larger and larger, and I feel more and more responsible to use my poetry and literature to express what that community is going through in whatever form that I can. I think that's a really important development with literature because in this country, for the most part, literature is separate from these kinds of issues that make it a personal thing. So the artist is a special person who goes around trying to create his own work. But I do just the opposite; the audience and community have created me, therefore I feel responsible for that. It doesn't mean that I can't get good at the art; it just means that I take that on my shoulders as part of what I do when I write. As far as what I would say to writers, you know, I think that the best thing to do is to look for the inner truth, to get to the heart of the matter and bring that out, to never lie about the heart of the matter. You can lie about other aspects, but never about the heart of what's going on. And I think more poets need to get closer to that truth. It's risky, it's dangerous ground; sometimes it's scary when you start walking that ground truth, but it's the best one right now. We have so many lies in politics and church; I mean it really is so many people telling you these lies and we need poetry to be the one place where people can find the truth of their times. So I would encourage writers to be open to that truth.

EBR: Speaking of truth and the heart of the matter, would you chance a definition or description of three things: truth, the heart of the matter, and poetry? You can weave 'em together if you like.

LR: Okay. You ask some difficult questions (laughing) in this short period of time that I have. But you know, what it is that you've got to get back to the fundamentals. This is a very complex society; we get so many images thrown at us, the media is more important, the pragmatic, and we've got to get back to some fundamentals. What are human beings here for on this Earth? Basically, we're here to reproduce ourselves, but that means that we're here for our children, that means that we've got to guarantee that the next generation has it better than us, and that's not what's happening. And so I think that everything – economics, politics, culture – has to start going back to preparing the way for a future in which every human being, every child, reaches his or her full, complete, creative being. That, I think, is a very important task that we've all got to do, and I find it in myself, the more that I try to do the most that I can; try to be as literate, as intelligent, as spiritual, and as literary as I can be. I'm trying to prove by example that anybody can do this – and do it a lot better than me. It's not a question of only certain talented, special, superior beings doing the art and poetry, and I'm proof of that. I tell people that my intelligence is average or below average, I got nothing special about me, I'm just a regular smoe, but I can do poetry because it's in me. It's not something I have to make up; it's there and I just need to find the outside world confidence to do it and learn from other people. So, I don't know, I think that – I don't know if that weaves in all the points you wanted to get into, but I think it's important. You know, I would say that we ought to get to the point where art and literature are not tied to marketplace values; it's not tied to the marketplace or whether you can make a profit. It's almost like food, clothing, housing – these things shouldn't be up to whether people can afford them or not. They should be things provided because we need them to survive. And literature and art are part of that. It's our survival that we're talking about, and if we don't take care of that, and give it to people because it's a necessity – rather than somebody who can afford to do it, we're going to lose our humanity.

EBR: Thank you, Luis Rodriguez, speaking to you while touring East St. Louis, affectionately known as "East Boogie," here on April 8th, 1992. We've enjoyed you, we love you, and we certainly want you to come back to us to continue to share your gifts and talents.

LR: Thank you.

P.S.:

Additional Questions & Answers

EBR: Crossing the Mississippi now from east to west, East St. Louis, East Boogie, to St. Louis, Missouri, looking at the Arch, at the PET Corporation, Ralston Purina, the Clarion Hotel, the St. Louis skyline. What is your favorite work by yourself, Luis, and why?

LR: Uh, that's a hard question because I usually like the last thing I'm working on. I like the response I get with "The Rooster's Poem: The Rooster Who Thinks He's a Dog." I think humor breaks down a lot of defenses and people connect all of a sudden, and then I can hit 'em with the more serious stuff. I like doing that one. But my most favorite is the last one I did, which is the memoirs. So the next thing I do, that'll be the most favorite.

EBR: Oh, okay. Thank you very much. What is the name of your memoirs, when will they be published, and who's the publisher?

LR: It's got a tentative name of "The Crazy Life." We might not go that way; we'll see what happens. The publisher is Curbstone Press out of Connecticut, and it'll probably be out next year, and it's the first book that I've ever gotten an advance for, so I'm really happy about that.

EBR: All right, excellent. Advances are always nice for writers. It's encouraging to know that writers get advances, because it says to the rest of us that maybe we can get advances. Let me ask you, Luis, are there any new, young, exciting writers on the scene now for you?

LR: Um, yeah, especially up in Chicago I've been working with this young Jamaican guy – Rohan B. Preston, who just published his work. There's a Native American woman in Wisconsin who's new and never been published before named Denise Sweet; I'm considering her work. So I'm coming across some pretty good new material that I'm really looking at; we'll see what happens. There's people out there now.

EBR: Okay. Thank you, thank you. It's good to hear new voices, new names, new people to look for. Thanks a lot. The name of your press is ...?

LR: (Tia Chucha Press.)

EBR: (Tia Chucha Press.) Named after your aunt, right?

LR: Named after my good, great, and lovely aunt who died a couple of years ago.

EBR: Okay. Thank you, thank you. You have a poem in her honor, right?

LR: Yes. It's called "Tia Chucha."

Rite #5

Hungers, Flowers, Sightings, Blood

Gwendolyn Brooks
Cornelius Eady
Mari Evans
Janice Mirikitani
Jeffrey Skoblow
Eric Stinus
Christina Springer

TO AN OLD BLACK WOMAN, HOMELESS AND INDISTINCT

Gwendolyn Brooks

1.

Your every day is a pilgrimage.
A blue hubbub.
Your days are collected bacchanals of fear and self-troubling.

And your nights! Your nights.
When you put you down in alley or cardboard or viaduct,
your lovers are rats, finding your secret places.

2.

When you rise in another morning,
you hit the street, your incessant enemy.

See? Here you are, in the so-busy world.
You walk. You walk.
You pass The People.
No. The People pass you.

Here's a Rich Girl marching briskly to her charms.
She is suede and scarf and belting and perfume.
She sees you not, she sees you very well.
At five in the afternoon Miss Rich Girl will go Home
to brooms and vacuum cleaner and carpeting,
two cats, two marble-top tables, two telephones,
shiny green peppers, flowers in impudent vases,
visitors.
Before all that there's luncheon to be known.
Lasagna, lobster salad, sandwiches.
All day there's coffee to be loved.
There are luxuries
of minor dissatisfaction, luxuries of Plan.

3.

That's *her* story.
You're going to vanish, not necessarily nicely, fairly soon.
Although essentially dignity itself a death

is not necessarily tidy, modest or discreet.
When they find you
your legs may not be tidy nor aligned.
Your mouth may be all crooked or destroyed.

Black old woman, homeless, indistinct
Your last and least adventure is Review.
          Folks used to celebrate your birthday!
Folks used to say "She's such a pretty little thing!"
Folks used to say "She draws such handsome horses, cows and
          houses."
Folks used to say "That child is going far."

PAPA WAS A ROLLING STONE

Cornelius Eady

A few weeks before my father died, my sister
tells me a fuzzy story about a young woman she'd learn
rumors about, a class or two ahead of her in high
school, who carried our unusual last name.

And when my niece goes through some of my father's
papers, she uncovers a small, laminated card, a birth
certificate from a mid-western state, for a boy, born
a year before I was, though it's a different last
name.

What about this? We want to know, and we badger
my father in the hospital, until he finally admits
to us that the woman my sister tried, but never got
to meet in high school was indeed our half-sister.

My father tells us that when my niece was just
an infant, and my sister was living away in Florida,
he'd bundle my niece up and take her to this woman's
apartment. He was that proud of being a grandfather,
and he knew my niece would be too young to remember.

She married a rich man, and they moved away to
Israel, is as far as he's willing to take us on this.
She's happy, and I don't want to bother her.

And the birth certificate? I see language in
the way the bones in his thin body twists; his mouth
says, *beats me.*

He's pissed-off that it's come down to this,
that his children would have enough time to try and
unravel a man's business.

And then he clucked, which I took to mean,
what makes you think I owe you this?

YOUNGBLOOD

Cornelius Eady

I'm sitting in this restaurant, having a very
serious discussion with my niece on eastern religion,
when suddenly, out of the corner of my eyes, I notice
a young woman as she crosses the street.

Oh, look at the way she walks as she tries on
for size what appears to be a new hairdo for her,
a white woman with dreadlocks. She's announcing the
changes to a friend who sits waiting for her on a
trash can.

And she stops just before she reaches the curb,
bends her head low like a wild mare and shakes her
new look, tossing the braids airborn like strange, intelligent rope.

How like the woman I used to read about in
Brautigan's books, the young spirit that had the power
to postpone a man from whatever he was thinking, urge
him to wipe his glasses for a closer look.

I'm thinking of him right now, as this woman
speaks young we're-hanging-out-on-a-summer's-afternoon
things to her girlfriend, and they cross back, leaving
the afternoon alert and softly wobbling off its axis.

Cornelius Eady, winner of the Academy of American Poets Lamont Poetry Prize and author of *Victims of the Latest Dance Craze*, ***reflects during lunch in Greenwigh Village, New York, August 1992. Eady read his poetry at Washington University, SIUE, and State Community College in East St. Louis during March-April 1993.***

HARD TIMES

Cornelius Eady

And this is for Etheridge, whom I never met,
but feel a certain kinship with. We share a long
distance story, a kind of bond by blue coincidence.

A few years before he died, he was homeless in
New York and living in a city shelter. He had just
finished teaching a workshop at the 63rd St. Y about
the time I was teaching there, and somehow, someone
from the *Voice* found out, tracked him down, and wrote
a feature on him.

When the article appeared, there was a head shot
of Etheridge. *Hard Times* was the caption.

How many of our songs are fleshed with what he
had to say? It was *Nobody Knows You When You're Down
and Out*. It was *Rollin' and Tumblin'*. It was *You
Can't Lose What You Ain't Never Had*, but he was still willing
to double-cross the trickster, still smiling and
laughing about dancing.

Roll on, Etheridge, roll on. He and I look nothing
alike, but our tongues do what they must, and our
skin's that dark river Langston writes of, and months
after that article ran, people'd walk up to me with
that barely hidden amazed-you're-still-walking-the-
face-of-the-earth expression on their faces and ask:
Didn't I read something about you in the Voice?

And these days, I'd lie and say *Yeah*, but I'm not
lying, even though I'll never be king of the dozens.

A MAN WITHOUT FOOD

Mari Evans

Resolute
icon of the revolution
the leader of the people
stubborn and stony
faced the cameras

He had swallowed his spittle
and could not wet his lips
"A man without food" he said
his lips parched and cracked
"is an animal"

"A man without food is an animal"
he said, confronting the cameras
his lips dry against his teeth

At the barre: Dance students enrolled in the Annual Katherine Dunham Seminar, held every August at the Center of Contemporary Arts in St. Louis, go through their paces in 1990.

HOW SUDDEN DIES THE BLOOMING
(For Paula Cooper and All The Other Children on Death Row)

Mari Evans

How sudden dies the blooming
An instant's crass confusion
An err of hand
and heart and head
A bent decision then
and now
one instant in the past as
constant present
Rarely out of reach the act
Tethered to some unrelenting
infinite recall
Today's reality
in yesterday's precise and fine
detail..

One moment's cruel confusion
carved forever in the spirit's
tender steel
How sudden dies the blooming
How withered lies the promise
lies the reach
the blind potential
All that lingers in the breathing
is a warp of understanding
a fist of clear confusion
and a desperate
a frightened
need. . ..
to live.

JOHNETTA BETCH COLE
(Spelman College, November 1988)

Mari Evans

Rising, striding, chin uptilted
Feet above earth
above earth
Throwing down a Road
the same yet
different
Guidelines, no parameters

Say y'all keep crossing over
On a useful level
Higher
Be strengthening traditions
straightening, smoothing
preserving...
No wrinkles, aaaah Lord
using a new iron

Remembering our wholeness
The one thread woven
into fine fabric
The strong translucence we
once were
This is a time for refashioning, the
ancient colors, the fragments pieced
The brilliant thread
A careful gathering

Reconciling Past with Future
A graceful work to be worked
The knuckles skinned
No magic metamorphosis
Straightening, preserving
no wrinkles
aaaah Lord
Using a new iron
this sistuh president

Sister
President

FOR MY FATHER

Janice Mirikitani

He came over the ocean
carrying Mt. Fuji
on his back/Tule Lake on his chest
hacked through the brush
of deserts
and made them grow
strawberries

we stole berries
from the stem
we could not afford them
for breakfast

his eyes held
nothing
as he whipped us
for stealing.

the desert had dried
his soul.

wordless
he sold
the rich,
full berries
to hakujines
whose children
pointed at our eyes

they ate fresh
strawberries
with cream.

Father,
I wanted to scream
at your silence.
Your strength
was a stranger
I could never touch.

iron
in your eyes
to shield
the pain
to shield desert-like wind
from patches
of strawberries
grown
from
tears.

DESERT FLOWERS

Janice Mirikitani

Flowers
faded
in the desert wind.
No flowers grow
where dust winds blow
and rain is like
a dry heave moan.

Mama, did You dream about that
beau who would take you
away from it all,
who would show you
in his '41 ford
and tell you how soft
your hands
like the silk kimono
you folded for the wedding?
Make you forget
about That place,
the back bending
wind that fell like a wall,
drowned all your geraniums
and flooded the shed
where you tried to sleep
away hyenas?
And mama,
bending in the candlelight,
after lights out in barracks,

an ageless shadow
grows victory flowers
made from crepe paper,
shaping those petals
like the tears
your eyes bled.
Your fingers
knotted at knuckles
wounded, winding around wire stems
the tiny, sloganed banner:

"america for americans".

Did you dream
of the shiny ford
(only always a dream)
ride your youth
like the wind
in the headless night?

Flowers
2¢ a dozen,
flowers for American Legions
worn like a badge
on america's lapel
made in post-concentration camps
by candlelight.
Flowers
watered
by the spit
of "no japs wanted here",
planted in poverty
of postwar relocations,
plucked by
victory's veterans.

Mama, do you dream
of the wall of wind

that falls
on your limbless desert,
on stems
brimming with petals/crushed
crepepaper
growing
from the crippled
mouth of your hand?

Your tears, mama,
have nourished us.
Your children
like pollen
scatter in the wind.

SALAD

Janice Mirikitani

The woman
did not mean to
offend me,

her blue eyes
blinking
at the glint
of my blade,

as I cut
precisely
like magic
the cucumber in
exact, even,
quick slices.

Do you orientals
do everything
so neatly ?

WE, THE DANGEROUS

Janice Mirikitani

I swore
it would not devour me
I swore
it would not humble me
I swore
it would not break me.

And they commanded we dwell in the desert
Our children be spawn of barbed wire and barracks

We, closer to the earth,
squat, short thighed,
knowing the dust better.

And they would have us make the garden
Rake the grass to soothe their feet

We, akin to the jungle,
plotting with the snake,
tails shedding in civilized America.

And they would have us skin their fish
Deft hands like blades / sliding back flesh / bloodless

We, who awake in the river
Ocean's child
Whale eater.

And they would have us strange scented women,
Round shouldered / strong and yellow / like the moon
to pull the thread to the cloth
to loosen their backs massaged in myth

We, who fill the secret bed,
the sweat shops
the launderies.

And they would dress us in napalm,
Skin shred to clothe the earth,
Bodies filling pock marked fields.
Dead fish bloating our harbors

We, the dangerous,
Dwelling in the ocean.
Akin to the jungle.
Close to the earth.

Hiroshima
Vietnam
Tule Lake

And yet we were not devoured.
And yet we were not humbled
And yet we are not broken.

World renowned achitect Gyo Obata is all smiles following his induction into the St. Louis Walk of Fame in May of 1992. Obata designed the Elijah P. Lovejoy Library on the campus of SIUE.

MOSQUITOS & POISON IVY

Jeffrey Skoblow

A nervous friend warmed our house
with a box for bats to simulate
a cave we hung upside a tree

We broke out first
in blotches then
in fear inhumanly
it seemed murderous

I went out and bought
plastic products of much
praised killing agency
and put them in a closet

SCREEN

Jeffrey Skoblow

The Mormons at my door

told me I seemed like
a spiritual guy

I said the Holy Spirit

tells you that
but my cat tells me

My cat was walking by

*

I saw them again at the supermarket

later looking frantic like spiritual
FBI agents casing the aisles

in a TV show

THELONIOUS DEDALUS

Jeffrey Skoblow

If a stone could sleep thus
Monk would creep in every
single where tickling
the bone of that beauty that
bone of your beauty
which has yet to
come into the
world

this world without
laughing stones
of tones and tomes
of homes to put
his tongue teems
of times to
the eyeless

Jeffrey Skoblow speaks at an October 1992 forum on Margaret Walker and Ralph Ellison at State Community College in East St. Louis (IL.).

CHILE DURING THE FIFTEENTH WINTER

Erik Stinus

On the walls we are painting our dreams.
We take our time over it - in broad daylight:
justice must be done to all the colours,
the whole poem must be there, no word missing
from the beginning to the future,
as in the kitchen all the strength and flavour
of onions, potatoes, beans, bread
must summon children
from every nook and cranny of the district
so that their dreams may be less painful,
so that they can get a bit of warmth by the fire
and on the day when the first peach tree blossoms
and the mimosas without bashfulness mirror the sun,
run out into the streets, into the gardens and fields
and never again let themselves be beaten.

Poblacion La Victoria, Santiago, July 1988

AN OLD PLAY RE-ENACTED

Erik Stinus

Today the earth is smelling of spring.
The door bell rings,
and with a blood-stained bandage on his forehead
the Emperor's messenger unfolds
a dispatch
from an arm's length above his head
to the rims of his bootlegs.
There
everything is written.
The old folks
stroke the frost off his hair,
addressing him fondly,
and the future rolls itself up
like a black curtain
with a crack letting in the light.

Today the earth is smelling of spring.
No one has died in my street,
I meet all of them:
bricklayer,
house painter and joiner,
the asthmatic secondary school student,
Miss Hansen and Miss Rasmussen,
the philosophical watchmaker,
the charwoman
and my father
taking the pipe out of his mouth
and his hat off to greet them.
I hear
my mother's brisk heels on the asphalt
and see her among the women
queueing up at the milk cart.
Something heavy is lifted
from their shoulders.

On such a morning
the popular front is practicable,
so think the two communists in the street,
Ingeborg and I.

The earth is smelling of spring today.
On the sky's inner vault,
seemingly blue:
the tilted moon
so white and pure
as if we had not set foot on it yet.

STOCKTAKING

Erik Stinus

Fortunate he who starved for only three days and nights.
Fortunate he who only twice was locked up
in a cell
and believed it would last longer,
and once placed under house arrest
in a derelict and kitchenless hotel, but the floor boards
blackened by the fires of people feeling hungry and cold,
thus inhabitable
because hope had not moved out,
and there was a well in the yard where women and sheep,
crows and sad looking guardsmen gathered at sunrise.
Fortunate he who never was a soldier, a partisan,
a saint,
yet in great danger and seldom afraid without reason. Fortunate
he who was able to recognize each island
he flew over
in reality and in dreams,
the harbours which like fragrant shadows or constellations
tugged nearer the ship at sea,
the cities and market towns
where the train stopped,
but always had to rediscover the known,
learn the languages afresh.
Fortunate the traveller whom it is granted to return,
to remember long his first road
and marvel at where it led,
remember
all the faces and just as clearly the handshakes
and the letters brimming with songs,
strive laboriously
at making a stanza, a chord, a single note
from the unexpectedly emerging songs
resound in every word,
often in vain.
Fortunate he who saw his trees outgrow him,
his crops turned into bread,
he who suddenly dejected,
the road gone,
at a last station meets another
last traveller asking him the news of distant places.

IN MY GARDEN

Christina Springer

There was a beginning.
In this beginning was not,
    a space
    a void
    or openings
especially not,
thought for flowers.

And each took root,
    in whatever way
    they had habit,
    on whichever patch,
in this heart
they found.

And each took nourishment,
    from my bleeding
    water soaked kisses
    into their grasping fingers,
flooding their souls
meticulously without routine.

And each one flourished,
    making space
    filling void
    created openings,
transforming flowers to smouldering
backward journeys of smiles creeping.

And each one jockeys for favor,
    in my mind
    rotating colors
    seasonal, harmonious,
out doing the previous one's
exquisite yielding to bloom.

And each one dies,
    with persistent regularity
    returning fresh
    pregnant with abundance,

I gladly have them all
again and again,

In my garden.

DAME'S ROCKET

Christina Springer

Spray the boundaries
of soul you ignite,
washing a hedonist
flare against all
instinct for practicality.

Thought succumbing
to flight of tender
fancy, the inhalation
intoxicates a moan,

and ricochets.

Visual artist Annabelle Lee explains her work during art exhibit and sale on St. Simons Island, Georgia, July 1991.

Rite #6

Appraisals, Testimonies, Fables, Folksay

AESTHETICS OF AFRO AMERICAN THEATER

Amiri Baraka

Aesthetics relates to the concept of Beauty. (Which I connect with Passion in Form & Feeling. The trail of Emotion, as sense and act.)

Raymond Wms in *Poetry & Marxism* calls Theater the most ambitious of the arts because it tries to represent, literally, real life. He says also that during periods of revolutionary social activity is when new and innovative drama develops.

He cites Shakespeare, the bourgeois revolutionary whose chronicle of the dying class The Feudal Kings and Queens he chronicles so well. *MacBeth, Richard The 3rd*, Hamlet's mother and uncle, &c.,&c. Shakespeare also covers the major themes that will remain within society as long as capitalism remains--*Hamlet*, the liberal; *Othello*, racism; *The Merchant of Venice*, Anti-Semitism; *Taming of the Shrew*, Women's Oppression and Male Chauvinism; *Coriolanus*, relationship between people and leaders; *Julius Caesar*, democracy and idealism.

Even the Bourgeoisie seldom does Shakespeare straight up shorn of the jingling Elizabethan verse that too often puts us to sleep and covers the real meanings of the plays. Now even tho they celebrate him they dont want you to know what he's talking about either.

If we wrote plays about the US rulers. Richard The Nix, Ronnie the Rage; George The Reefer; we would not be called classical. The plays would not be done, just like they are not done now. (I've never had a play on bdway. No play even in major offbroadway house in 10 years.)

Feeling – Emotion, the trail of form and feeling. What is most important. The content. So the content of our lives, whose form is also part of that content is what is most important. What has produced and been produced by feeling.

Slavery & White Supremacy have not only oppressed us (50,000,000 middlepassage--how's that for a holocaust?? and we hadn't even got here yet. They have also oppressed our culture (the entire entity of our lives and history).

Wm Wells Brown's "1st Afro American play," *The Escape* was about, you guessed it, escape from slavery. The abolitionists did it, read it. But there should not be too much question as to why Brown cdnt get it done on the great white way. It has not changed very much in the 127 years since we got loose (Jan 1 1863).

Our creations carry and speak from our lives. If we are sincere, and deliver the depth of our feelings, then obviously our enemies cannot abide what we say. Our observations are accusations. Our aesthetic, what is beautiful, must carry, in essence, our will to freedom, our will to self determination, self-respect and self-defense.

Our songs and dances, our paintings and books, our entire cultural projection at base, in essence, speaks constantly to the desire for freedom. Even our drums had to be banned – and who does not understand that the drums are an intensely political instrument--our drums were banned because they spoke very functionally of freedom! (demonstrate.)

So the aesthetic, our concept of beauty, must revolve around the concept of freedom and at the same time, dialectically, against the concept of slavery. Jazz, Monk said, is about Freedom, to say more is to complicate it.

Free jazz, *Freedom Suite*, *BeBop*, *Improvisation*, even the old blind funkateers in the recent slave south, always pushing freedom, "... the sun gonna shine on my back door one day." "I maybe wrong, but i wont be wrong always."

In the slave society, naturally our creations are always measured, by the slave master and their sycophants by the intentions and desires, the interests and Devil Reefer Bush whacks, of the slave master. As Douglass said, when the slave master stopped him from learning to read. What they hate we love, what we love they hate.

Like Devil Reefer Bush designating Jan 15, the birthday of our prince of peace, MLK, as the day of death and greedy murder in the middle east. DECLARING WAR ON DR KINGS BIRTHDAY IS A WAR CRIME! AN INSULT TO THE AFRICAN AMERICAN PEOPLE AND THE PEACE LOVING PEOPLES OF THE WORLD!

We are obstructed by a national oppression which includes, as WEB pointed out, a **Double Consciousness,** where even our so-called intellectuals and artists too often see the world through the eyes of people that hate them.

But if we look historically at our artists, people of the theater, say Brown, DuBois, Hughes, Childress, Hansberry, Baldwin, Ward, Peterson, Branch, we will see that the overriding emotional projection of the work, the aesthetic, the form and feeling of passion, ultimate concern from the work, is about freedom.

Do Hughes' *Mulatto*, or *The Sun Do Move (Don't You Want To Be Free?)*, or *Raisin* or *Blues for Mr Charlie*, or *Big White Fog*, and check the concerns, the attention to both history and day to day life, and the bottom line of feeling, emotional registration about those lives.

Our theater, like our art, must strive to be emotionally powerful and politically revolutionary. To paraphrase Mao. We must be writing to change ourselves and the world, most particularly to free the people in the world, as part of the whole evolutionary process of human development.

The entire educational system in the slave society (and this is still part of it) teaches submission to slavery. That any action or idea opposed to slavery is terrible and backward. Certainly any thing created carrying such ideas could not be art or scholarship!

The reason for the opposition to multicultural curricula is that our inclusion and most of the peoples of the world (say, the Native Americans – what does their art say, does it paint pretty pictures of the "white eyes" who committed genocide on them and banished them to reservations (plantations, bantustans, concentration camps). Panamanian and Grenadan art, would they paint pretty pictures of white supremacy and imperialism?

In the Black Arts movement we said we wanted our art to do three things. 1. Be identifiably African American. 2. Be mass oriented; to come out the libraries and seminars and boogaloo out there with Malcolm and Dr. King, The Panthers,

Rob Wms, Fannie Lou and The Deacons. 3. To Be Revolutionary, to be part of the world force of change.

We had dug that you did not have to be backward to be an artist. That we could create works that were artistically powerful and politically revolutionary. That is what we meant by Black Art! That was our aesthetic.

Where we made our mistake, being nationalists, was in not seeing clearly the class nature of society and oppression. We had known, of course, about niggero toms, but we were unprepared for the new wave of backwardness neo colonialism would bring in. And that now we would see a black middleclass arise who were no longer even physically connected (living in the same neighborhood with other blacks) for whom black was an abstraction. Like the sinister creeps Stanford Univ keeps manufacturing and the other negro factories telling us we are our own worst enemies, like Thomas Sowell, Shelby Steele, plus Walter Williams, Ann Wortham (the physically sick female slug who said on the Bill Moyers' show-- "the founding fathers told us what to do") and the Stanley Crouches, Playtoy Benyesmens and Frankenstein monsters like this negro Michael Williams in the education dept who finishes Bush's one-two punch of not only vetoing the civil rights bill but now even taking away minority scholarships yet sending us in great numbers to Saudi Arabia to die in the sand!!

There is even a small coterie of negroes, part of the retrograde trend that emerged after the revolutionary up surge of the 60's–From Flash Gordone the first negro pulitzer winner, (in drama), telling us black power (weeping in drag) was a drag. Now there has been developed a full-fledged group of negro playwrongs and movie dismakers whose bottom line is not only to attack the revolutionary 60's, as if all black people were rebelling about is a handshake, a haircut, some African clothes and the right to put down white people.

These people tell us the 60's were ridiculous, especially any militance. They tell us money is what it be. That history and the real lives of the African American people dont matter. And they are made instant neon numbers in our consciousness. They tell us our women got to have it. That our schools are for copulation and rock and roll. That our struggle is to put photos in pizza parlors and that our leaders are bugged out, and the Yusef Hawkins and Philip Patells and Eleanor Bumpers and Howard Beach victims were killed because they played their radios too loud.

They are in Living Color, or live at the Negro Museum or they think our children are Zoomen and urge us to have enough balls to kill them. They tell us we shd become good soldiers in the mans army and turn in the militants, because they're the reason we got troubles, besides if we bust them we can become negro officers.

But we can see from the youth, the Public Enemies, and KRS Ones and X-Clans, among the rappers, and many more, and the USO's and Nia Forces, high school and college militant student groups that more and more of us are finding out, "What time it is." We used to say, "It's Nation Time!" in the 60's, but now its InterNation Time, time for the world's people to self-consciously tune in to their fundamental and instinctive aesthetic, freedom and creativity! Which is to say time to remobilize and reorganize against imperialism, which is the most creative act there is.

Ancestor/genius Henry Dumas, circa 1953, around the time he graduated from Commerce High School in New York City. At Commerce, Dumas wrote poems and stories, ran track, and studied photography.

PRELUDE TO A MAGNIFICENT HAPPENING: [SHORT STORY (MIRROR: FABLE)]

Doctor E. Pelikan Chalto

The abstract-registrations and feelings of a kid (middle-teens) *awkward*, *ignorant* and *square*, (mainly *square*) can be a frightening affair, repeated endlessly through numberless births and rebirths, wherein the properties of monotony and repetition get mixed up and become misconstrued, as an unhappy excuse for trendy life-style. Every kid senses these things, and knows these feelings Intuitively. It's usually called the awkward age. (The transition period.) The only possible cure known to man, is instant hipness. However, before you can be hip, you must have a hap. The opposite of what a square would automatically think, and thereby misconstrue.

(2)

Therefore, an unhappy and unfulfilled kid would naturally seek out a Hap, in order to test himself (usually), in some cases even test herself. Nevertheless, in most so-called democratic societies, the male of the species is usually thrown to the wolves and foxes at a very early age. Particularly, in Black societies, coast to coast, internationally and continentally.

(3)

The youthful would-be Hipster clads himself in whatever quality symbol replica he is most likely attempting to attract in like-kind, that hopefully will lead him to the scene of the happening.

Although, initially, he does not know or even understand the jargon or vernacular of the idiom he is seeking. Feeling kind of strange and weird inside, he places the dark sun-glasses on his face to cover his eyes and consequently to hide his shame. His laments at not knowing what's going on, only feeling inwardly that he must succeed somehow in this living adventure in order to gain (what?) of that he knows not, and yet it must be obtained.

Somehow, someway, methodically conniving, he finagles himself into an invitation at some vogue teen-friend's party.

(4)

Next, with stingy-brim, shades, peg-leg pants, zoot-coat or bell bottoms?, double-breasted coat with vest (naturally chalk-striped) cold blue silk shirt with peach colored silk scarf, pointed hanky in pocket and knob-toed shoes, he's off and flying, heading for the taxi cab, with a pint of gin in his inside coat flask.

It is late-spring-early-summer evening, and the weather is breezy, wind is wavy and the juice is flowing with the juices.

(5)

Trees and telephone poles swish in and out amongst the buildings, the houses, the churches and schools.

The abrupt stops and pauses while the lights change at the various intersections heighten the suspense!

Fortunately, it is mid-evening and traffic is light, so that the transaction from Point A to point B is made without unnecessary difficulty. Now, the kid is thinking to himself, "(mind-quote) How different and exclusive is this section of town, from my home in the ghetto. I suppose this is what is meant by the middle-class. (mind-unquote)"

(6)

Abruptly at that moment, the taxi driver eases down on the brakes and brings the vehicle to a halt. "How much do I owe you?" asks the kid nervously, reaching for his wallet.

"That will be three dollars and eighty-five cents," chimes the driver. The kid hands him a fiver and tells him to keep the change.

Stepping out of the taxi and removing his flask for a swig of gin, and the driver scurries off in a cloud of dust. The kid shivers and shakes himself, feeling grown up and Hip.

(7)

He rings the front-doorbell at the place of the Hap, excitedly anticipating the Joy of the Party. Casually, looking cool (to himself) 3-piece chalk-stripe double-breasted suit with bell-bottoms and two inch cuff, cold blue silk shirt and shades. "So this is Saturday night in the Universe." A bespectacled face peeks out from the left side front window, as the kid returns his flask to his inside coat pocket.

The front door flies open in a blare of blues and party noise. "Hey, you're right on Time, Guy, the party is just beginning," announces the jubilant host.

(8)

The kid steps into the house, somewhat cautiously, acknowledging the host with a little polite bow. "What a slick-black middle class party this is going to be," thought the kid. All the black kids at this party seemed to be well-scrubbed Ipana-clean with Ebony magazine smiles, the pride of negrodom. The kid felt more than a trifle out of place here, out of context, so to speak. The lights in the room where the music was playing on the phonograph suddenly changed from white and became muted and blue, and there was even a mellow green light in the room, on the way to the john.

(9)

The faces that the kid encountered were young, mutable and bathed in rainbow (impressionistic) hues of profound black technicolor.

Either the liquor was working overtime, the way his gait was sliding, that is, the angle he was leaning at, as he coolly strolled on the way to the john.

The golden amber light in the john was an extra special touch of beauty in tonal aesthetics, marvelous and bewildering to a youthful man-child.

(10)

There was an aroma in that room with the green light, the mixture of olfactory textures, subtle star of venus oils and perfumes blending with indescribably pleasant odors of bath-soap, coupled with aroma of after-shave lotion and hypnotic incense burning along with some unimaginable fume that made the kid's heart skip a few beats. "Was that actually music emanating from that juke-box or victrola, or whatever?" Seemingly, it was Voodooistic.

In somnambulistic cadence, the kid walked out of the john, into the large blue room. At this point all the people seemed voodooistic and were sitting on pillars on the floor in a circle.

(11)

The kid found himself in the center of the circle, and now the group no longer appeared like children. More so now, they seemed likened unto aboriginal pygmies. About four or five people at each end of the circle began firing up cigarettes, taking 2 or 3 deep drags and passing it on to their neighbor. This motion caused a bewildering reaction in the mind of the kid. Yet before he could speak out in protest, a number of people forcefully exhaled the smoke into his face, literally blowing him away.

The kid was coughing uncontrollably, and someone was pounding him on the back. "Spit it out. Spit it out," they kept shouting.

(12)

Regaining his composure, the kid hoarsely whispered, "I'm o.k., I'm cool, man." Then taking out his flask, he took a short swig that (incidentally) made him feel as though his brain was couched upon a warm mellow revolving pillow and his eyes seemed to be spinning. Suddenly he became aware of a variety of scales of laughter, and without even wondering why, he immediately broke-up and began laughing with such great freedom and abandon, unlike any he had ever known. Next, all the voices in the circle chanted mystically; "*It's all about you, man. It's all about you, man*," over and over.

(13)

From a deep resonant chant to a fading whisper, "*It's all about you man, because now you're high. Yes of course, Amen. Now you are high.*" And the kid laughed resonantly, as a king would, being praised highly by his circle of ministers.

"It's quite true you know, you are high," an innermost voice as mellow as a celestial flute spoke to the kid. "Of course it was true," and irrevocable besides.

The music didn't matter anymore, the people didn't matter either. This was life on the outskirts, fulfillment in the existence realm.

(14)

Now all the laughter was musical, and mutual besides, because the understanding was perfect. People had gathered here from various places to accomplish something valuable, and obviously, this was it. The perfect Aesthetic. The balance of beauty and the glorious. Then this *was* the Happening. Magnificent Happening.

The kid barely realized that he was the only person wearing shades.

S'POSED-TO-BE DADDY
A Ten-Minute Play

J. e. Franklin

CHARACTERS IN ORDER OF APPEARANCE

GIDEON (A Black elder, aged 80)
GUSSIE LEE (His wife, aged 50)
CAREY (Their son, aged 25)

A back yard with a picket fence.

The back of the house can be seen, with its porch sitting low on the bald earth. A few things are on the porch: wash tub, mop, broom, bucket ... and most prominent, a shotgun.

GIDEON ... aged 80, is nailing a horseshoe over the door of the house. Then he digs into the nearby bucket and begins scattering "black cat powder" over the yard.

GUSSIE LEE, around 50, comes into the yard, a letter in her hand.

GUSSIE LEE: Gideon ... you look like you setting a trap for a rat!

GIDEON: He is a rat ... a two-legged rat.

GUSSIE LEE: He's my child and yours, too ... and you ain't got no right to do this!

GIDEON: Why the hell you keep calling him a child? He ain't no damn child. He might'a been one when he left here, but he grown now.

GUSSIE LEE: You didn't even give me a chance to finish reading the letter...

GIDEON: I don't wanna hear it! He had a good home and he left.

GUSSIE LEE: He ain't asking to come back home to live ...

GIDEON: I know what he coming for. My left eye been jumping all day yes'tiddy and the Obeah-woman told me that bastard coming to put a fix on me.

GUSSIE LEE: You and that Obeah-woman, both, talk like somebody with a wooden head! Don't nobody believe in that mess but somebody ig'nant.

GIDEON: That's what you say. That woman called my friends and my enemies by name! And never laid eyes on me before!

GUSSIE LEE: Carey ain't coming back here to hurt you ... he say he low-sick. What can he do to you?

GIDEON: Yeah, you thought his heart was 'bout to give out when you spent all that money for that operation that time. What was that boy doing when we got to that hors'pital? Jumping up and down in the bed ... all the nurses kissing on him and playing with him.

GUSSIE LEE: I know what them doctors told me ... he was born with a bad heart.

GIDEON: His heart was working pretty good when he left here ... his arm, too ... strong enough to raise up and hit me up'side the head.

GUSSIE LEE: He know he was wrong ... he asking to come back and beg your forgiveness for what he did.

GIDEON: He ain't gotta come beg me nothing ... keep his ass on out there in whatever den he in if he know what's good for him.

GUSSIE LEE: Lord, my po' son! If I knew where he was, I'd go to him, but he didn't leave no number or nothing!

GIDEON: He ain't nowhere but in that pen'ten'tia for something he ain't had no business doing.

GUSSIE LEE: How can he be in the pen if he's on his way home?

GIDEON: He been in the pen. That is why he ain't wrote all these years ... scared you'd find out where he was.

GUSSIE LEE: He say he been working in strawberry fields and on hog farms ...

GIDEON: She-it! You believe that shit if you wanna! How come he ain't sent you no money if he been working?

GUSSIE LEE: Some men jumped him, he claim ... stripped him of all his money and clothes and left him for dead, and some hoboes found and nursed him ...

GIDEON: That's what he get! Didn't wanna listen to me. I told him a hard head make a soft ass!

GUSSIE LEE: Gideon ... just let him come back long enough for me to see if he's all right ...

GIDEON: He made his bed ... let him lay in it.

(Gideon gets the rifle and begins cleaning it.)

GUSSIE LEE: Now, you know I'm not gonna stand by and let you hurt my child, Gideon, so I don't know why you got that gun.

GIDEON: He come back here trying to run over me, don't tell me I won't put a bullet up his ass.

GUSSIE LEE: This all gonna come back on you one'a these days, Gideon, cause God ain't sleep and who knows if the same thing might not happen to you?

GIDEON: If it do, he wouldn't open the door to me ... told me one time if he pass by on a dark road and seen me laying in a gulley bleeding to death, he'd walk on by and let me die.

GUSSIE LEE: He was a child then, Gideon ... speaking like a child, acting like a child and understanding like a child. Now that he's a man, he know better.

GIDEON: Then let him act like a man! I didn't go crawling back to be under my daddy's roof when I left home.

GUSSIE LEE: He ain't asking to stay, I'm telling you! After he lost everything, he been working sick and weak in the cold to make enough money to bring and give you.

GIDEON: Aw, git-away, git-away!

GUSSIE LEE: That's what the letter is saying, Gideon!

GIDEON: What the hell I want with his money now? The time he should-a been bringing me his money, he took and give it to that teacher at that school to put up and save for him. It wasn't even enough to buy a pocket-han'che'ker ... he just didn't wanna see me with it. I'd-a put it up for him ... I was his daddy ... s'posed-to-be daddy. He was living under my roof, eating my food. Now he on his ass, he wanna come back here with a handfull'a gimme. Shit on that shit! Let him go live with that teacher.

GUSSIE LEE: I never heard of judging somebody's whole life by one wrong. Y'awl used to go fishing and hunting together ... I didn't think nothing in the world could come between you. Folks used to call the child your shadow. Soon as he opened his eyes in the morning, he'd run put your house slippers on and flop around the house in 'em til you woke up ... cry if I wouldn't let him wait for you out in that front yard so he could run meet you after work. He'd jump all up in your arms.

GIDEON: He ain't run to me after he started going to that school and thought he had more sense than me. Shit, I done forgot more'n he'll ever know! I'd go over to that school to see 'bout him and he didn't even want them other chill'un to know I was his daddy, acted like he didn't even have no daddy. I reckon he must-a thought he was born by a virgin or something.

GUSSIE LEE: I'm gonna go'on like I didn't even hear you say that, cause I know you don't know what you just said.

GIDEON: I know what I'm saying. Do you know what you saying?

GUSSIE LEE: I know one thing, if the sheep stray it's the shepherd's fault. If you hadn't been trying to beat that child for something, he never would'a struck out at you like that.

GIDEON: That Bible say spare the rod, spoil the child. That's what was wrong with him ... I'd try to get on him 'bout something, he'd run to you and you hide him 'hind your skirt-tail.

GUSSIE LEE: When he said he didn't do it.

GIDEON: He didn't never do nothing, to let you tell it.

GUSSIE LEE: You need to go to that church sometime, that's what ... and pray, that's what.

GIDEON: You think you the only one done prayed? I done prayed before. I used to go out in them woods and pray til my prayers choked up in my throat. I lifted up my eyes, too ... all I ever got was bird-shit in my face! God ain't never gave me nothing!

GUSSIE LEE: You got four living children. Who gave you them?

GIDEON: I got three chil'lun and a dog I raised that bit me, and I ain't gonna get bit twice by the same dog.

GUSSIE LEE: Them other children come here when they on they ass ... and all your people do ... don't never hear from 'em til they want something.

GIDEON: They ain't hit me up'side the head, trying to kill me.

GUSSIE LEE: If you knew how to read and could read this letter, you'd know that child wasn't trying to kill you!

GIDEON: Liked ta'kilt me just the same. You want him to finish the job.

GUSSIE LEE: I'm just gonna leave you to God, Gideon, cause can't nobody down here on this earth tell you nothing.

(GUSSIE LEE is about to leave, resignedly, when CAREY appears at the corner of the yard ... disheveled, unshaven, gaunt, subdued, and with his pockets turned inside-out.)

GUSSIE LEE (Straining to recognize her son): That look like my child coming yonder ...!

(A soul-rending wail of agony and recognition fills the air. GUSSIE LEE runs to CAREY, who is torn between reaching out to his father and going to comfort his mother.)

GIDEON readies the rifle, but holds it at an angle toward the ground.)

CAREY: Mama ... Mama, I'm all right!

GUSSIE LEE: My baby! My baby! Thank you, Lord! God is so good! God is so good!

(Father and son face each other, with GUSSIE LEE sobbing and clinging to CAREY and being a barrier between the men.)

GIDEON: Well, look what the cat done drug in!

CAREY: Hey, daddy.

GIDEON: I told you if you ever come back here I was gonna kill you, didn't I?

GUSSIE LEE: Gideon, for God's sake ...!

CAREY: Yes-sir, daddy, I remember.

GIDEON: You don't believe I'll shoot you, do you?

CAREY: Yes-sir, I believe you'll do it, daddy.

GUSSIE LEE: Lord, Lord ...! What did we do wrong ...?!

GIDEON: I don't know why you calling me "daddy"... you ain't been no kind-a son to me.

GUSSIE LEE: Gideon ... can't you see he's humbling his'self to you!? He ain't come here to hurt you!

CAREY: Mama, I don't blame him ... he's right! I ain't fit to be called his son. I ain't even fit to tell him I love him, but I'm gonna say it, anyhow. I love you, daddy. I declare it.

GUSSIE LEE: See there, Gideon? Lord, Lord! How can you turn from him?

(GIDEON Averts his face, struggling with his emotions, but still holding onto the rifle.)

GIDEON: He turn from me. I'd go to that school to see 'bout him and he'd done told them people I was his grand-daddy! Shame-a me cause I was old.

CAREY: I know how much I must-a hurt you, daddy, and I was wrong. But it wasn't you I was shamed of... it was me ... shamed of being poor, wearing mix-match socks and the same clothes to school ... just shame-a myself! I had to hear this from a hobo before I could come to my senses and realize what you were trying to teach me.

GIDEON: See there! I told you, didn't I?!

CAREY: Yes-sir, daddy, you told me ... I was hard-headed.

GIDEON: I said that!

GUSSIE LEE: Bless his heart! See there, Gideon?!

CAREY: Move, mama ... let me get down on my knees to my father ... and if he can't forgive me, he'll never see me again in this life ...

GUSSIE LEE: Oh, son, don't talk like that!

CAREY: At first I wished them hoboes had'a let me die ... then I asked God to just let me live long enough to make it home and ask you to forgive me for hurting you, daddy ...

GUSSIE LEE: Bless your heart! Your daddy wanna forgive you ... I know he do!

(CAREY goes down on his knees and waits humbly for a sign from his father.

GIDEON keeps the rifle in its position but hesitates to give a sign.)

GUSSIE LEE: Gideon, give him a sign! Can't you see he's changed?!

GIDEON: How come you stayed away all this time ... without writing your mama? You know she was worried about you.

CAREY: I started a lot-a letters, but I wanted to mail me in 'em ... and I wanted to come back sooner, but I was scared you wouldn't forgive me, and even more scared you'd still believe I'd lied to you that time, and I hadn't, daddy. I raise my right hand to God! I was telling you the truth. All these years I kept saying, "If only my father would believe me." Now it ain't as important as you forgiving me, cause if you don't I know I'll never be a man.

GUSSIE LEE: Your daddy's good-hearted in his heart, deep down in him ... he just set in his ways.

GIDEON (lowering the rifle): Sometime I had asked myself was I right or wrong.

CAREY: I know I was wrong for raising my hand to you.

GIDEON: What hurt'ed me more'n that stick, I put my "X" on your r'portcard, and I see'd where you had done spit'd on the pencil and rubbed it off.

(CAREY lowers his head in shame.)

GUSSIE LEE: He didn't know no better, Gideon ...

CAREY: Yes, I did mama ... I was old enough to know better. I saw that cardboard in the bottom of my father's shoes ... who did I think he was sacrificing for? I wasn't thinking about nobody but myself ... and I wish them hoboes had'a let me die!

GUSSIE LEE: Hush now!

CAREY: I'm leaving now, mama... I got my sign.

GUSSIE LEE: Leaving for where?! You wanna kill your po' mama talking like that?!

CAREY (Getting up from the ground): I got my sign and I wanna go.

GUSSIE LEE: Gideon, don't let him do this! Don't y'awl know what this do to a mother's heart?!

GIDEON (throwing the rifle down): I ain't said he had to go nowhere ... he know he ain't ate nothing ...

CAREY: I'm full now, daddy. I have to go now ... I want to ...

GUSSIE LEE: Carey ... Lord ha'mercy, don't just run off again like this!

CAREY: I'll write you and let you know where I am this time, mama ... I promise. I just wanna put my arms around my father before I go, though I know I don't deserve it.

(GIDEON sinks down onto an old tree stump, unable to hold back the storm of emotions.)

GUSSIE LEE: Gideon, let him do it! Bless your heart!

(GIDEON is unable to hold back his tears, CAREY moves hesitantly toward his father until he reaches him and they embrace painfully.)

CAREY: My father ... my father!

CURTAIN

BODIES IN SILENCE: THE MISSING DIASPORA IN AFRICAN LITERATURE

Tess Onwueme

> Forgetting is essential to action of any kind, just as not only light but darkness too is essential for the life of everything organic. A man who wanted to feel historically through and through would be like one forcibly deprived of sleep or an animal that had to live only by rumination and ever repeated rumination: Thus, it is possible to live almost without memory ... but it is altogether impossible to "live" at all without forgetting ... So there is a degree of sleeplessness, of rumination, of the historical sense, which is harmful and ultimately fatal to the living thing, whether this living thing be a man or people or a culture.
>
> Frederich Nietzsche, *Untimely Meditations* 60-61.

Forgetfulness? Amnesia? Have we been dreaming so long we no longer remember? Can one talk about the politics of remembering? And silence, even over missing bodies of one's kin? It is from this threshold of questioning that our discourse begins. It is designed to focus on African literature to reveal what so far constitutes its main body and why certain parts or features have gained prominence while others have been distorted, masked, or even amputated from that body. Our overall aim here is speculative, pelting questions that might enable us to decode silence(s) belying the rational constructs that become choice schemata in the modern bowl of African literature.

In this regard, a critical look at the physiology of African literature reveals the following:

1. Distinct outlines or bodies of the African in the continent burdened and groping for meaning from *Fragments*, the result of Africa's *Ambiguous Adventure* with the West, determined to ensure in Africa that *Things Fall Apart* into Western pockets.

2. The "been-to" elite African who has gone over to the West and made a *Sudden Return* to find himself/herself *No Longer At Ease*, or faced with the *Dilemma of a Ghost*,[1] or in Sembenian metaphor, gripped with the *Xala*[2].

3. The white from the West groping in the mystic space and soul of Africa, as does Clarence in Camara Laye's *Radiance of the King* (1971), or the demonic angel of God and man, like Captain Winterbottom and Livingstone in the novels of Achebe and Ngugi Wa Thiongo, respectively.[3] Looking through these phases (or faces, rather), it is obvious that one feature, the African Diaspora--which should have been a major component of African soul and body--is generally missing, and yet *appears not to be missed*! As Lemuel Johnson rightly observes, "Until the politics of post-independence provoked contemporary African authors to outrage and to

near-fatalistic vision of history, the motif [Black Diaspora] had been literally absent from modern African literature ...." (63). It is this mystifying silence concerning the missing portrait of the black diaspora in African literature that has fueled my curiosity, and therefore, has become my charge in this discourse.

What is the character of this silence? What factors inform the astute resolve to silence? How much longer must the conscience hold forth in the trap of this silence, especially in view of current revisions of canons, alliances, global convergences, and anticipated integrations in the twenty-first century? These questions are meant not only to provoke more thoughts on the current discourses on "Afrocentrism" (especially to involve African writers and scholars in the mother-land in the discourse) but also to broaden canons of literary aesthetics that speak to collective identity from an *Afro-global* perspective.

The subject of collectivism could not have been more appropriate at any time than now when to reconnect has not just become fashionable, but is being inscribed and impressed by white, in white, on white and is already being executed by evidence of recent convergences (e.g., East and West Germany, and the Mitterand/ Gorbachev/ Yeltsin/ Bush/ Thatcher connection during the Desert Storm offensive), convergences which are conspiracies contrived and designed by the cabal of Western hegemony for the continued hoarding of power to stifle the discordant other--the rest of us. How are we, as Africans, preparing to face Japan and the West to dialogue on equal terms on economic, social, political and technological matters affecting us when all the evidence of history (especially since the leprous contact with the West) reveals to us only stories of our disorientation, socioeconomic indisposition, fragmentation and distortion of all that gave us any sense of identity, dignity, and wholeness as a people? And where does the writer, as witness of this melee from the beginning to the close of this century, come into this? Ngugi's words might be instructive to us at this point:

> What has been, especially for the vast majority of submerged, exploited mass in Africa, Asia and Black America, is bound up with what might be: our vision of the future, of diverse possibilities of life and human potential, has roots in our experience of the past.... The novelist is haunted by the past. His work is often an attempt to come to terms with "the thing that has been," a struggle, as it were, to sensitively register his encounter with history, his people's history. And the novelist at his best, must feel heir to a continuous tradition .... At the same time, he must be able to stand aside and contemplate the currents. He must do both simultaneously, swim, struggle and also watch, on the shore. But occasionally with the process, he feels that his feet are unsteady, that he has been uprooted, that he is not heir to a continuous culture. Where do I stand in the mainstream, he asks. Has there been a mainstream, any way? (*Homecoming* 39).

How, as African scholars and artists, do we respond to the above pricking questions from one of us? Has there been a mainstream, or merely streams without common source flowing along different or parallel courses? Can there be a point of confluence? Let these questions simmer in silence until we return to them later. For now, let the mind scavenge on the anatomy of silence.

A Brief Anatomy of Silence

Silence, which defies verbal communication, has, ironically, been generating controversy among scholars who concern themselves with epistemological questions regarding its true character. From a laywoman's point-of-view, silence entails words intimidated to submissiveness: silence implies the "death" of words, and, vicariously, action. However, for a scholar such as Leslie Kane, "Silence is a moment in language" (11). Kane argues that silence is imbued with a vast, superior authoritative power "to express the unspoken and the unspeakable" (17). George Steiner has this to say for silence:

> We live inside the act of discourse. But we should not assume that a verbal matrix is the only one in which the articulations and conduct of the mind are conceivable ..... And there are actions of the spirit rooted in silence. It is difficult to speak of these, for how should speech justly convey the shape and vitality of silence? ..... The highest, purest reach of the contemplative act is that which has learned to leave language behind it. The ineffable lies beyond the frontiers of the word (12).

Traditional Ubulu-uku people of Nigeria have not read Steiner or exchanged ideas with him, but they share similar views on the overwhelming power and profundity of silence in one of their local expressions, "*Ude ya bulu okwu*" ("let the heavy weight of silence bear the burden of speech"). Silence thus has its profundity, its multi-dimensional character, defying any restrictive confinement to linguistic and semantic boundaries. Silence functions as that turbulent space or rocking-bridge where action and thought (word) collide, rebounding in the chasm until new frontiers are broken, and thus silence is the aggressive interplay between affirmation and negation. In all, silence resides at the margin or border and can be broken to take root in word or action. In a paradoxical sense, silence draws attention to itself because there has been a presence: a voice, a body, that is no longer physically resident but whose echo or shadow burdens space in the present. Silence like absence, is noticed because a body *has been present* and is still lingering. Silence signifies the presence of absence, not the absence of presence, and it is from this vantage point that we would attempt to conceptualize silence regarding the missing bodies of the Diaspora in African Literature.

But first, what is the nature of this silence in African literature? Specifically, I am urging you at this point to speculate with me on the socio-historical, as well as the political, imperatives that have curiously dictated or decreed the isolation, or amputation, of the portrait of the Black Diaspora from the body of African literature, thus oppressing ones that seek reconnection with such an odoriferous trail of silence. My argument here is that this silencing of the voice of the Black Diaspora has inscribed markers of space to void the all-too-necessary link between the Black Diaspora as a genuine, indispensable component for restoring health and wholeness to the battered body, soul, and identity of the African household, and consequently, has impeded the progress of collective vision.

An Outline of the History of African Literature

A brief excursion into the history of written African literature is instructive at this juncture. In this regard, Omafume Onoge's seminal article on the "Crisis of Consciousness in Modern African Literature" provides us with a succinct account of the historical evolution of modern (written) African Literature. In his analysis, there have been four identifiable phases revealing the shifting rhythms of consciousness and, by implication, emphasizing bodies in the life of the literature.

First, alongside the vibration in the political struggle for independence especially in the 1950's, was literature that revealed Nationalist consciousness, by which African writers and scholars contributed to the prevalent political struggle for national independence. This they performed through constant protest against colonialism, and through the assertion of the culture, identity, and uniqueness of the African personality in the literature. This literature was characterized by protest and conflict, the African person being presented as one grounded and rooted in his socio-cultural milieu that was not just different, but conflicting with the superimposed socio-cultural, political, and economic order of Western imperialist hegemony. This is the phase Onoge identifies as the "Affirmative Consciousness"(23), developing concurrently with Aime Cesaire's march towards "Revolutionary consciousness"(23). The most remarkable current of "Affirmative Consciousness" was the controversial NEGRITUDE, which was championed by Leopold Senghor. Negritude affirmed African cultural identity, emotional rhythm, and spiritual sensibility. Negritude tended to fall back on the abstract rooting of the distant, rather fossilized past rather than on the brittle, immediate present which still bore the brimming inscriptions of slavery, and colonialism. Like every other movement in the history of African literature, Negritude, too, safely steered away from facing the current of the Black Diaspora.

Thematically, the literary works significantly corresponding to the phase of Negritude as well as to the period of cultural Nationalism and "Affirmative Consciousness" dealt with the resurgence of the past, which, in more ways than one, was generally romanticized, idealized, and mythologized. One recalls, for example, such works as *Things Fall Apart* (Achebe 1958), *Arrow of God* (Achebe 1964), *Weep Not Child* (Ngugi 1964), *The River Between* (Ngugi 1965), *Dilemma of a Ghost* (Aidoo 1965), and *Song of Lawino* (P'Bitek 1964). In these works, the past not only stood out in its monolithic majesty, it sometimes became so conceptually reconditioned and romanticized that its seeming perfection evoked questioning, especially since this could not be reconciled with evidence of the African fall to the invading Islamic and Christian entrepreneurs. For some time in the 1960's, therefore, this issue stirred controversy even among the patriotic practitioners of African literature. One recalls here in particular Chinua Achebe's defense of his sentimental representation of the past in his famous essay on "The Novelist As A Teacher." In this essay Achebe states, "I would be quite satisfied if my novels, especially those set in the past, did nothing else but teach my readers that their past, with all its imperfections was not one long night of savagery from which the first Europeans, acting on God's behalf, delivered them" (45). Perhaps it was in direct response to this conscious (re)-presentation of the past that Wole Soyinka also made his now famous cynical remark on the Tiger not going about singing about his "Tigritude," and opted instead for a critical interpretation of the African world, particularly the myth of an ideal past. This introgression was in keeping with the prevalent mood of disillusionment, betrayal, and pessimism in Africa after the attainment of political independence and the failure of the new African leaders to deliver the promised goods of freedom. The literature captured this mood, reflecting it through "Critical Realism"(35), Onoge's second phase resonating the hollow echoes of independence as a result of the betrayal and reckless consumption of the fruits of independence by the chosen elite, the Westernized African middle class now turning into indigenous predators.

The period of the 1960s and '70s in Africa was thus preoccupied by literature that questioned the values of independence such that the ordinary people especially became critical of their treacherous elite who inherited power from the Western imperialist only to compound the crises of consciousness and identity of the African. This fever of consciousness and skepticism writers recorded through satirical works that underlined the despondent and pessimistic mood of the new nation-states of Africa. Examples of such works are: Ayi Kwei Armah's *The Beautyful Ones Are Not Yet Born* (1968), *Fragments* (1969), Ngugi Wa Thiongo's *A Grain of Wheat* (1967), Chinua Achebe's *A Man of The People*, Nkem Nwankwo's *My Mercedes Is Bigger Than Yours* (1975), and Meja Mwangi's *Going Down River Road* (1976). Notably, too, these works, as significant, realistic, and critical as they are in marking the African people's post-independence fever (except Aidoo's *Dilemma Of A Ghost*, 1965), bypassed the portrait of the Black Diaspora in the literature.

The third phase identifiable in the literature has been characterized as Onoge's "Socialist Realism"(36), with its hand-maiden "Feminist Realism,"[4] by which writers like Ngugi Wa Thiongo (*Petals of Blood*, 1978), Sembene Ousmane (*God's Bits of Wood*, 1971, and *Xala*, 1973), Femi Osofisan (*Morountodun and Other Plays*), Buchi Emecheta (*In The Ditch*, 1972, and *Second Class Citizen*, 1975), and other writers[5] have not just been critical of the tragic social condition in Africa, but employ the literature to confront and to redress their exploitation and relegation, while forging new frontiers of consciousness for collective survival, progress and continuity for the common people.

None of the literary issues, phases, or movements, including Negritude with its Affirmative Consciousness of African culture, myth, identity, and being, assigned any significant, memorable position to the portrait of the Black Diaspora in the realm of things. To begin with, the PAST generally lacked concrete definition or character, and was usually vaguely sketched in space, in African time. This too has problematized the already beclouded issue of vision, or lack of it, and has continued to spread its mist on the urge for collective consciousness and vision among Africans from the motherland to the diaspora.

More significant about this history is that African literature has tended to centre on immediate national issues rather than on global, Pan-African sentiment and problems. Specifically, literary scholars and writers, like everyone else in Africa since the '50s, have been responding to the imperatives of colonialism, post-colonialism and now, neo-colonialism, particularly as these affect their nation-states, thus eclipsing a Pan-Africanist, global-African collective vision and consciousness. Recalling here the words of Abiola Irele concerning this lack of connection between African peoples, it is indeed ironic that:

> The very Political success of nationalism has created the condition for a limited national as against a continental, or even regional feeling and loyalty. This situation is further complicated by the fact that practically every African State is in reality multi-national, so that African leaders have been more absorbed by the political problems of ethnic relations in their countries and their efforts towards the promotion of unity at the territorial level, than by the question of realizing an effective form of continental unity. (118)

The African writer is not only a product of his/her time, but also speaks to that time. It is, therefore, to be expected that the African writer who has witnessed the ravages of colonialism and its consequences should attest to these experiences. What is surprising, however, is that these writers succumb to the hypnotic spell of reality instead of transcending it with the formulation of a comprehensive, collective vision that will include not just Africans in the continent but in the Diaspora as well.

This is not to say, however, that there has never been any streak of light in this beclouded landscape of collective vision through African literature. A few literary works such as *Bound to Violence* (Ouologuem 1968), *A Dance of the Forests* (Soyinka 1960), *Two Thousand Seasons* (Armah 1973), and *Legacies* (Onwueme 1989) twinkle as distant stars in the murky horizon, giving a glimpse of the Diaspora in African literature. In Soyinka's *A Dance of the Forests*, the Diasporan body surfaces through a flashback to the court of Mata Kharibu. In that historical scene, Mata Kharibu decrees that the intransigent army Captain be sold into slavery. In *Bound To Violence*, Yambo Ouologuem also documents the shameful history of slavery and violence in the African past which has continued to burden the present. However, even in *Bound To Violence*, the focus is not on recalling the lost image of the Black Diaspora and restoring wholeness to Africa, but on the gruesome character of violence and tragedy that have ensnared the people.

Permit me to point out a disturbing inference here again. It would seem from *A Dance of the Forests* and *Bound To Violence* that those sacrificed in the "Middle Passage" were the undesirable "carriers" ritualistically sacrificed for renewal and continuity of those living in the continent. But I very much doubt this was so. The auctioning of the rebellious soldier to the slave merchant in Soyinka's novel would tend to reinforce the myth created in certain quarters to brow-beat posterity into believing that "those who left deserved to go, and are not missed." This is blatantly untrue, deceptive, and self-destructive, for based on more recent tragic social and economic developments in Africa, it is not uncommon to hear people grunt about the luck of the Black in the Diaspora as "the lucky ones who left." Who are really the lucky ones? The one alienated inside HERE or the one outside THERE? How do we define who is "here" and who is "there"? These are some of the seemingly inconsequential but relevant questions that must be brought forward if we must frankly strive towards collective vision and consciousness. In *Two Thousand Seasons*, Armah is as uncompromising in apportioning blame to both the Islamic/ Arabic Christian/European invaders as he is in blaming the Africans themselves, whose propensity for greed and gullibility facilitated the process of annihilation of the place, identity, economy, and political integrity of the African. Although evidence of negative reactions to Armah's portrayal and representation of the African condition is not uncommon and even though respectable people like Chinua Achebe may get away with labeling *The Beautyful Ones Are Not Yet Born* a "sick book" ("Africa" 624-25), such cultural purists lose deposit when they chide Armah for "washing our dirty linen in public" in *Two Thousand Seasons* (Achebe, *Novelist* 44).

It is here, within this history of African literature, that my own questioning begins. What precisely is our problem? What problem does African literature experience in relating its identity to, or rather claiming kinship with, the Black Diaspora? Why has African literature so conspicuously hidden away and sentenced to silence the Black Diaspora in the literature? If we must truthfully address the issue of collective vision, this taboo must be broken, and the knots of kinship and renewal be retied through self-questioning, commitment to collectivism, envisioning of a new order, and re-definition of who we are, where we are, where we have been, and where we are going. Is Africa (and by implication, the Black Diaspora) prepared to face its own spectra? I am not necessarily concerned with questions as to what went wrong--and as Achebe states, "where the rain began to beat us" (625)--but more crucially, why since the rain stopped, Africans have not considered it necessary to regroup, assess the damage, take stock collectively, and reaffirm our zeal and commitment for continuity. Perhaps you may snap at me here and ask, "Who says the rain is over?" I must confess that even as optimistic as I am, I cannot dare say that the rain is truly over. But I certainly think that it will be over only if we commit ourselves to the truth of our being, our collective reality and existence as a people.

Recalling again traces of dominant bodies in the history of African literature, it is implicit that, so far, the focus at each phase of development has been a parochial preoccupation with national issues, problems of the moment and the burden of the present, without any concerted effort to view reality from Black-global future reconnections and linkages rooted in the past. I believe this is unhealthy for growth and must be reassessed, and it is this that brings us to the crucial question: Why is there this silence on the Black Diaspora in African literature?

Silence and the Politics of Remembering in African Literature

> The animal lives unhistorically: for it is contained in the present ... Man, on the other hand, braces himself against the great and ever greater pressure of what is past: it pushes him down or bends him sideways, it encumbers his steps as a dark, invisible burden which he would like to disown and which in traffic with his fellow men he does disown ... (Nietzsche, *Untimely Meditations* 61).

We have already hinted that one possible factor decreeing silence on the Diaspora is the catalog of problems facing African nations themselves from colonial to post-colonial times. Africa has been under constant bombardment from the West beginning with the use of "slave trade" as a euphemism for the plundering of Africa's humane essence, dignity, and population. Slavery was soon followed by colonialism, another euphemism for the legalized theft of African space sanctioned at the Berlin conference of 1884, by which Western nations were empowered to "Scramble for Africa," slice it up into pieces, and take the loot; after all, "the winner takes all." Africa has suffered economic, political, cultural, social, and psychological dislocation, staggering from assault to assault. But the tragic blow came with political independence, with the African elite's taking over power from the colonialist and perpetuating, with even more criminality, the oppression, injustice, and dehumanization of the people begun by the Western missionary entrepreneur. It should not, therefore, be too surprising that, in this margin between despair and hope, silence inscribes the marker of space between word (thought) and action. As an Aniocha-Igbo saying goes, "onye fu be odana oju asia ife wa mee" ("It is only when you have found a place to sit on that you can question why you have been kept standing"). For good reason Africa is wary of staring deeply either into the past or into the future from this precarious borderline of the present. This wariness is even more understandable now when the sceptre of International Monetary Fund is hovering menacingly around Africa to pluck out and scavenge the last relics of any soul in the continent.

Another major factor in this game of silence and remembering is alienation. Alienation in this context is synonymous with loss of identity, lack of self-confidence, self-denial, or even self-hate, and a frustrating desire to belong to an order outside the self and determined by the other. The colonialist scheme not only appropriated African space and traditional order, but also devalued and disintegrated the African personality and epistemological order, so as to reinforce the propaganda of Western superior hegemonic order. For this reason, the colonized strives to belong to and acquire the powers of the normative order mostly by negating the distinctive features of "self," thus marginalizing self as the price to pay for getting into the "centre" and being classified as "same." V. Y. Mudimbe gives an incisive analysis of this phenomenon as he quotes Bigo:

> There is no doubt that direct or indirect colonialism always provokes in the countries that experience its cultural constraint, a contamination the more profound as it is hidden. Life styles and modes of thinking of the dominant nations tend to impose themselves on the dominated nation. Moreover, they are accepted, even sought after. Models spring up, alienating factors for the people who adopt them (5).

Gripped with this feverish anxiety to belong, to become a member of the new centre, the "Born-Again-African" deliberately attempts to dissociate self from the African tradition and mode of being now stigmatized as inferior and lacking any sense of order. With the shift of centre from self power now lies with the other: the unlike pole which attracts, while the like pole of self repels, lacking the power to pull towards itself that is now fragmentary, reified and decentred. The colonized African no longer thrives on being for the self, but instead on "being for the other." Frantz Fanon dramatically states this phenomenon of alienation in "The fact of Blackness":

> Sealed into that crushing objecthood, I turned beseechingly to others. Their attention was liberation, running over my body suddenly abraded into non-being, endowing me once more with an agility that I had thought lost, and taking me out of the world, restoring me to it. But just as I reached the other side, I stumbled, and the movements, the attitudes, the glances of the other fixed me there ... I was indignant; I demanded an explanation. Nothing happened. I burst apart. Now the fragments have been put together by another self (109).

Magubane also echoes this tragic lament when he discusses the status of the African-Americans in white American society:

> The loss of identity ... ultimately leads the individual to a state of alienation both from himself and from the larger society. He is then constantly preoccupied with seeking of the self, and black nationalism in its search for roots becomes inextricably conscious of, even though ambivalent about, Africa (3).

Slavery and colonialism have ensured disorientation in the Displacement of the African (both in the motherland and in Diaspora); rather than claim kinship with the African kind, the strategy is to evade "Africanity" now associated with inferiority as a way of deodorizing self, a price for being admitted into the normative order. The irony, however, is that this African "reborn" into the ambience of a Europhyllic world never succeeds in getting to the desired centre. He has to hover at the margin, a wanderer/exile, forced to reject self for the other, and yet never accepted by the other. Seeking an "I-Thou" relationship, he ends up reified in an "I-IT" relationship, where he is distanced, an alien to all "others," including self.

How does the alienated African remember self or even the other side of self? The combined force of slavery and colonialism, with its malevolent scheme for creating sociopathic dysfunction in the colonized, plays a role in the politics of silence about and remembering of the Black Diaspora in African literature. Does not the anguish of alienation inform the silence on missing bodies of the black Diaspora in African literature?

In front of the mirror, the self confronts self – self at the margin between affirmation and negation. The impact of the self-confrontation reveals blemishes, the fragments of self as it is now charged with anguish, the tension of presence(s) of the double that is potently here but intractable. The self becomes trapped in the paradox of being. And though we know that the other self in the mirror is not real but a reflection, the self is shocked by the truth of its own lie, out there, beyond the mirrors. The problem is not the "lie," but the "truth" of the lie, and no matter the attempt to dismiss it as fiction or dream, it is all too potently close to the truth of being and existence that the truth of the lie is bound to awaken even the somnambulist. It is this stark revelation of truth and the self's failure to kill that truth in the mirror (even by attempting to smash it, he multiplies it) that forces the self to become prisoner of it (self). The self-censored suffers the epileptic seizure of silence. From time to time, it stutters and foams in the mouth because it is trapped in self-generated heat. Rather than confront this truth of its own impotence and challenge the soul of being, the African character chooses instead to flee into silence as a statement of denial of the truth of its own being, its own self. Public censorship is destructive, but when censorship is self-imposed, it becomes deadly! And that appears to me to have been the case with African literature and its potent silence on the Black Diaspora.

Depending on the degree of curvature, the mirror can reveal various images of self. A plain two-dimensional mirror will represent an image reflected as "truthfully" as possible without any obvious design for distortion. The subject views self here as it is, in reality, for the mirror shows it no more and no less than it is--in the PRESENT!! But the self too is transposed in a double present, the true-self existing in reality and the other-self present in the mirror. Perhaps this point has a bearing on why African literature has tended to dwell on the weight of the "double present" as against rethinking the past or future, and hence the seeming success of masking the face of the Diaspora in the literature. The weight of a double-present will more likely stifle the urge for action to change reality.

The mirror, too, may have some curvature, say, as in the case of a concave mirror, which may distort, enlarge, or reveal other dimensions of the image which the plain mirror cannot reveal. But the most provocative charge to action arises when two mirrors are brought face to face, to produce an infinite number of "selves" that are linked in tandem, and thus expose the transformational capacities of the selves for collectivity. This is ultimately what bringing together the split images, bodies and fragments of ourselves in Africa and the Diaspora can achieve. Through the literature, the self would have re-discovered its other; the Diaspora too would have rediscovered its African body, and thus the coalescence or convergence would foster the re-birth of collective visions. It is this vision that informs Armah's philosophy of "The Way" in *Two Thousand Seasons*. In the prologue, the author's intrusive voice resonates: "A people losing sight of origin are dead" (111).

My concern here is not so much to sing apocalypse as it is to exhort our writers, the creators of our images in literature, to strive towards convergence of mirror reflections of us here and elsewhere. It is tragic enough that one loses a portrait of one's self, but it is more tragic when one fails to recognize one's own self-portrait with the inexcusable reason that one is suffering from amnesia, disorientation, or being broken. The problem is not so much that dreams are broken, but that the ability to reconnect the broken chain and resume living in wholeness is lost. Is it that we (Africans) have lost that ability to wake up from dream, resume the dialogue with existence and translate our dream into reality? Or have we been dreaming so long that we can no longer remember?

What can African literature contribute to the politics of remembering and self-renewal of peoples of African descent who must bear witness to other people's convergences and ethnic solidarity in the 21st century? Focussing on missing links, missing bodies of the Black Diaspora trapped in silence in African literature provokes images at the margin of the mirror into confrontation of selves. This should make it possible for Africans to discern the infinite transformational possibilities in resemblances between the person and his or her portrait. Molefi Asante and others are currently sounding the drumbeat of "Afrocentricism." Where is the African centre? Or are there many centres, and if there are, how do we harmonize these centres? Writers and scholars in Africa must contribute to the dialogue on Afrocentricism, redefining the centre, canon, and consciousness from an Afro-global perspective if the 21st century is to come without passing us by as fragments.

Senegalese filmmaker Ousmane Sembene (left) signs autograph for admirer during reception for film directors at National Black Arts Festival, Atlanta, August 1992.

NOTES

[1] *Ama Ata Aidoo* dramatizes the theme of cultural disorientation and crisis of identity through the conflicts faced by Ato Yawson and his African-American wife as western and African values meet.

[2] "*Xala*" is used as a metaphor for impotence: cultural, economic, social, and political.

[3] Captain Winterbottom, in Achebe's *Things Fall Apart*, is an example of a stereotypic characterization of the white man as colonialist in African literature, while Livingstone, in Ngugi's *The River*, is an example of the white missionary in African literature.

[4] This is the category of African literary works that gives prominence to women as agents of social reconstruction.

[5] My plays, *The Reign of Wazobia* (Ibadan: Heinemann, 1988) and *Go Tell It To Women* (Newark: African Heritage Press, 1992), fall within this category.

WORKS CITED

Achebe, Chinua. *Africa and Her Writers*. (Massachusetts Review, XIV 1973).

_____. *No Longer at Ease*. (London: Heinemann, 1964).

_____. "Novelist as Teacher," in *Morning Yet on Creation Day: Essays*. (London: Heinemann, 1975).

_____. *Things Fall Apart*. (London: Heinemann, 1958).

Aidoo, Ama Ata. *Dilemma of a Ghost*. (London: Longman, 1965).

Armah, Ayi Kwei. *Fragments*. (London: Heinemann, 1969).

Asante, Molefi. *Afrocentricity*. (Trenton: Africa World Press, 1988).

_____. *African Culture: The Rhythms of Unity*. ed. Molefi K. Asante and Kariamu Welsh Asante (Trenton: Africa World Press, 1990).

Buber, Martin. "I and Thou," in *The Way of Response Martin Buber: Selection from His Writings*. ed. N. N. Glatzer (New York: Schocken Books, 1966).

Fanon, Frantz. *White Masks, Black Skins*. (New York: Grove Press, 1967).

Irele, Abiola. *The African Experience in Literature and Ideology*. (Indiana: Indiana University Press, 1981, 1990).

Johnson, Lemuel. "Middle Passage in African Literature: Wole Soyinka, Yambo Ouloguem, and Ayi Kwei Armah," in *African Literature Today*, 1980.

Kane, Cheik Hamidou. *The Ambiguous Adventure*. Trans. Katherine Woods. (Oxford: Heinemann, 1963).

Kane, Leslie. *The Language of Silence: On the Unspoken and Unspeakable in Modern Drama*. (New Jersey: Associated University Presses, 1954).

Laye Camara. *Radiance of the King*. Trans. James Kirkup. (Glasgow: Fontana Books, 1965).

Mugubane, Bernard. *The Ties That Bind: African-American Consciousness of Africa.* (Indiana: Indiana University Press, 1987).

Ngugi Wa Thiongo. *The River Between.* (London: Heinemann, 1965).

Nietzsche, Friedrich. *Untimely Meditations.* Trans. R. J. Hollingdale. (Cambridge: Cambridge University Press, 1983).

Onoge, Omafume. *The Crisis of Consciousness in Modern African Literature.* ed. Georg M. Gugelberger. (Trenton: African World Press, 1985).

Onwueme, Tess. *Legacies.* (Ibadan: Heinemann, 1989).

Ousmane, Sembene. *Xala.* Trans. Clive Wake. (Chicago: Lawrence Hill Books, 1974).

Owusou, Martin. *The Sudden Return.* (London: Heinemann, 1973).

Steiner, George. "Retreat World," in *Language and Silence: Essays on Language, Literature and the Inhuman.* (New York: Atheneum, 1967).

Critics Joanne T. Gabbin and Joyce Ann Joyce join novelist John A. Williams at the June 1991 Shooting Star Writers Conference at the University of Pittsburgh. At right is Dr. Gloria Spencer, member of Pittsburgh's Board of Education. Other conferees were Amiri Baraka, Molefi Asante, and Ntozake Shange.

A VAMP ON TONI MORRISON'S *JAZZ*

Robert Earl Price

"Writing and reading are not that distinct. Both require being alert and ready for unaccountable beauty, for the intricateness or simple elegance of the writer's imagination, for the world that imagination evokes ... Writing and reading mean being aware of the writer's notions of risk and safety, the serene achievement of, or sweaty fight for, meaning and response-ability."

Toni Morrison, *Playing in the Dark*,
Cambridge, MA, and London, England:
Harvard University Press,
1992, page XI.

"...I can't tell anyone that I have been waiting for this all my life and that being chosen to wait is the reason I can. If I were able I'd say it. Say make me, remake me. You are free to do it and I am free to let you because look, look. Look where your hands are. Now."

Toni Morrison, *Jazz*,
New York: Alfred A. Knopf,
1992, page 229.

By the time we read the above lines in Toni Morrison's new novel, *Jazz*, she has so entangled us in its "unaccountable beauty and intricateness" that we feel transformed from mere readers into co-creators. *Jazz*, the book, seems designed to function in much the same way as Jazz, the music. It is created by providing space for the audience to "respond" to the leader's "call." The style of this daring book allows the reader space to sit-in with one of the hardest working writers in the novel business. Rather than maintain a guarded and unwarranted control, Morrison exhibits a serene respect for the world that imagination evokes, while remaining mindful of, and alert to, the unexpected magic in every imagination. This writing approaches the fluidity and flexibility of jazz music.

Legend has it that Charlie Parker was able to explore totally new musical improvisations with such imaginative logic that his audiences/listeners would hum the closing lines before he actually played them. Imagine this and we get some idea of the opportunities for the imaginative participation that *Jazz* presents.

A straight ahead jazz composition usually opens with the group, often a quintet, playing the melody in a clear, recognizable fashion. This "head" is often followed by a slight time shift as the rhythm section makes its presence felt. The drummer lays in a bottom of sizzle and cymbals for the other players to ride. The bass expands and contracts the rhythmic tension seeming to viscerally modulate our pulse. Then the piano becomes a percussive signifier, vamping on the melody in terse phrases, implying possibilities and suggesting points of departure. The trumpet accepts one of the piano's dares by taking one of the musical ideas implied in the melody and rewriting it on the spot, riding the rocket of improvisational imagination out to the limit of its skills before falling back into the waiting arms of the rhythm section. And as the trumpet fades the saxophone steps from behind a cloud and rains sonic logic on a melody that has been rearranged a dozen ways in the time it takes to expel a column of breath. Soon the audience gets into the act by responding to the players with physical and verbal signs of approval as the other players re-enter the fray and when this demonstration of imagination, improvisation and cooperation has transformed a simple composition into an uplifting communal ritual, the wily musicians take us home, smiling and applauding the healing magic of Jazz.

Jazz lures us into a hyperspace-like freedom where comforting, familiar structures have been transformed. Morrison writes like a one-person quintet, leading us to places where we, as readers, must engage the material and select from the possibilities that suit our personal view of the world. *Jazz*, as the title implies, owes much of its structure and style to the influence and implications of African artists on western music, i.e. jazz music. But this is more than a stylistic experiment or a show of respect for artistic roots. This is a master work by an experienced author and, although the rhythms of jazz have been implied in past literary works, few have created a narrative experience that approaches the literary equivalent of jazz found here. In this new work Morrison builds a strong case for a genre called the Jazz Novel; not to be confused with a novel having jazz as the subject, but rather a novel that uses the musical structure described above as a scaffolding for sustained literary expression.

The very structure of this book seems based upon the subtle organization of classical jazz compositions. Like any great jazz composer, Morrison opens with a simple plot/melody, a plot so common and so bluesy that we all feel familiar with it; Violet and Joe are married when Joe falls for Dorcas. "...He fell for an eighteen-year-old with one of those deepdown spooky loves that made him so sad and happy he shot her to keep the feeling going" *(Jazz* page 3). Next she employs a device straight out of the jazz musicians' handbook. That is, she begins to introduce subtle shifts in time to manipulate the story's tension. "...Way, way before that, before Joe ever laid eyes on the girl, Violet sat down in the middle of the street. She didn't stumble, wasn't pushed; she just sat down..." *(Jazz* page 17). These understated references to other times eventually link the characters to slavery, miscegenation and the [East] St. Louis riots. New York, "the City" of *Jazz*, plays on the "bottom" of this writing like an accomplished drummer. "Do what you please in the city, it is there to BACK and FRAME you no matter what you do ... all you have to do is HEED THE DESIGN--the way it's laid out for you..." *(Jazz* pages 8-9) [emphasis mine].

If "the City" functions as a literary drummer in this work, then the elusive narrator plays our imagination the way a hip bass player thumps our pulse, one unexpected beat at a time. Like any good bass player, the ethereal narrator enables us to shift effortlessly through time and space. Then, without our realizing it, Violet begins to feed us piano-like phrasing. She steals a baby, frees the birds, interviews the dead girl's guardian and places Dorcas' picture on her mantle. Each action verges on total madness and charges the narrative with explosive energy similar to the way a piano shapes a jazz composition.

The trumpet function is performed by Joe, first soft and disinterestedly, but when he does step center stage to solo we realize that he is a hunter, still tracking the mother that denied and abandoned him. "... I chose you. Nobody gave you to me. Nobody said that's the one for you. I picked you out. Wrong time, yep, and doing wrong by my wife. But the picking out, the choosing. Don't ever think I fell for you, or fell over you. I didn't fall in love, I rose in it. I saw you and made up my mind. My mind. And I made up my mind to follow you too. That's something I know how to do from way back..." *(Jazz* page 135).

It is the dead Dorcas that imitates the spiritual chanting of an inspired saxophone. With the dead girl swirling in the center like a string of breath, the last forty pages read like an inspired improvisational solo, and as a participatory audience we deconstruct and reconstruct our imagination to fit the fluid flow of human emotions as Morrison finally brings what can only be described as a literary jam session to a close. "... that I have loved only you, surrendered my whole self reckless to you and nobody else. That I want you to love me back and show it to me. That I love the way you hold me, how close you let me be to you. I like your fingers on and on, lifting, turning. I have watched your face for a long time now, and missed your eyes when you went away from me. Talking to you and hearing you answer--that's the kick..." *(Jazz* page 229).

With Morrison we are in the presence of a seasoned master innovator. *Jazz* takes an ordinary love triangle and murder for a melody and plays it like those brass bands play a New Orleans 2nd line. What could have easily turned into a soap opera is kept afloat by language, symbol and image combined and arranged in such fascinating, yet familiar patterns that we are willing to hear voices and see visions in ways that force us to rethink the term "reader." She takes us from the Buddy Bolden-like swing of Ellison to implied Bebop passages of her own invention. She uses narrative ideas as instruments that modulate our pulse rate the way Elvin Jones used to set us up so Trane could deliver his saxophone sermons.

Jazz forces us to rethink history, fate, coincidence, our morals and our ethics. We choose the narrator and point of view. The reader must engage *Jazz* because like the music it reflects, this book is interactive in a way that demands our response and like all great innovators, Morrison risks alienating those of us who are not ready to be response-able. For those who recognize the skill and craft required to produce this work, *Jazz* is a literary jam session with room for all of us to sit in as the writer sets out to transform the art of fiction into a collective act of faith, a ceremony and a ritual. A ritual that leaves us wondering how the author has managed to read our minds, predict our imaginative responses and remake characters that we have always known.

In retrospect, Morrison's evolution to the creation of this complex work seems obvious and logical, especially when we look at her literary ancestors and contemporaries. She has woodshedded with the work of Henry Dumas, Zora Neale Hurston and Joyce. She sat in with literary preachers like Killens, Baldwin, etc, and jammed after hours amid the sweet dangers of Chester Himes. With her traditional church/blues roots we can trace the evolution of Morrison's chops from the tender solos gently explored in *The Bluest Eye* to the independent confidence of *Sula* and on to the churchy *Song of Solomon* and the carnal *Tar Baby*. She even throws in a salsa-like Latin influence of magical realism in the much acclaimed *Beloved.* These are all risky, courageous and powerful works, but not until this aptly titled novel has she demonstrated a narrative virtuosity and a mastery that approaches the literary equivalent of the musical contributions of Bird or Trane, who each could take simple tunes and turn them into spiritual experiences. After people had heard Bebop, they could never hear swing in the same way again. And, after reading this novel few of us will be able to read Pre-*Jazz* novels without the urge to participate in their shape and direction.

Jazz is a score that seems to work in opposition to the lonely ivory tower school of literature; an approach that often leaves the reader outside of the work watching the writer flaunt his knowledge of obscure places and language. Brecht said, "a spectator is less than a man" in that spectators give up their right to respond. But, Toni Morrison refuses to allow us to remain literary spectators. She summons Joe, Violet and Dorcas, sketches a thin plot line and then lays out, allowing our imaginations to fill in the implied passages. *Jazz* is the assured, confident work of a writer that respects us and trusts us to come to the work ready to jam and free to remake her vision into one that fits our hands.

FROM THE "CHAOSMOS" TO SELF-KNOWLEDGE

Charles Johnson. *Middle Passage*. New York: Atheneum, 1990. 209 pp. $17.95.

Reviewed by Eugene B. Redmond

This funny-gloomy novel will dazzle and distance readers with its syntactical gymnastics, philosophical sparring matches, word wizardry, rich flights of imagination, cultural cross-fertilizations, modal/cyclical time tables and intimate incursions into the nether-regions of human psyches--both contemporary and ancestral. But these deep currents are buoyed by a high-sea and low-land adventure story of hero (word used guardedly) Rutherford Calhoun and the misfitted cast of Creoles, American Blacks, European-Americans, Africans, gods, half-men (or "halved" men) and animals he encounters.

"Middle Passage," a loaded (loded) phrase, refers to the stretch of sea (now the Atlantic Ocean, but called the Ethiopian Ocean before 1650) between the West Coast of Africa and the New World. Forty years ago, Robert Hayden's great poem, "Middle Passage," surveyed the emotional and psychological horror of this sea-stretch, trafficked legally by slave ships between 1619 and 1804 and used illegally for decades afterwards.

Middle Passage, the novel, is set in 1830 in three places: New Orleans, aboard the slave ship *Republic* and in the Senegambia area of West Africa (with flashbacks to life under slavery in Southern Illinois).

Rutherford Calhoun, a 22-year-old manumitted slave, hustler and petty thief, makes a pilgrimage from Makanda, Illinois to New Orleans, where he unsuccessfully attempts to navigate the marginal social stream between the underworld, represented by Creole gangster Phillippe Zeringue, and the upperworld of Boston-bred (and husband-hunting) school teacher Isadora Bailey. Miss Bailey, to Calhoun's thinking, wants him to "be a credit to the race" and a "gentleman of color." However, for iconoclastic, irreverent Calhoun, this last phrase evokes the "image of an Englishman, round of belly, balding, who'd been slightly brushed with brown watercolor or cinnamon."

Caught between an army of creditors, unscrupulous Papa Zeringue (who doesn't "mind gettin' rid of people who have the bad manners to cut me off in mid-sentence"), too scrupulous Isadora ("...Isadora had remained innocent. There was no hatred in her. Or selfishness. No vanity, or negativism.") and the deep blue sea, our man opts for the latter, stowing away aboard the *Republic*--itself a multi-story within a story, and a horror story at that.

And what, by turn (and by God!), a stage, mirror, battlefield, tomb, metaphor, fortress, menagerie, asylum, desert, altar of angst *cum* catharsis the *Republic* turns out to be!

Told serially, by way of daily entries in a captain's log, this first-person narrative unfolds as a tale of grit, greed, misogyny, cannibalism, sodomy, murder, suicide, love, hate, mutiny, love-hate, treachery, cultural dismemberment, social mongrels, dispossession, dislocation and the mental/physical destruction [and re-creation] of its inhabitants. While this latter transmogrification occurs in Africans-made-slaves in particular, everyone gets hellishly re-wrought during the roller-coaster-like "passage" through the eye of the "chaosmos."

Once the *Republic* is launched, sticky-fingered/split-tongued Calhoun becomes cook's mate to Josiah Squibb, an alcoholic (who on the ship isn't) and polygamist, who is crippled of body but not of spirit, and has "perfectly balanced crosscurrents of culture in him, each a pool of possibilities from which he was unconsciously drawing, moment by moment, to solve whatever problem was at hand."

And the problems were multitudinous, beginning with the ship's doom-fated voyage from New Orleans to Senegambia to pick up hides, ivory, gold, rice, animals, beeswax and 40 "slaves" (called "black gold, black ivory, black seed" by Hayden) of Allmuseri stock--"the most sought after blacks in the world."

As the novel builds to and relaxes from its various peaks of suspense, violence, philosophical combat and compression, character sketches--major and minor--along with flashbacks to land (Isadora, Calhoun's family's slave-master relationships in Southern Illinois, Madame Marie Toulouse, Papa Zeringue) and brilliant descriptions of man, ship and sea help to sustain its buoyancy. Buoyancy, yes, even in the denseness of cruelty, suffering and madness.

The *Republic*'s Captain Ebenezer Falcon, possessed by a Napoleon Complex ("Aye, small enough to miss in a crowd, but with the bantam spirit for fighting and overcompensating that many men of slight stature possess."), is the hated, despised would be power-builder, turned out to sea by a plague of egomania, Eurocentric dualism, womanlessness and Afro-phobia. He "possessed a few of the solitary virtues and the entire twisted will of Puritanism ... perfection ... loneliness, self-punishment, and bouts of suicide it brings; and a profound disdain for anyone who failed to meet his nearly superhuman standards." Falcon, a human time-bomb and paranoia personified, was a "leader who lived the principle of Never Explain and Never Apologize." By contrast, First Mate Peter Cringle, "the only one [of the crew] not pitted by small-pox, split by Saturday night knifescar, disfigured by Polynesian tattoos, or distorted by dropsy," was one whose "whole air spoke of New England gentility." Cringle "stood tall and straight as a ship's door."

Helping further to flesh out the stage of this "chaosmos" is the elusive, foreboding mosaic of Allmuseri men, women, children, and one of their "captured" (and shape-shifting) gods, all epically incarnated in Ngonyama, their leader and spokesman. According to Calhoun, this African, the oral repository of his people's history, "was coolness itself."

Feared and hated for their "devil-worshipping, spell-casting" ways and desired and admired for their intelligence, fortitude and dependability, the Allmuseri became a necessary evil aboard the slave ship *Republic*. During the ship's return voyage, events leading up the Allmuseri's mutiny and occupation of the ship make it clear that they are part of a curse--like the albatross around the neck of the Ancient Mariner--dooming crew, themselves and the *Republic*. As Calhoun observes: "This was not a ship; it was a coffin."

Minor figures, treated with the believable depth and precision one finds among supporting casts of Dickens, Ellison, McPherson and Morrison, parade, flawed and flailed, before our literal and figurative eyes: adolescent Allmuseri girl Baleka, thief of hearts and survivor; cabin boy Tom, sodomized by Falcon and driven crazy by the Allmuseri "godhead in the hold;" fellow tribesman Diamelo, an Iago-like figure, plotting to turn mutinied Allmuseri against Ngonyama (whose "stare" was "so fierce," it was like "sparks from a blacksmith's forge"); and ship barber-surgeon Nathaniel Meadows, who, "for all the talk of his being an ex-murderer," looked "Biblically meek."

Subplots and mini-tales abound, and are tossed about like storm-driven waves or the *Republic* thrown off-course. Though this is a male-centered novel, women haunt *Middle Passage*--from beginning to end--just as slavery, guilt, material obsession and dogged faith haunt the crew. Mothers and wives are constantly invoked by the womanless, landless men aboard this ship of *fools*, *fortune-hunters*, *ghouls*, *ghosts* and *blues*.

"Of all the things that drive men to sea, the most common disaster, I've come to learn is women," Calhoun announces in the very first sentence of the novel. Indeed, most of the Stateside players aboard the *Republic* have been set out to sea by women. However, Calhoun, after experiencing his "middle passage" ("one long hangover"), with its "storms," mutinies, intermittent bursts of violence, sinking of the ship, and survival, is re-united with none other than Isadora--in a bizarre twist of fate--who, presumably, will help him raise the orphaned Baleka.

Of the women characters, Madame Toulouse of New Orleans--Isadora's landlady--makes the most exciting cameo appearance. Married four times to a banker, actor, preacher and mortician respectively, the wealthy widow explains that "she'd used the principle of "'one for the money, two for the show, three to get ready and four to go."

Like other major works of art in any genre or era, *Middle Passage*--a metaphor for *rites de passage*--has its centers of density, intimidating brilliance, indiscretions, technical complexities and often inaccessible or unbreakable codes. Falcon's fetish for philosophical meander, for example, may dismay some readers; though his ramblings aid in setting the stage for this, among other things, a philosophical novel. At the same time, Johnson's apparent stiff-arm approach to the emotional throes induced by slavery ("middle passage") and the innumerable ensuing degradations may enrage and estrange the race-burdened reader.

However, it appears that the author leans more towards clinician and philosopher-observer than racial excoriator. The most heinous hurts, too, are often handled with humor, as opposed to gut-level sentiments. Humor aids in authorial response, restraint and control. Three examples illustrate the latter:

1) Told he has a choice of marriage (to Isadora), jail or death,

Calhoun wanders off into a New Orleans world where he encounters "a den of Chinese Assassins, scowling Moors, English scoundrels, Yankee adventurers, and evil-looking Arabs." Calhoun's response: "Naturally, I felt pretty much right at home."

2) Falcon: "We've captured an African God."
Calhoun: "I said nothing. Surely you can understand why."

3) Falcon: "Then we underestimated the blacks. They're smarter than I thought." Calhoun: "They'd have to be."

So, brave reader, there you have it. *Middle Passage*, a rite of passage during which boys grow to men, men regress to boys and beasts, and women wait, wail and wane. A horror story. A philosophical stand-off. A tale of severest discipline (to bring one through a "middle *cum* rites of passage"). A treatise on the creolization of ethnicities and ideas. A meditation on Eurocentricism vs. Afrocentrism (e.g., Falcon's preoccupation with the "duality of mind" alongside Calhoun's observation that the "failure to experience the unity of Being everywhere was the Allmuseri vision of hell."). A Romance (Rutherford and Isadora/Man and Sea). A testimony of resilience. A text of defiance and rebel-criminality ("...for was I not, as a Negro in the New World, *born* to be a thief?" [Calhoun]). A joltingly brilliant ritual of revelations, cultural self-discovery and personal hunger/thirst. For, to quote the protagonist: "As I live, they so shamed me I wanted their [Allmuseri] ageless culture to be my own."

Much of this painfully comic novel is about how too many people become anchorless when they are willingly or unwillingly estranged from their own "ageless" selves.

African-centered gathering: Renowned scholars Asa Hilliard, left, and Theophile Obenga (right) flank St. Louisan Michelle Lowery at the First Annual Conference on the Infusion of African and African-American Culture in the curriculum, Atlanta, November 1990.

OF POETRY, MEN AND TIME

Men of Our Time: An Anthology of Male Poetry in Contemporary America. Eds. Fred Moramarco and Al Zolynas. Athens: U of Georgia P: 1992. paperback: $19.95

Reviewed by Richard Stimac

Poets as poets do not exist in movements. Critics create the categories, forcing the fashion onto the art. It is for this reason that a book claiming to chronicle "a quiet revolution . . . in men's poetry" is suspect. In the 1990s, a men's movement claiming to examine masculinity honestly for the first time is too little too late at best, or a ploy to gain a moment of social sympathy at worst. Unfortunately, *Men of our Time*'s introduction, written by editors Fred Moramarco and Al Zolynas, is more of the latter. They claim the new male poetry in *Men of Our Time* is not a reaction to feminism, but an action towards a new definition of masculinity, a positive happening where men finally begin to learn themselves. Yet, Charles Bukowski's "sticks and stones" is included:

> complaint is often the result of an insufficient
> ability
> to live within
> the obvious restrictions of this
> god damned cage.
> complaint is a common deficiency
> more prevalent than
> hemorrhoids
> and as these lady writers hurl their spiked shoes
> at me
> wailing that
> their poems will never be promulgated
> all that I can say to them
> is
> show me more leg
> show me more ass –
> that's all you (or I) have
> while
> it lasts
>
> and for this common and obvious truth
> they screech at me:
> MOTHERFUCKER SEXIST PIG!

If Bukowski is not reacting to feminism, then he is doing nothing at all.

But this poem is only one out of more than 250 in this anthology, and the introduction is just the introduction. Moramarco and Zolynas should have forgotten "quiet revolutions" and "psychological transformations" and focused solely on editing, of which they did an excellent job. *Men of Our Time* is divided into topical sections such as "Boys Becoming Men," "Fathers and Their Sons," and "Men and Women." Each section has its own enlivening identity that fits into the greater whole of the book, showing that this anthology was not piecemealed together, but actually edited. Often, the poems are arranged in point and counterpoint, such as Charles Simic's "Breasts" and Bin Ranke's "Turning Forty in Denver." Simic begins his poem:

> I love breasts, hard
> Full breasts [,]

which is followed by Ranke's poem, with this opening:

> I wonder what they think, women, of men's
> obsession with breasts

It may be an uneven topic, but the play between one poem and the next offers a glimpse of a fuller experience, and the total arrangement of the anthology offers many such instances. It is difficult to finish reading this book and believe "contemporary male poetry" signifies anything. Moramarco and Zolynas have arranged a wide selection of poems in such a way that the reader becomes aware of the breadth of life recorded here. The general terms "male," masculinity," and "man" almost become nonsensical in relation to the specifics of the lives in these verses.

The first section of *Men Of Our Time* is titled "Boys Becoming Men" and in many ways prepares the reader for what follows in the entire book: brutality, honesty and insight. Most ot these first poems dwell on male maturation rites, or their unsanctioned equivalent. Cyrus Cassels' "The Lesson (*from* Stoic Pose)" is a good example:

> At dawn, they splashed his cheeks with cold sake.
> Then they led him to a room – brusquely
> sliding back the panels –
> where a man's, a peasant's body
> lay on the mat, naked
> except for stripes of shadow
> across the flesh;
> This was his introduction
> to death.
> They positioned him near the corpse, saying:
> *The boy is samurai;*

he must learn.
In his hands they placed
the heavy sword,
as quietly he began to cry . . .

Later, they hung his small, blood-flecked kimono
on a bamboo pole:
He was five when they taught him
to quarter the bodies.

The boy, a future man, is taught by men how to dismember men, suggesting a sort of fratricide/suicide, one of the themes that runs throughout many of the poems in this first section and across the entire anthology.

In the section "Men and Women," there is an obvious juxtaposition between poetry that emphasizes gross sexuality, as if by using the words "fuck" and "cunt" a poet is tapping into some sort of primordial sexuality, and poetry that sublimates the sexual experience, making it more of a means than an end. Paul Zimmer's "The Great House" is an example of the latter:

At night, after lingering dinner and wine,
Lieder and string quartets by candle glow,
We ascend the tower, open the skylight
And turn the huge reflector into position.
The shimmer that we see has traveled for eons.
Under the circling stars, the birds against
The moon, with the vast rooms breathing
Beneath us, we know that the only sadness
In the world will be to leave this house.

The poem suggests an intimacy that is given between two people almost in an unconscious, maybe even primordial, sense. The important aspect to consider is not sex by itself but the context in which sex is defined and experienced. Ishmael Reed's ".05" works in ways similar to Zimmer's "The Great House":

If i had a nickel
For all the women who've
Rejected me in my life
I would be the head of the
World Bank with a flunkie
To hold my derby as i
Prepared to fly chartered
Jet to sign a check
Giving India a new lease
on life.

If i had a nickel for
All the women who've loved
Me in my life i would be
The World Bank's assistant
Janitor and wouldn't need
To wear a derby
All i'd think about would
Be going home

These two men are so at ease with their sexuality that they can talk about it without mentioning it. It is a given aspect of their adult lives, not needing to be waved around like a penis in a locker room. Meeting men like these is one of the joys of this book.

Men of Our Time is an excellent compilation. The poetry is sharp, well written, sometimes blunt and crude, often lucid, and always fresh and lively. Moramarco and Zolynas have done a thorough job of collecting and arranging a broad spectrum of verse by poets from a wide variety of backgrounds. They should have forgotten movements, though. Trying to define a group that includes whites, blacks, Bly, Bellamy, Asians, Native Americans, Hayden, Latinos, Ginsberg, Dickey, Catholics, Carver, Protestants, Atheists, Buddhists, Troupe, war veterans, war protesters, Major, gays, Gonzalez, straights, Redmond, and everyone else is as difficult as deciding on which politically correct label to use. With so much diversity, labels just do not fit. *Men of Our Time* is not a chronicle or manifesto for anything larger than itseif. *Men of Our Time* is a collection of poetry, almost all good, some exceptional, written by men. Nothing more, nothing less.

New York City poet Sekou Sundiata, left, and theologian Cornel West talk after a May 1992 forum on "Writing in a Racialized Society." Participants included Toni Morrison, John Edgar Wideman, Paula Giddings, and Hazel Carby.

KEEPING THE SPIRIT WHOLE UNDER WOLVES' TEETH *

Clyde Taylor

Some folks have even declared it a miracle that Black poetry exists at all. Like Countee Cullen, who called it a marvel of God "to make a poet black and bid him sing." But there are wrinkles in that line. Poetry is not some Supertreat people get to after they've driven the wolves of hunger, cold and despair from the door. Poetry is a fundamental act of man. You will find it everywhere people are, especially in that corner where the fight to keep that spirit whole takes place under wolves' teeth.

Everywhere. Attica, the death camps of Europe, the stenching bays of sea-borne slavers all prove, by the dirges and lyrics that have risen from them, that poetry is a way of signalling and testifying to one's humanhood. The tight grip Black people have kept on their humanity down the long gauntlet of history may be miraculous. But once you accept that, you can take the poetry as a natural, something to be looked for, a sign from the skies or pits that we've come through one more once, like the familiar whistle of a long-missed friend. It is the feather in Chicken George's battered derby.

If Black poetry is a natural process, then a pressing question is, what makes Black poetry *Black*? Can a white writer write Black poetry? Is a poem Black if it is written by a Black person who has turned his back on all or part of his cultural identity? Can you spot an Afro poem shuffled in a mixed batch? These and related questions are being probed thoughtfully in these years of awakened identity among Afro-Americans. The reader might gain from a review of these questions as they are explored in Stephen Henderson's *Understanding the New Black Poetry* or in Eugene Redmond's *Drumvoices*, a book that will be a companion to Afro verse for a long time to come.

Answers to these questions should not be allowed to become beehives in the way of the enjoyment of the poems themselves. At least we should not demand a tighter, more perfect definition of the *Blackness* in Black poetry than we ask of the *Englishness* of English poetry, the *Americanness* of American poetry or the *womanness* of women's poetry.

The best commentaries help most by pointing out those features that *sometimes* give the work of Afro poets their special flavoring. There is, for example, the influence of Black song (the poems sometimes being the lyrics), the response to Black dance, the echo of the drum in the poet's rhythm. Much could be said about each of these. But you should also keep an ear open for the power of Black speech in its generous vitality, from street talk to pulpit eloquence, the grand institution of Afro oral repertory and the heritage it offers the Black poet with its forms of signifying, testifying, its tall tales and folk ballads, its trickster stories, blues and

---

*Editor's note: This essay originally appeared as the Introduction to ***Griefs of Joy: Anthology of Contemporary African-American Poetry for Students***. Ed. Eugene B. Redmond. East St. Louis: Black River Writers, 1977.

spirituals, its boasts, toasts and other word games and adventures. The apprecia-tion of the poems in *Griefs of Joy* will be enriched if the tune and tone of these signs and traditions of the Black experience are kept in the back of the mind.

There are also some foundations beneath Black poetry that I want to risk describing to the reader as a way of introducing this brilliant band of Black singers. Poetry, in the extended African sense, is a verbal display of the intense presence of life. A powerful salute in Jamaican slang talk is "Heights!", meaning, "the heights of love to you." The heights of love, of fear, of crises overcome, the heights of mourning and respect and of laughter, the heights of *being* are the goals of African-based poetry. They carry, more than the dull routine of everyday, the awareness of the quick presence of spirit. So a poem is a spirit. Technically, it is like a mask or ritual dance, passionate sermon or gospel hymn, a vehicle through which a spirit, *the* spirit, can be summoned and reaffirmed. A kind of signifying about the soul of things is usually going on in Black poems. What's said up front is only a part of what's going down. The rest, the important part, is left for the ear of feeling and imagination to catch, the inner, intimate conversation that Afro listeners habitually pick up from their music. In "A Late Monsoon Rain," James Kilgore is talking about more than a backache, and the storm he predicts is a good deal more than a weather report. Weather, in fact, is a significant vehicle, in Black rhetorical style, for conveying heavier meanings.

The best way to get your bearings on poems from the Afro tradition is to look *through* the windowpane of the poem's surface into the interior chamber of the collective lives of the people. When in doubt about a reference, try it in the context of the historical experience of the Black folks. Behind the surface plane you can see the outlines of what used to be called the Negro quarters. Here, children are hostages to history and sacred trusts to the future; low ceilings cramp the reach of men; women balance orphaned love and feelings with poise and composure. Mementos of gone heroes crowd this room. And there are many warm reminders of places where the spirit listed, and of friends and loved ones, an extended family almost global in its reach: the idea of ancestry. If you miss the stereo in the corner and the giant speakers, you cannot miss the *sound* of the music. As Willie Kgositsile said to Hugh Masekela, "Home is where the music is." And yes, more than you notice at first, there are books in this room, dusty but proud, Zora Neale Hurston, DuBois, John Mbiti, Chester Himes, Jean Toomer ...

Yet and still, you need two eyes to read these poems, one for the spiritual undermessage that comes from the room inside, and one for the surface of the windowpane, often not badly decorated itself. Because the frame and structure provided by images and metaphors, stanzas and sections, the rhythm patterns, the alliterations and repetitions, the personifications, allusions, the selections of voices and tones and points of view all help to prepare a setting in which some genial emanation can appear majestically.

Mind you, this is no chinchy, monotonous rock, this scene where the more eternal personalities of Afro poetry hang out. The universe of spirit celebrated in this poetry is, as Henry Dumas says, "a coat of many colors." There is comfort here for poems that bury their spiritual communication deep under a worldly exterior as well as for poems like Joyce Carol Thomas' "You Can Not Kill A Spirit" where spirit rises to the surface of discussion. Equally, poems belong here like the quiet, personal introspection of Pinkie Gordon Lane's "Me," the giant pilgrim verses of Lance Jeffers and public, national odes like Dumas' "Black Star Line."

So there is room for variety, differences, in the spirit house of Afro verse, and for something more; let's call it an acceptance of the contrariness of life. In Black speech, we say something is *bad* when we mean it's good, wonderful. True, but part of the wonder is that the energy in the beautiful object we are talking about is also capable of awesome, destructive as well as life-giving force. *Griefs of Joy* recalls to us the powerhouse of the blues, where you find elation in the middle of troubles. Redmond calls it "sugarpain." Josh White asks in his song, "how can you get a baby without no crying?" From back before Duke Ellington, Black musicians have been loyal to the deeper, more comprehensive tones of the minor key. The refusal to separate the sweet from the rough comes out of the background of Afro poetic imagination, whence the poem emerges as a flag of the human spirit (which we sometimes call *soul*) over the bring-me-downs of anti-life. But it is also connected to the African philosophical assumption of the oneness of being.

It is this oneness that generously gives us all our place and character. All true poetry partakes of it, a universal, humanizing energy. But here, now, on this very stage, you are invited to witness a performance of that energy by a contingent from the Afro division of the human creative enterprise, who have their own tough sweet, proud way of getting here.

Detroit poet-playwright Bill Harris (foreground) and Tufts University critic Clyde Taylor tune into a speaker at Shooting Star Writers Conference, Carnegie Mellon University, Pittsburgh, September 1992.

THE DEVIL'S PICK

(from the novel, *Once Upon A Sambo*)

Charles Wartts, Jr.

"I DECLARE, LIL BUDDY," Sam crowed as he baptized the crisp-baked pork snout in a shower of "Lousey Anna" hot sauce, "Ma Cindy made a believer outta me that day!"

It was Friday night and the eagle was flying high. The clock was stretching past 1 a.m. and me and Sam had already mounted what was to become our routine raid on Crown's Soul Food and Lucky's Chinese Food Shops, and had beat a retreat back to Gamble Street with our booty of barbecued snouts, fried tripe sandwiches, a whole order of pork fried rice and two gleaming 16-ounce bottles of Orange Whistle.

It was Sam's first payday, and our celebration of the eagle's arrival was in full swing as we sat out on the front, feeling the bite of the breeze, huddled into our respective corners of the bench, feet propped up, soles almost touching. Sam seemed reluctant to let go of the tale of Ma Cindy and the butterbean arbor. His demon still had a hold on him and my back dug deeper into the pickets as I zipped my light windbreaker up to the neck, knowing there was more to come.

"Come to thank of it," Sam chomped down on the pork rind, frowned as the hot sauce bit into his tongue, then washed it down with a big gulp of "pop" as he called it, "Ma Cindy was the cause of me joinin church soon as I did." He swung his feet onto the concrete walkway and hunched forward, facing me, as a medley of voices from other diehard clusters along the street warbled by on the spring air.

"Yeah, Lil Buddy, I had chills for a week – everytime I thought about the way that 'oman fastened them muddy green eyes on me that day. Didn't miss Sunday school for the next six months," he guffawed. "So I couldn't wait to git on the mourners' bench when revival meetin rolled round, but Big Mama Rachel wouldn't let me. Said her and Mama be carryin what little sins I had til I was twelve.

"Anyway, I worried her so bad til she let me go soon as I turned ten – but I still didn't git nothin. Wasn't til I was eleven – and come eyeball to eyeball wid my Great Uncle Pearl Turner – that I got in earnest. Uncle Pearl was a strange sorta fellah, never did talk much to nobody except his horses. Always kept a stable full of prime horseflesh, and look like he'd be ridin a different one everytime you see him. He could lomo ride em too, podnuh. Musta been one of the last gen-u-wine cowboys. He had a full head of curly white hair with a face that looked like Geronimo or Cochise or one of them other Injun chiefs, except there was so much red and black mixed up in it, til it looked almost raspberry.

"Well, one day I was settin out on the porch of our house on Refuge when Uncle Pearl come ridin down off the levee like the U.S. Calvary was on his tail. I was by myself that day cause Mama was up at the big house and Big Mama Rachel had gone off to the sweet potato patch.

"I knowed who he was right off by the way he was laid down in that saddle. You couldn't hardly tell the difference between the horse's mane and that long, snow-white hair of his ropin in the wind. And to boot, he was ridin that coal-black stallion of his – I bleeve he called him Midnite. Only thang white on him was his mane and his two front paws. Anyway, that day ole Midnite was wet and glistenin like black gold as he come bearin down on me. I'd already scrambled up onto my knees and made it to the far side of the porch when he come to a full stop, his hoofs pawin the front steps. Matter of fact, they made it to the steps at about the same time, cause Uncle Pearl had already swung down outta the saddle and was trottin right long beside him.

"Straightaway, he went about his business, tying the reins to one of the porch beams. Then he looked me up and down pretty good like he usually did, his eyes still squintin from the wind. 'Boy, go git yo Uncle a cold glass of ice water,' he said in a gruff, gravelly voice that seemed too low and quiet for his looks. I was back in a flash. Then stood there like a dumbwaiter while he gulped down half a fruit jar of water without ever takin them hawkish eyes off me.

"'When you gon quit wearin out the seat of yo britches at dese revival meetins and gone git yo'self some 'ligion?' he asked, gazin straight through me.

"'Well ... ahm doin my ... I mean ... ahm prayin hard as I kin, suh,' I stumbled over my words, tryin to keep from bitin my tongue off.

"'How old you, son?'

"'Ahm 'leven ... be twelve come October,' I blurted out, my chest swelling up. Meanwhile, he slipped them beat-up calfskin gloves off his hands, fingered the stubble on his chin and looked out over the pastures.

"'You know, hit ain't seemly fuh the Good Lawd to keep passin over a willin soul jes drylongso .... Boy you jes might be the devil's pick!' he let out quiet as the Judgement as he raised the fruit jar and drank it dry.

"I'm tellin you a chill went all through me, Lil Buddy. Had to lean aginst the porch to steady myself I got so weak.

"'You ever been burnt, boy?' he looked down at me kinda curious like. Meanwhile, I'm still tryin to collect myself.

"'Yassuh!'

"'Wharbouts?'

"'I stumbled and fell aginst the stove one time and burnt my arm.'

"'Did it hurt bad?'

"'Yassuh! You kin still see the mark now....' I held the back of my left arm up for him to see. But he took hold of my elbow without even lookin to see where I was pointin.

"'You ever been up in the quarters, round the 'chine shop, whar dey works on dem broke down tractors and plows and thangs?'

"'Yassuh!'

"'Den you done seed yo gawddaddy, Deacon Brooks, when he weldin sumpthin r'other back together?'

"I bowed my head to save breath.

"'Dat little piece of tube he hold in his hand spits out a streak of blue fahr hot enough to melt iron jes lak butter. Did you know dat? Well...they tell me dat's some of the hottest fahr on earth,' he said, grippin my arm tighter as he stooped down to look me dead in the eye.

"'Now son, I want you to thank about a fahr seben times hotter'n dat ... seben times! Thank about what it feels lak to have a fahr lak dat – whitehot and quicker-'n a water moccasin's tongue – lickin its way up yo legs, yo arms, yo chest,' he said, grabbin hold of each part of my body as he went along.' Even yo hair and eyes – flamin, scorchin, blisterin, makin yo blood boil and yo eyes pop. And not jes for a few seconds lak wid dis heah arm, awhhh nawhhh! But fuhevermo'! Dat's what hellfire is lak, son. You thank you ready for a taste of dat?'

"'Nawsuh!' I whispered through parched lips, feelin my skin meltin under the heat of his hands.

"'You thank you gon git yo'self some 'ligion dis time round?'

"'Yassuh!'

"He still stood there, crouched on one knee, his breath steamin aginst my face.

"'Git 'way from round all dese folk. Find yo'self a prayin ground somewheres. Git in earnest and the Lawd will heah yo prayer. Cuz if you don't,' he raised up, lookin down at me from on high, 'come October when you turn twelve yeahs old and sumpthin happen to take you way fum dis world, in hell you gon lift up yo eyes.'

"Lil Buddy I musta stood there for the longest time befo I could even move, just gazin after my uncle and that devilish stallion of his til they wasn't nothin but a oily black streak on the horizon.

"Come evenin time, I didn't want no supper even though we was havin my favorite – rabbit 'n rice – and Big Mama had gone and baked a lemon meringue pie for dessert. I could see both of em lookin under-eyed at me as I shook my head and passed on by the table. I could even hear what they was thankin: 'If dat boy turnin down rabbit 'n rice and lemon pie, the Lawd sho nuff must be done troubled his heart.' And back then, even grownfolk would git outta yo way when they thought the Lawd was workin wid you.

"Bright and early the next mornin, I went searchin out me a prayin ground. Wasn't long befo I stumbled upon the corn crib a little ways down the road from the house. It was right across from the hogpen, and I had to go there every evenin to get feed for em. I figgered it would make a good prayin ground since it be bout the last place anybody'd expect to find me, bad as I hated havin to shuck corn for them pigs. So right away I cleared out one of the back corners of the crib and piled it up with cornshucks – enough to hide under if I had to. Then I set down Injun-style wid my back restin in the corner, and offered up a prayer for the Good Lawd to consecrate it for me.

"Over the next few days, I rooted down in them shucks like a sow stretched out in the fattenin pen. Big Mama had made me a present of my own copy of the New Testament, and I'd set there studying over different verses and prayin bits and pieces of prayers I'd heard the Old Folks say, mixin em in wid my own. Then I'd go to revival meetin at night and watch all *my* friends crossin over one by one

– dancin and shoutin and testifyin to the congregation bout how they'd shook hands wid Jesus.

"Now, all the time I'm settin there waitin and wonderin what was takin the Good Lawd so long to move me *up* off that bench. Hard as I'd been prayin, I figgered any minute the Holy Ghost was due to straddle my back and ride me like a Georgia mule. But no sich a thing happened. Pretty soon, wasn't nobody but me and ole mean Doreen left warmin the bench, and everybody knowed she'd been the devil's daughter ever since her mama nursed her on milk from a nanny goat when she was nothin but a baby.

"When I left outta church that night, I was lomo draggin, podnuh, cause look like the devil had me wrapped up, tied up and tangled up so tight til the Lawd just couldn't git ahold to me. The next day was Friday, and I remember I got up outta the bed real early. Had a wanderin sperrit on me. Didn't want no breakfast, even though Big Mama Rachel had the whole house smellin up sumpthin awful wid fresh-baked cracklin bread, grits, eggs, and crisp poke jowl. Yet 'n still, I couldn't wait to get outta the house and set my feet down on the road.

"No sooner'n my bare feet hit the dirt, I commenced to walkin like a big piece of lodestone was drawin me off somewheres. Walked right past the corn crib like it wasn't even there. Almost stumbled over one of Big Mama's settin hens. There she was cluckin round the hogpen wid a fresh-hatched brood of nine baby chicks trailin behind her. She had a dark, reddish-brown color to her, and nary a one of her biddies favored her a'tall. Some of em was yellow, some speckled, and the rest jet black. And yet they was all cheepin right long under her wings, stumblin over each other, tryin they best to keep close to her as they could. Now, that wasn't nothin new to me, Lil Buddy, but look like on that partic'lar mornin, it was a marvel and a wonder that turned my mind as sweet and mellow as a honeydew as I stood there gazin at em.

"But the road was callin to me and I couldn't stop for long. And all the while I was walkin, I was lookin out over the canebrake and wheatfields, and over the meadows where the cows and sheep and goats was grazin peacefully. I could feel the beads of sweat makin my hand slippery on the big Bible I'd hauled long wid me, and my mind kept runnin back over the different passages I had been studying.

"I thought about David sleepin out in the pastures, keepin watch over his flock. And how Gawd had raised him up in faith and grace from a lowly shepherd boy and give him the courage to slay Goliath and become the pick of King Saul. Then I thought about Shadrack, Meshack and Abenego, the three Hebrew boys who'd been thrown into the fiery furnace and how Gawd had dispatched an angel from heaven to plunge hisself into the fire and draw out the heat til it wasn't nothin but a blast of friendly sunshine. Thought on how ole Lazareth had stood hongry and raggily at the rich man's gate when the attack dogs bore down on him and licked him wid healin tongues.

"But the thone that kept prickin my mind the most was what the presidin minister, Elder Powell, had said last revival meetin. He'd talked about how ole Lucifier was a crafty ole devil. How he could dress hisself up into the very image of the thang you desired most in the world and come promenadin up to the door of yo heart. And once you open it, how he could bore his head in like a tick and suck out all the humbleness, til he turn yo heart hard as stone.

"That got me to thankin about by own heart and how hard it must be that everybody else could git religion except me. I could feel a chill run through me everytime I thought about what Uncle Pearl had said: '*Boy, you jes might be the devil's pick*!' In fact, every since my feet hit the floor that mornin I'd been thankin on a way to soften up my heart so Jesus could come in and save me. Just then, as I was walkin long wid my mind all tangled up, sumpthin that one of the old white-haired mothers of the church had spoke to me that night befo, come back to me.

"I remembered how Mother Daisy Mae Taylor had crept over to me while I was settin there on the bench wid my head swung low. She'd laid both her hands on my shoulders and smiled the sweetest ole snaggled-toothed smile I ever seen as she bent down and whispered to me: 'Sammy, hit don't take but one prayer. You jes keep on sayin ham mussy, Lawd. Let dat be yo *onliest* prayer, and I gahr'tee de Lawd will heah yah!' So all the while I was walkin, I just kept on prayin that prayer: 'Have mercy, Lawd! Lawd have mercy on me!"

"Befo long, I come up beside a little pond just across the barbed wire fence of the pastures, where a knot of cows led by a testy ole bull, had stopped to drink. I stopped and stood there lookin, not knowin rightly what I was lookin at, when words started droppin from my lips: *He maketh me to lie down in green pastures; He leadeth me beside the still waters; He restoreth my soul.* Look like no sooner'n I'd said em, the knot in my mind came untangled and I just stood there for the longest, smilin at them cows. And look like to me they was smilin back as some of em turned they spotted faces toward me.

"Then all at once that ole red bull, whose backside had been turned to me all the while he was suckin up a belly full, flicked his tail and turned all the way round. Then he raised his head, looked me dead in the face, and bawled: '*Have mercy, Lawd*!' No sooner'n he let it out, the throng around him lifted they heads and bellowed: '*Have mercy, Lawd! Have mercy, Lawd*!' Then from all cross the pasture – from the calves to the young heifers to the fullgrown breedin cows – all of em was cryin out: '*Have mercy, Lawd*!'

"Lil Buddy, it scared me so bad til I liketa croaked. I jumped back from that fence like somebody'd just juiced it, and broke a trot on down the road without lookin back. Kept my eyes trained on the cornfield to the other side of the road where a big flock of crows was holdin court bout sumpthin or other. Then just as I went to hurry on past, they all pointed they beaks up in the air and got to squawkin and screamin: '*Have mercy, Lawd*!'

"That's when I got in the wind sho nuff. Didn't even thank about easin up til I'd left them fields and pastures behind. By then, I'd made it to the lip of the slough where the road dipped down and wound its way round the edges of the swamp, then come out agin near the foot of the levee. It was thick wid all kinda trees and bushes and wildflowers, and I slowed up my pace pretty good when my eye fell on a bright patch of field lilies growin near the swamp's edge.

"I figgered if I could just stop a while to meditate on the lilies, maybe I could git hold of myself. But soon as I started to relax good, a strong breeze stirred up off the swamp and troubled the branches of the weepin willow trees, and they started whimperin: '*Have mercy, Lawd*!' Then it was in the tops of the oaks and the cottonwoods; in the mulberry and dewberry bushes; the lilies and the sunflowers; and they all swooned together in a mighty chorus, chantin: '*Have mercy, Lawd*!' I was beside myself by then, Lil Buddy, and I struck out for the other side of the slough as fast as I could. But now everytime I made a step, I could hear the redhot soles of my feet pantin and pleadin to the road: '*Have mercy, Lawd*!' "I declare, Lil Buddy, I didn't know what to do wid myself. Didn't know whether to praise the Lawd or cuss the devil. By then I'd come up outta the slough, and I raised my eyes up to the sky. I didn't have nothin to do wid it. The words come outta my mouth all by theyselves, and I heard myself shoutin: 'Hallelujah! Thank you, Jesus!' over and over til it filled me up from my head clean down to the soles of my feet. When I looked up agin, the sun was shoutin all over the place. Then the clouds joined in and started clappin they hands and pattin they feet and fannin theyselves round sumpthin scandalous. That's when I lit out back down the road goin a mile a minute, not stoppin til I'd spread the news all over the quarters."

Madame Katherine Dunham talks to a March 1992 audience at Washington University during her 47-day fast for the plight of Haitian refugees. At right are dancers Theo Jamison and Sylvester "Sunshine" Lee.

ALICE WALKER AS MESSENGER IN HER LATEST SAGA

Possessing the Secret of Joy. Harcourt Brace Jovanovich: 1992. 286 pp. Hardback: $19.95.

Reviewed by Andrea M. Wren

Possessing the Secret of Joy is Alice Walker's most recent offering. Thematically, it's a courageous effort; but the text reads like a research paper with characters. *Possessing*... is dispassionate, didactic, maddeningly lackluster, prosaic and pedestrian. The characters seem mute or shy. Tashi sounds like Adam. Adam sounds like Olivia. No voice ever emerges distinct. However, Walker has chosen a subject that should be anything but lackluster: clitoridectomy.

Clitoridectomy is a brutal rite undergone by some eighty million African women. It involves the mutilation of the external genital organs. There are several "reasons" for this practice. It is believed to insure fidelity by lessening the pleasure of the wife through the removal of her clitoris. Secondly, the removal of the clitoris is supposed to end the androgyny of childhood. These procedures are performed under the most hideous conditions: without anesthesia and using unsterile objects--if you consider a rusty razor an operating object. The procedure often leads to life-threatening loss of blood, infection and sometimes loss of life. It can also lead to infertility, difficult childbirth and painful intercourse.

There are three methods of the procedure. Sunna is the most traditional. It involves removing the tip of the clitoris. Excision is another form and involves the removal of the clitoris and the labia minora. Infibulation is the most insidious of the procedures. This form involves the removal of the clitoris, the labia minora and labia majora. With infibulation, the pubic area is stitched up after the genitals are removed, leaving a small opening for urination and menstruation. Imagine volunteering for such a procedure. Tashi's mother refuses to let her daughter undergo the "operation" at the proper age because of religious beliefs. Walker undermines the brutality of the rite by having Tashi "volunteer" after she has already come of age.

Regarding this subject, Walker raised an important question in a recent issue of *Ebony* magazine: "I'm saying that if you mutilate 100 million women and make it so hard for them to give birth that many of them will die trying or their children will be born deformed or crippled, how can you expect the continent to be healthy?" In one of the more real moments in the book, Tashi aborts a would-be daughter rather than let her live to experience clitoridectomy. This revolutionary act is reminiscent of captive mothers who would kill their children rather than let them be enslaved. Walker simultaneously addresses a similar crisis in America. Though not an actual ritual in America, mutilation and assassination of women occurs daily. For Walker, the locale of the mutilation is unimportant. The discontinuation of abuse and oppression is the pressing issue.

Walker is to be commended for bringing this insanity to light and for continuing to speak for the disenfranchised. However, her agenda seems shaky from the beginning. The title of the book evolves from "a white colonialist author" who says: "Black people are natural, they possess the secret of joy, which is why they can survive the suffering and humiliation inflicted upon them." Near the end of the novel, a character tells us that the author of the quote is faulty but one wonders why Walker would name her precious novel after such an illogical theory. The reader learns "the secret of joy" towards the end of the novel but the denouement, like the disclosure of "the secret," is unfulfilling and unrealistic in its tragic, ebullient ending.

Some readers found fault with Walker for getting on a podium and preaching in *The Temple of My Familiar*. Such preaching is an overt reality in *Possessing*. Religion, sexism and misogyny continue to be subjects sermonized throughout the novel. There are other more suspect assertions such as this one: "Negro women ... can never be analyzed effectively because they can never bring themselves to blame their mothers." Perhaps responding to the backlash that the movie and novel *The Color Purple* received, we "hear" a response from Adam that stirs old memories: "As soon as he utters the word 'ritual' there is a furor in the court...This is our business you would put into the streets! We cannot publicly discuss this taboo."

The author assumes an annoying persona throughout the novel. There are moments when the dialogue reads like an interview and the same illogical assumptions that shadow the title, shadow the pages. One look at the note "to the reader" and you realize that the writer has not obtained enough distance from her life to leave the majority of it out of the text.

It's difficult to believe that the same person who penned *The Color Purple* wrote this series of sentences. I suppose it's hard to keep the momentum and passion of a *Meridian* and *Third Life of Grange Copeland* going. The "third life" is Walker's. And it is outlandish and cosmic, sometimes unbelievably unreal, but most of all, it is an intruder on the page.

Novelists Walter Mosley (*Devil in a Blue Dress*) and Octavia Butler (*Wild Seed*) listen to audience responses following their panel on mystery and science fiction at Shooting Star Writers Conference, Carnegie Mellon University, September 1992.

Rite #7

St. Louis and Otherwheres: Urban Wordscapes

Jabari Asim
Bob Holman
Ira B. Jones
Debra F. Meadows
Carla Moody
Christopher Stanard

From THE PLACE WHERE YOU LIVE

Jabari Asim

cracksters

in the shadow of the school
commerce is their rule:

say dude, you lookin?
yo bro, ah got it ovah heah.
my man, wanna piece uh the rock?
dis stuff so good it's bettah than pussy.
c'mon slick. your first taste is free.

wish the earth would open up and eat them.
wish cold death would come and keep them.

family in a nutshell

oaken hands circling the dinner table
form an urgent prayer cable
calling on God most high
to prove He is alive and able.
mother prays for descending wings
to end her husband's smashing things.
sister prays for wisdom past her years
and words to dry her mother's tears.
father prays for escape from life
and its ensuing hateful strife.
brother prays for a gun
to get the job done.

jermaine's rap

crack broke the old man's back
then he dropped from a heart attack
mom's for sale on Sarah Street
how in hell am Ah s'pozed ta eat?
y'all know who Ah am
Jermaine Jones – who gives a damn?

just raise yo hands in the air
keep 'em up while Ah strip you bare
give up that goddam chain
or you gonna feel a lotta pain
Ah gotta switchblade anna gun
an' Ahm damn good wit eitha one
scream, bitch, Ah don't care
it turns me on when you git scared
the cops know who Ah am
Jermaine Jones – who gives a damn?

blowin at the Moose

In a nightspot called the Moose
a bebop band is bustin loose.

As glasses clink and saxes roar,
a sexy dancer takes the floor.
Her breasts are round.
Her waist is lean,
Nefertari garbed in green.
Jazzers lick their lips
and watch her swaying hips.

In a nightspot called the Moose
a bebop band is bustin loose.

WE ARE THE DINOSAUR

Bob Holman

Blast open the gates to kingdom come
Whoops what happened to everyone
Planted a seed – Grew into a gun
Dum de dum dum dum dum dum dumb

Life was so much easier livin in a cartoon
Ice-age in a dumpster – that's our living room
Set fire to yr roof – get a better view
Global warmin' is a warnin' – toodle-oo

We are the dinosaur
We don't live here anymore
We got what we were askin for
Follow the dinosaur

Ho ho homo sapiens
Ain't so smart
Ka ka kamikazi, Friend
Which way is the ark?

The world is dialin 911
The don't walk sign just changed so ya better run
What we are waiting for has long since come
Dum-de-dum dum dumm dum dum

Cross the scorchin sands w/ my big fat feet
It's hard becomin diesel fuel with nothin to eat
We're prewinged birds & tend to disappear
Better catch us quick – we're outta here

We are the dinosaur
We don't live here anymore
We got what we were askin for
Follow the dinosaur

Hurry! We're disappearing back into the past
Did you really think the Future was gonna last
It's endin with a bang so let's have a blast
Let's go cannibal – it makes a nice contrast

Chauffeured ambulances race to the prom
Santa, please bring me a neutron bomb
Recycle the planet before the earth is a grave
Excuse me, I have to get back to my cave

We are the dinosaur
We don't live here anymore
We got what we were askin for
Follow the dinosaur

Ch-ch-ch Chinese chance
It's all a joke
M-m-m-may I have this dance
Th-That's all folks

Writer and Neo-Hoodoo pioneer Ishmael Reed relaxes between panels during the Literary Celebration of the Second National Black Arts Festival in Atlanta, August 1990.

ALLEY GAMES 13

Ira B. Jones

my father spins vintage vinyl against the turn table
soloing at seventy-eight speed
john coltrane rhythms into my memories
as i take *Giant Steps*
not as large as his or Trane's
Giant Steps for me just the same
remembering not to double dribble inside
or slam the back screen door
my young legs jump down the flight of five stairs
streak through the early afternoon of the spring of '71
bursting with endless energy across the walkway
with one smooth dribble behind and between my legs
propelling myself against the weight of life's gravity
airborne above the gate built by my father's hands
touching down in the alley with wings spread
like the posturing young black birds sitting on the schoolyard fence
crooning the *Temptations'* tune
young flesh fills with fresh lyrics licking like fire in the air
tasting like black licorice and bloody street beats

Organizers of the new Black Literary Guild gather on the campus of Southern Illinois University at Edwardsville for a spring 1992 photograph. Members include (l-to-r, seated): Juble Hairston and Jazell Dailey. Standing: Eugene B. Redmond (faculty advisor), Michelle Foster (secretary), Ramona Jones, Marcus Atkins (president), Yvette Bean (treasurer), Harold Austin, Crystal Goff, Jamal Isaac (vice president), Marcia Hunt, and Janice Gregory.

&/HE'S GOT A MUSIC/MAGIC

Debra F. Meadows

"She has a way about her . . .
Makes me want to kick off my shoes
'n dance all nite" – Layding
Lumumba Kaliba

". . . Come and dance the Lover's
Dance! In an old remembered way..."
– Countee Cullen

i told him
i cd do w/out the
clutter of subways/&
tobacco streets
manhattan sky/scapes &
city boys w/silk
scarves/& empty pockets . . .

but how i
miss mother harlem's
sunday kitchen – –
the soul food fumes
& fruit/stands
w/fresh picked flowers
the songs that
exude from his
spirit
the moons that
dawn in his
eyes
the poems that
flow from his
perfect/pen

& the smooth
special/gentle
manly kind-of-way
claude mckay's metaphors
melt on his tongue/& how
countee cullen's copper
suns pale next to his

he spoke of
rainbow/images
still life/&
b flat
broken dreams/&
purpled/hearts
blue mondays at
baby grand's
shades of cotton
in harlem/&
dark-skinned
prima/donnas . . .

i told him
i cd do w/out the
iron/horse
& asphalt/jungles
urban dreams/&
new york city/slickers
but he's got a
music/magic –
silver ribbons/tied
round nomadic/trystings
porcelain love
warmed/wrapped in
red/cotton
gingham –

a music/magic –
duke ellington's adagio
agile/pirouettes in the night –
regal/ballerinas dancing
on boogie-woogie
paper/mates

a smooth
special/gentle
manly/music kind-of-magic
that baritones a
sweet/potato inspiration
whenever he flicks his
bic

FORTUNATE

Carla Moody

Fortunately,
my imperfections and inclinations
are well-known, well-publicized
by people who apparently know
or at least think/say so
there is nothing deep about me
and that makes it easy on everybody.
I am so obvious
so one dimensional
that I don't need much time to think
for or about myself
and neither does anybody else.
And it is fortunate.
I don't take much
to dissect or explain.
It seems brief and surface observations
readily reveal my limitations
and potential (such as it is).
Don't spend too much time
trying to find out
what I am really about.
Obviously, surviving has taught me nothing.
Watching my own "self" fragment
has left me none the wiser?
Meeting the coldest eyes
and the most degrading sighs –
walking through fire
has not deepened me?
Me?
One of history's earliest robots.
One of technology's earliest machines.
Well, I'm not one to reject
the experts
(people commissioned and paid
to find the truth of things)
so I guess they do know my
dreams and ambitions better
than I do.
And I guess, it's fortunate
although, it seems to me

you've got to do a lot of dying
living by this plan
and it's just fortunate
I'm a black woman
and suffering comes easy.

A SHORT POEM

Carla Moody

It doesn't matter

in the end

how many

dark ladies

board buses

on late autumn

evenings

teeth clenched.

MINDIN' YOUR BUSINESS

Christopher Stanard

Maybe you should stop calling your sisters
"bitches and 'hos,"
and show some respect
for your mother.
Maybe you should stop treating your sisters like
"sluts and 'hos,"
and take care of that baby girl who needs you –
or maybe she's just another 'ho to you.
Maybe you should show some respect
for your father;
act like one.
Maybe you should truly mind your business
and show some respect
for yourself.
Go ahead and mind your business.
I'm just tryin' to mind my own.

KRS-1

Christopher Stanard

He fought a stereo-
type of stupidity
by reading a book
becoming a bibliophile
then blasting knowledge
back from the past.
Relevant now,
his story
is in the future
today.

RAINDROPS

Christopher Stanard

My love
fell like raindrops
splashing atop the crystal ceiling
she had built over her heart
to keep the flower inside
from drowning.
tap tap tap.
I see the petals withering.
tap tap tap.
Don't let the flower die.

HEADLINE NEWS

Christopher Stanard

Chuck D.,
Gil Scott-Heron,
and the Last Poets were wrong –

The revolution *will* be televised,
shot on a camcorder,
and viewed worldwide on CNN.

NOT that a camcorder means a damn thing –
just ask Rodney King.

Rite #8

'Whereabouts Known': Apropos Ancestors

ALL BLUES

for Miles Dewey Davis

Baron James Ashanti

Yeah
In the Big Apple
1944
dressed in zoot suit
pork pie hat
was ready
to jump jam & jive
The Street was hot to trot
but
Minton's cooked feasts
for the masses!

while the okey doke
was on death row
anxious for execution
there was this young blood
from East St Louis
who used big muddy for
electric current
During the wake
he joined the greater good
with fierce aggression
and
genius baptized in war water

becoming accomplice
to red hot series
of cutting sessions
that spent life
like chump change
thrown to robust winds
of innovation
where uninitiated
ran for cover

on the one
on the one
where danger did
boucoup damage
cruising high on hog

grease on rail
Miles as
Gabriel's bad tempered child
came up from privilege
with smooth onyx tinct skin
as breaklight

*"You gotta bring ass
to get ass !"*

hard & cold venture
neon sweating echoes
rode chordal changes
like bug eyed loa
lost between ceremony
'sitting shivah'*
for normal shit
cut short by frantic quest
for special sound
that splits rocks
creates myths
and makes fine women
weep for lost gods!

Smoke from another fire
draped all over
the real deal
gone down jagged like
shattered glass
Miles was unaware
hanging out with legends
would make you
see strange things
and speak in tongues

Be-Bop suckling at
the breast of fluent rage
c flat
goose bump riff
shuffling arrogance
in the glare from
spotlight conk

---

*Shivah (Heb-seven) mourning period of seven days

Miles grew up
with a lyricism
fragile in its sensuality
cool by probe leading
to an alchemy of sound
that left squares
sucking corpse gas

yet and still
chanting a spell
the wrong way
will fuck your shit up

drunk from
misogynic nightshade
Miles stumbled
because
sometimes dreams
don't hold tight
and
artists fall short
of what they create

after 10 years
'in a silent way'
he felt
grains of sand's method
marking time
so he came back
for an encore
before the set closed
using raspy voiced
vibretto as testament
to his last number
an 8 bar slow drag as
lascivious bulge
in flatline transforms
heart thumping
sequined death rattle
into wings
across river styx

with history as mistress
now
Miles can chord and score
for the angels!

LIKE MILES SAID

Alvin Aubert

my memory ain't too good
i trouble the past, like, crazy
maybe i'm crazy like they say miles was
maybe i don't half know what i'm doing

like miles said if you don't know what you're
doing chances are you ain't doing nothin'

quoting the old drummer he played with
when he first started playin'
who was dead when miles said that about him

now miles is dead and i'm sure every mf
and his mama is going to be lyin'
about stuff miles said like maybe i'm doin'
right now but miles won't mind

miles was hip to all that shit
like every time you put a mouthpiece
to your lips you bound to lie some.

Alvin Aubert, founding editor of Obsidian, *at Modern Language Association conference in Chicago, December 1990.*

MALCOLM X

For Dudley Randall

Gwendolyn Brooks

Original.
Ragged-round.
Rich-robust.

He had the hawk-man's eyes.
We gasped. We saw the maleness.
The maleness raking out and making guttural the air
and pushing us to walls.

And in a soft and fundamental hour
a sorcery devout and vertical
beguiled the world.

He opened us –
who was a key,

who was a man.

"CHILDREN OF THE SUN"

Henry Dumas

... Jubal's shadow stretched across the ground where all the pine needles lay like a brown quilt. His shadow made a small cross over the cardboard box, and in the box the dead dog lay – its face covered with foam and blood. We were all waiting for Jubal to say something. But we didn't know what he was going to say. And since none of us knew what to say, we just waited.

Nathan's dog was going to die anyway. A mad dog always dies. But most of the time a mad dog has to be shot, and if Lance hadn't grabbed Nathan's gun and shot it, maybe Jubal would have, maybe I would have. I don't know. Even Hoodoo Brown might have, and I guess Nathan would have even though it was his dog. We felt more sorry for Nathan than for his dog. Lance and Hoodoo Brown were sitting behind me on the mound of dirt that had piled up in front of the cave. Pieces of the roof of the cave were still falling, now and then, as if another cave-in were coming. We knew that if we wanted to keep coming to that cave we'd have to get some logs and two-by-fours to support the entrance. I looked at Lance and Hoodoo. They weren't saying anything.

Up the hill, through the high pines, the mist from the waterfall made a rainbow in the morning sun ... and as the waves of mist hung in the stillness of the pine grove, moving like a ghost wearing a bright band of red, blue and yellow around its neck. I seemed to hear the echo of that shot which Lance had fired. It was funny trying to think about seeing that dirt tumbling down in front of us and blocking the entrance to the cave. It was funny because I was trembling still as if we all weren't free from the hole yet and Jubal was still digging us out with that stick.

Hoodoo Brown had eased himself down from the mound so that he was standing directly behind Jubal. He leaned as if he were going to say something. Knowing Hoodoo I knew he was going to try something funny to make us laugh, and while we were laughing he would make a speech or something and take the attention away from Jubal, who was standing nearer than any of us to the brown cardboard box with the dead dog in it. But he didn't say a word. Only his mouth fell open and hung when he sensed that he didn't know what to say. None of us had planned on who would say the prayer over the dead dog. Hoodoo bowed his head. His shadow merged with Jubal's in the morning sun. And a drool of saliva began to develop from the center crevice in Hoodoo's round lips, a drool that hung there in the light, building up slowly like an icicle does in the winter time from the cold rain that rolls off of our barn across from my window. I watched him. And I knew that he wanted to say something. But he couldn't.

The sun fell through upon Jubal, whose blackness seemed to reflect the light, seemed to thrust itself out at the light and shine...as if he were sweating – and sometimes he was – and the light and Jubal's skin seemed to grab on to each other like two forces grappling ... and as we stood there around the box with Nathan's dead dog in it, stood there trying to pretend we were grownups having a very proper funeral, something about Jubal's manner caught us and halted us, drained us of all the horseplay and laughing and made us look at what we were really doing. We sensed vaguely that somehow he knew what he was doing, or at least felt it. I doubt now if I knew what we were really doing then. How could a group of kids know about the terror and pain of dying...and yet we did know, we did sense something. Jubal made us. I don't know what it was, but we sensed it. Hoodoo Brown sensed it too. His mouth hung, dropped and stayed .... If we had planned on mocking Reverend Flare, if we had dared plan – without any of us saying it either – if we had dared to mock Nathan's dead dog because Nathan was a white boy and that made his puppy also kind of white, despite the fact that it was reddish brown – indeed, if we had dared to mock death, to ridicule a funeral, then I know we would have all felt hideously ashamed. Somehow Jubal sensed this. That's why we were all waiting for him to speak, waiting for him to save us again. And Nathan, who had not asked us to pray over his dog, sensed it too. He mumbled something about going, but bowed his head in anticipation, his blond hair flopping over into his face like a veil. I watched him and I wondered if he were going to cry.

Lance was cocking and recocking Nathan's twenty-two rifle, cocking it and aiming it here, there, and over and around. I could feel him, feel his indifference in back of me. I wanted to turn around. For some reason I thought I felt him aiming the gun at one of us, just for fun, and I was hoping it wasn't loaded. Out of the corner of my eye I saw Lance jerk sideways. I couldn't help but turn to look. I saw him aiming the rifle down the road, through the pine trees, following some target! Hoodoo looked, Nathan glanced up past Jubal who was looking at Lance, and then we were all looking at what Lance was aiming at and it was a road runner! The wingless bird was racing along, just passing by. Soon it would be out of sight behind the trees. If Lance was going to shoot ... ! It had a snake in its beak, and the snake was flopping back like hair ... and then before we could all breathe in and out, the bird was gone, racing into the wind. Lance leaped up and ran a couple of paces, pretending to follow the target and firing, "Whuck! whuck! whuck!" As he was making the sounds with his mouth the sound seemed to fill the whole place. Why didn't he shut up? I felt like telling him something, but I knew if I did we'd be in an argument, and Lance was bigger than me and always won the fights. Then Jubal pointed with his finger. His arm jerked up toward the trees. The only one of us that didn't know what he was pointing at was Lance. We looked. And there sitting on a pine limb high in the tree over Nathan's head was a red bird, and it was watching us. We had seen it before but paid no attention. Now Jubal was pointing at it. Lance turned and saw Jubal's arm retreating and he looked into the trees, and when he did, the red bird flew away, and the sun broke through upon us more ... and beat down upon us standing there beside the mound, and Jubal stepped upon the rock and he spoke ....

CIRCLES

(for Malcolm X on the 66th anniversary of his birth)

Darryl Holmes

my son is six, so full of questions
I was eight when you fell in the audubon
a nation went down in the silence
gasping for air.
what would I have said if I knew you then
how many questions would I have asked my father
before I cried?
the more I see the more I want to close my eyes
and swallow your death, echoing off of mountains.

I have gone from punching the walls to praying at night
from kneeling in a cloud of dust to knowing my darkness.
I am not a silent fist or a face in the crowd
not one of the boys swallowing an innocent beer.

where did we go when you left us
how many sunsets passed us by
while we counted the circles of blood?
sometimes I see myself leading an entire army into war
riding shotgun in the back seat of a southern car.
sometimes I find myself kneeling in a forest
scraping the face of a bludgeoned enemy from my hands.

where does the madness stop Malcolm
how do I press my mouth to a woman's tongue
swallow the water without looking past her eyes?
how do I tell my son, somewhere the bullets are waiting
a badge is on fire
everywhere the country has his name
and I can only carry him so far?

why do the faces haunt me
why do I see the same dark man everyday
rocking on the steps of a building?
why do I carry his eyes in my pocket
think of his hair as tight knotted
in coils of dust and tar?
his lips stretched out like a runway.

once I wanted to change the world
once I wore dashikis over my ties to work
once I married a woman who I pushed too far
and now I am here alone
standing near the lines I will never cross.

was it too much weight for one man Malcolm?
is it too much now that you hear my voice
and all of the other voices
all of the other fists and guns
that grow out of our mouths?

all of the silent moments when we question our lives
the things we let go by?

last summer I took my son on a boat
the sun burned down on the lake
a family of ducks moved in our direction.
I watched them stay in line
I watched them swim so easily through the water.
I learned what freedom is like
and why I have so much faith in my son.

it is simple isn't it? it is also very hard
to join the fragmented voices
to spring our feet from the vice
to slow down long enough to listen
to the earth sounds that Edwin talks about,
the beautiful earth sounds.

I heard Philip Harper the other night in New Orleans
I heard him blow a song for his daughter Dakini.
I saw my cousin Keith with an ankh around his neck
Clifford Brown clapping for Philip as he screamed
through 1239A.
the young alto player wailed like Charlie Parker
and the first time I ever heard Kevin Powell
read a poem, it blew me away.

all of this within us
all that america wants to take away.

is it too much weight for one man Malcolm?
have you turned to Allah with all of our eyes
spilling from your hands
have you gotten any rest since you left us
should I leave some water out by the road?

WAITING FOR MALCOLM

Ja A. Jahannes

Somebody said they were impressed by how Dan Quayle handled himself in the vice presidential debate. He was "aggressive" they said, with approval. Funny no one approves of my assertive behavior as a black man. Funny no one gives me rave reviews for not acting like a wimp.

Whenever I speak up, I am too outspoken. Whenever I am forceful, I am too strident. Whenever I am passionate, I am too emotional. Whenever I am assertive, I am too aggressive. Strange how aggressiveness wears better on Dan Quayle, who really is a wimp trying to act like a tiger.

The difference between Dan Quayle and me is why I was waiting for Malcolm X on a January evening in the Mary Dodd Memorial Chapel in 1963.

Somebody said kill the honkies. I was a twenty year old black man-child. I put my head down. Savagery embarrassed me. Murder is different from assassination. Murder is what they say happened to Martin Luther King while John Kennedy was assassinated. Murder is what happened to Patrice Lumumba as Dag Hammarskjold was assassinated. Aggressive is what is wrong with me and right with Dan Quayle. Assertiveness is aggressive with me and applauded by name in Dan Quayle.

I waited for Malcolm to bring together those ideas I had been taught in the schools of America and on the streets.

I was not falling. I was not sinking. I was not feeling. It was not like anything I could describe. It was like none of those sensations I remembered in the bad dreams of my youth. It was like breathing water. Like standing still as the world jerked to a halt. All sound was snuffed out. All fear anesthetized. Suddenly I could hear the train. Not hear as I was used to hearing. A knowing. A beyond sense reckoning of the presence of the train and its inevitable move in my direction. The inescapable pull of the train in my direction was a statement transcending universes of truth. The train was coming like a monster of possession let loose to rendezvous with this moment.

Malcolm was speaking. My life retreated to a punctuation mark. I was perfectly conscious.

I was at the center of the hurricane. I felt its power, gargantuan and unchained, dancing majestically. I was choking with the unearthly fury of passion. It heaved and ebbed. Ebbed and heaved. An implosion of my being was set at odds with the force of the planet bearing down on me.

Malcolm was speaking.

The train was steady on its destination. Time and circumstance were being reduced to an equation outside of science. Doubt ran like a mad dog howling at the chaos in the universe.

It hit me. The unalterable truth hit me. I had known it all my life. It was written in the root of my existence on the planet. It was a fundamental truth older than written history. It was superordinary to all the rituals that had been devised to keep the people in check through all the millennia. It was an unalterable truth. Black folks would not commit genocide.

Malcolm was speaking. His voice was actually pleasant. It was inviting. It did not threaten. It was a firm perch. The train was coming.

Now I hear Spike Lee's voice on the television inside the room. Spike. Nobody calls him Mr. Lee. Spike was asking that black people not go to work or school to support the opening of his movie Malcolm X. Sale of Malcolm X T-shirts would boom now. Malcolm, the pop image icon of the new generation of conscious blacks, would be looking out at the world from an oversized face on the front of the new fashion, eyes blazing.

Malcolm's face was bold with hatred. The hatred of a man denied the opportunity to feast fully at the tree of life. A whole man. Malcolm's eyes seared. They were full of the hurt that generation of blacks had felt in America. Deprivation. Spiritual defeat. The acquiescence to hatred. A hatred that cost one his humanity. Malcolm would be on more T-shirts than Martin and the athletes – Michael Jordan and Magic Johnson – and the court entertainers – Michael Jackson and Prince.

Malcolm would peer out on an ugly, unaccepting, and uncaring world. A world that had rejected him because he was too prone to speak the truth even under penalty of death. Malcolm's eyes would also reflect a deep love. The very power of the man was love. The extraordinary love for self. That self-love that is fundamental to the ability to love your brothers and sisters, to love your neighbor as yourself.

Spike's voice was whining now in that little brainy boy sound that was characteristic of him. What was Spike up to? Was he trying to hustle the people to support his movie that he had made in spite of financial fighting with his Hollywood producers? Was he trying to prove something to the ethnic conspiracy that controls images on the big screen? Or was he just trying to save some of the people some of the time by giving them realities that they could relate to, images that expanded that sense of what they could become by showing them that what they know is legitimate?

Was Spike (someday he may be called Mr. Lee) celebrating the long hard struggle of being black in America? Was this his essential genius? Was this his gift of love? Despite his petulance, the man seems too talented and too committed to be insincere. He could not even contrive insincerity in that voice.

Suddenly nothing happened. Suddenly the train stopped. It was absurdly quiet.

Then I heard the train. It was coming through Mary Dodd Memorial Chapel. It was coming through the walls. It was coming down on me. It was coming through my brain.

This train don't carry no passengers, this train.

Malcolm stood at the podium fully in command of himself and his audience.

This train is bound for Glory, this train.

The next evening my English professor asked me what I thought of

Malcolm. Did I think it was wise to bring such a hatemonger to the university?

"I agreed with everything he said," I responded. "He was right on the money." While I sat there eating this white professor's food and drinking his sherry, I confessed that Malcolm had inspired me as no other man in my life. Why? Because Malcolm was so damn bold with the truth.

Malcolm had done his homework before he came to the university. He had cased the joint. Or somebody had gotten the scoop on the situation for him. It didn't matter. The point was he knew what the hell was going on, not just in a broad view, but in the context of his audience. So many public speakers have only one speech. The rhetoric might be good. The oratory might be good. But the message ain't worth spit because it is out there somewhere other than where the audience lives. Malcolm wasn't like that.

From the moment Malcolm started speaking my soul was on fire. I was bewitched. Those eyes. That voice. The train. Malcolm mesmerized me with his sureness – borne of living on the edge of alienation. He enthralled me with his prophecy. Prophets are supposed to be without honor in their own country. I honored Malcolm in the country of my soul.

I felt Malcolm's prophecy. It was a sacred drum beating in my soul. It aligned with my vision of America's racial situation. America was messed up because white folks messed over black folks. As a result, the whole of modern civilization suffered. America could only begin to become healthy when Black folks rescued their psyches. Then Black folks would learn to negotiate their economic freedom. It was as simple as that. A whole lot of people knew this to be the truth, but they were afraid of the repercussions of admitting it to themselves or letting it pass their lips.

There was Malcolm boldly proclaiming the truth. He was some bad ass brother. And he had started by mocking the civil rights work I had busted my butt doing in the harsh winter cold.

Mind you, I did not think Malcolm was some quintessential orator. I had heard great orators regularly – especially at Lincoln University – that would put Malcolm to shame. I had heard Rabbi Martin Weitz, whose orations were Coltrane rhapsodies, painted in word tapestries that were pure art. I had heard oratorical elegance. And weekly I was privileged to hear university professors soar in the old school oratory that owed its wing to the best traditions of the Negro preacher and the Princeton-Yale forensic style. I had heard real oratory. Malcolm was only an above average speaker by comparison. But he had one power over the others. Truth. His truth was like a sword. It unsheathed itself and cut into the heart.

He stood there and questioned the sense of the weekly protest movement which I had been leading to desegregate the movie theaters and public facilities in Wilmington, Delaware. It would have made more sense for the university students to be trying to educate the black citizens of Wilmington and the other surrounding cities on U.S. Route 40 on how they could pull themselves out of the poverty that engulfed their ghetto neighborhoods, he said. As he pointed out the ridiculousness of the students' efforts – those poor black folks could barely afford to go to those movie houses even if they were admitted – I grasped the truth of what he was saying. Teach Malcolm. Teach Malcolm. I kept hearing the train, Teach Malcolm.

"You would be one of the first ones I would have to kill," I heard myself saying in even tones to my English professor. His wife looked on in amazement. Intuitively, I felt her thinking, you see you cannot do too much for these Negroes; they will never appreciate it, they will betray you. I never felt that she was committed to her husband's relationship with me or the other black students at the university. Especially with me. It was a kind of gut feeling. Sometimes you just know in your gut that the vibe isn't right.

"And why would that be?" the professor had asked, showing his irritation despite himself. I could see that the professor was controlling his anger. What had made me so damn bold? What had made me say things that would hurt this man who was truly my friend, my teacher, my mentor? It was Malcolm's truth. Truth boarded itself.

I was feeling uneasy too. Truth often makes us feel that way. That is why we avoid it. But truth does not go away. The more you stray from truth the greater the danger of losing your mind. This is what Malcolm had given me on that cold January evening in 1963. He had given me the vision to see the truth from which I could never again hide. Nothing can destroy Malcolm's truth.

"Because you are the most dangerous to me," I said calmly, "If the revolution came, which Malcolm X is calling for, it would be wise if we 'offed' all our good white friends first so that we would not lose our resolve."

He looked at me like I was crazy. I did not remember the rest of the evening. It became blurred. Somewhere before the evening was over I tried to explain the logic of Malcolm's speech in the pure intellectual terms of world history, how other people had thrown off their oppressors. Intellectualism was out of the window now to my teacher. And the wife never forgave me.

It was a quiet, uneasy ride in the professor's car back to the dormitory. I had often been invited to dinner at his house, more often on Sunday afternoon. I wondered now if the invitation this weekday evening following Malcolm's speech was an attempt to help the professor get a handle on Malcolm. It certainly was a turning point for me. I realized how afraid white folks are of the truth.

I loved the professor. He was a good man. His heart was in the right place. He really did enjoy empowering me with knowledge. Unfortunately, he was limited by the circumstances of his own life. I later came to believe my freedom was limited by his ignorance of the conditions of black people in America. The professor could not understand that such ignorance was dangerous to my existence. What I really needed from him was his example. He should have been attacking his own kind who treated black people unjustly. He could have stood with Malcolm. He could have stood with truth. Justice is not compassion. It is fairness.

Malcolm taught me that if a man does not know what killed his father he will die of the same thing.

I had been waiting for the train. Truth was on the rails.

This train don't carry no passengers, this train.

Novelists Leon Forrest, left, and Ralph Ellison at a June 1992 reception for the latter at the Harold Washington Library in Chicago. Ellison received the Harold Washington Literary Prize which is awarded annually.

Educator and entrepreneur Ruth B. Love and late author Alex Haley during March 1988 "Maya Angelou Weekend" at Haley's estate near Knoxville, Tennessee. Other guests included Lerone Bennett, Jr., Jessica Mitford, Calvin Hernton, Dolly McPherson, Vivian Baxter, and Tom Feelings.

I know their dark eyes, they know mine.
I know their style, they know mine. I am all of them,
they are all of me; they are farmers, I am a thief,
I am me, they are thee...

– Etheridge Knight
From "The idea of ancestry"

WHEREABOUTS KNOWN
A FAREWELL TO ETHERIDGE KNIGHT

An Interview By Seneca Turner

I ran into Etheridge Knight in the Fall of 1988, when he was conducting a workshop at the Westside YMCA in New York city. We had met during the mid-1970s in Chicago, recognized that we knew some of the same people, and immediately established a camaraderie. Our relationship endured until his death, March 10th 1991.

I visited him in his native Indianapolis on two occasions, once in the summer of 1989 and again on his 59th birthday, April 19th 1990. The Etheridge I came to know was a caring, wise, sensitive, and perceptive man. He had a great love for his family, especially his mother, Mrs. Belzora Knight. He remained close to her throughout his life.

There was something about Etheridge that connected who he was to what he did. In many ways he was the personification of Black manhood; his walk, the way he talked, indeed, his essence was that of a brother from the street. But that was merely one aspect of this poet who derived much of his art and style from the verbal combat in the Black community called "playing the dozens" or "toasting" and what he referred to as "just plain old rappin'." Etheridge was a Rap Master who predated contemporary young rap musicians. Of all the Black poets I have known and interacted with, he, in my judgment, is the best forerunner to the "Rap Movement." He considered himself a revolutionary/man of the people. In an interview with *Black Scholar* (Fall 1988) he concluded that: "I think it's a valid ambition to want the words you strung together to live on the lips of ordinary people."

At the time of this last interview we spent five days in his apartment. We laughed a lot between expressions of profound love and concern for our people-culture. We talked about "free-doom," his expression, his years in prison, his transgressions and excesses. And about his poetry:

SENECA TURNER: Etheridge, what writers have most profoundly influenced your work?

ETHERIDGE KNIGHT: Gwendolyn Brooks, Dudley Randall, Langston Hughes (work and biography), and Amiri Baraka (LeRoi Jones). I think the two major influences were Brooks and Randall. The writings of Richard Wright and James Baldwin.

ST: What piece of literature?

EK: *The Autobiography of Malcolm X.* I read that while I was in prison. Robert Bly, a poet from Minnesota, used to publish a magazine called *The Fifties and the Sixties.* The essays on poetry influenced me because he dealt with a lot of the older aspects of poetry.

ST: How would you describe the political nature of your work?

EK: That's difficult. I use the term "Black people" for us as a people. My politics stem basically from the reality that we are not an ethnic group. History has evolved in such a way ... we are an oppressed people. My art and my work come out of that reality ... stems from my experience as a Black man and a part of an oppressed people. I address my poetry mainly to Black people.

ST: What, more than anything else, motivates you to write?

EK: Wanting to be free.

ST: When I was in your workshop, you said that the writer has to find his or her voice. How would you describe your own voice?

EK: I hope it's a caring voice. I hope my voice reflects my love and respect for Black people. Sometimes my voice might become strident. If you're walking down the street with your sister and a guy jumps out of the bushes and attacks her and you kill him, you kill him because you hate him or because you love your sister. Some Black critics, but especially White critics, label the work of a lot of Black poets as "protest poetry." But as long as the voice is one of concern, as long as the motivation for creating is out of love, it isn't a protest. When the art of the work is a threat to the oppressor, hoping he'll understand ... how niggers go ... then I guess you can say that is protest poetry. When you are addressing your own people art is a liberating force.

What I hope I'm saying to Black people is that we're good, we're beautiful and once we understand that we are not going to allow ourselves to be oppressed too long.

ST: In our conversation yesterday you mentioned that a man's life is defined by his relationships with women. Could you expound a little on your ideas regarding the "ascendancy of female dominance," as you referred to it previously?

EK: As a poet and a person I am not apocalyptic. I don't subscribe to that suicide school. I cannot imagine the world not being. I don't operate on the fear that the White boys are going to blow up the world. I don't think that's within their power. The masculine consciousness that, uh, permeates this culture from religion to economics is lineal. That is, the perpetuation of a land, its racism and radicalism, comes from The Man wanting to see his image perpetuated. I don't think that this concerns Black people as much, because I don't think we operate under the fear that we will never be/that our image will be eradicated. No matter how many Blue-Eyes come on the scene, gods and all.

Male consciousness is derived from violence or the threat of violence. We see that in personal situations; the father as disciplinarian. And in our political system: when all else fails we've got to have our army and our bombs. Our god tells us to bomb you if you don't behave like we tell you. You're going to burn in hell or I'm going to hurl a thunderbolt down.

ST: Punitive.

EK: Yeah. And the feminine consciousness says that if you don't behave like I want you to behave I will withdraw from you. I'll turn my back on you in the bed or I'll pull out of the circle. It's not based on violence or the threat of violence. And I think that's the consciousness which will save the world. Since I don't see Russia, the U.S. – all of these big superpowers blowing up the world. I see the rise of feminine consciousness. We have evidence of that in art, music, religion. We have the whole idea of nonviolence as a way of making people behave. It is now beginning to creep into the literature. In most Western literature the climax of any story, any movie, any television program is the (male) resolution of conflict/violence. John Wayne has a shoot-out with the bad guys.

ST: Yeah. Prevails.

EK: I think that feminine thought is going to invade the councils where the world is run and that the idea of violence as a way of solving things is just going to become old hat.

ST: What is your position on the criticism leveled at Black women writers by certain Black men for painting unfavorable pictures of the brothers in their novels and poetry. For example, Alice Walker's *The Color Purple.* It received a Pulitzer but many felt that this kind of "airing of dirt" was another attempt to perpetuate the negative images of Black men.

EK: I think that any writer should write from his/her particular pool of passion. If incest exists in the Black community, and it does, then it should be written about. And anything else that the writer finds in his or her pool of passion. Because you can only get so much from each pool, you see.

ST: You once said that any poet or writer worth his craft must have some generalized sense of genealogy and it should be reflected in his writing. Could you elaborate?

EK: Well, what I meant, Seneca, is that a poet operates on personal authority. A poet does not become a poet because of a college degree or those kinds of credentials. The authority of any artist comes from tradition. And we understand that in laying out one's personal genealogy it reveals where he or she is coming from. It reveals the context, what history has shaped his or her life and therefore shapes his or her art. All of that's purely subjective. History itself is personal.

ST: His-story.

EK: Yeah. It's all according to who writes it. I don't trust the politics of what's inherent in art if I don't know that artist's personal genealogy – if I don't know where he or she is coming from.

ST: You have expressed a desire to travel abroad but haven't. Why is it that you've never gotten off these shores? Certainly you've had the opportunity to travel.

EK: I'm at the age, now, that I'm pretty well set in my ways. I've been reluctant. So much is going on here. This is where my people are. This is where my world is. I also felt I'd be more effective here. I feel, as a poet, that when one gets too far from one's source of language it dims. And one's voice will dim. I want to travel but I never want to stay away from Black American people too long. So much has been happening to keep me here. But now I understand that our liberation, our history is connected with the world and all that.

ST: One time I read that you'd said poetry was a dance. Can you explain that?

EK: What I meant was that there is always a constant examination, an awareness of my own feelings. What's going on inside my world and what's going on in my world outside and being caught up in feelings, my feelings and those of others. Relating to that makes the boogie that's poetry. Poetry is ultimately celebratory. Like an old delta blues says "trouble of mine, I'm blue but I won't be blue always." No matter how bad things get there is always this power to take pain and suffering and make it into a song, a dance. In Western literature there's this school of thought that the only good art comes out of suffering. It also comes out of joy and celebration. I think that our Black people produce a lot of this kind of art. So to me being a poet falls into both these traditions. There is the poet who is alone, woe is me/suffering in the universe. There's the poet who's connected up with his own people where there's always this affirmation going/this applause that causes this singing/this dancing.

ST: You also said it's the same song, the same line – it's how you sing the song.

EK: Shakespeare made up plays and poems for the English people, for their time. Burns made up poems for the Scottish people, in their time. Even though what they addressed was the same – you know, the eternal themes: death, birth, war, lost love, new love, they're all particular.

ST: What advice would you give to young Black writers?

EK: Marry rich. Seriously – understand that the artist is not separate from his or her people. Listen and examine people. People are the only game in town. Learn the language. Pay attention to the feelings. We often hear that reading and writing go together. For a poet, for an artist, reading, writing, talking and listening go together. Young poets should understand their traditions, that they are not unique, are operating on the backs of a lot of poets who've gone before them.

ST: We talked about the question of transcending race and what that means. You said that as a Black person in America it would be impossible to transcend the reality of being Black and what that means. The concept of universalism has been implied by many intellectuals and poets. I interpret this to mean moving beyond that question.

EK: Sure, the feelings are universal. Everybody feels sadness, joy, pain and all that. But I don't think young Black poets or any artist should be concerned with addressing everybody in the world. The concept of universalism is a bullshit aesthetic put forth by the dominant culture. Usually when White boys talk about universalism they're saying "write what we say under our circumstances."

ST: The example you gave was between the grief felt by a White woman whose son was killed on a football field and the grief felt by Emmett Till's mother when she found her son had been lynched and castrated.

EK: Where's the universalism there? The duty of the artist is to stay with the specific, the subjective. I think it's a waste of time for a young artist to be concerned with this universal thing. There is no universal. There is no universalism. Until we have a universal political system, a universal economical system, a universal language, a universal history and universal art.

FOR ETHERIDGE
By Seneca Turner

Renegade/flimflam man
Wordsmith/bebop slim
Blackman/soothsayer/wailer
Your voice and spirit
Rose from the bowels
of a prison cell
Echoing throughout this land

Tall and Black like a crow
Talked as much stuff as the radio
High Priest of the Word
Signifying Storyteller
King for a day and a nite
Smiling that knowing smile
Dazzling Master's children at every turn
Mississippi mojo man

Your words like 10-carat diamonds
on big Black Mississippi fingers
Your pen chopping cotton that was
to be weighed on the scales of Truth
Stiletto tongue/cutting across the grain
And the money went and came
While you did it again/just one more time
Polka dots and moonbeams and the pain
Against the backdrop of white thighs

Brother/man Kikuyu warrior
Professor of the College of Life
Singing your Knight song every hour of the day
Taking what you wanted/whenever you wanted

Driven by the pain and the Spirits of the Tribe

Traveling/turning corners
The road beckoned and twisted and turned
While we took the A-train to the Bronx of oblivion
New York City never tried to judge you
And sweat ran down your neck in the middle
of January/and we both heard the sound of
Clapping hands intrude upon the ritual
of white flesh and canceled checks

Seer/prophet Tribal Griot
Peoples' poet/Keeper of the Flame
Lonely hunter/alien
Conjure Man/dancing on the
penetrating edge
Your old enemies rose up to meet you
Pall Malls and the hot point
And VA hospitals and detox and skin grafts
and the pain, the diabolical pain of redemption
While you talked about Free/doom

Keeper of the Record
Rapmaster/maker of songs
shooting dice with the Devil
Hoodoo dancer,/dancing/dancing
Dance Etheridge, dance, dance

This is of remembrance
For Shorty Moe!, Black Frank, Three-Finger Bill
Willie Earl and Freckled-Faced Gerald
For the Big Yard and the Big Wall
Those that came and those that went
And for you my brother

Be free.

The last words Etheridge spoke to me, shortly before his death, were "Keep the song-and-dance, keep on boogie-ing."

A casual Etheridge Knight (1931-1991) pictured with the land and water (the inspiration for many of his poems) that he loved.

Poet-playwright Mari Evans sings praises to sister-bard Gwendolyn Brooks during a June 1987 birthday party for Brooks in Chicago.

At Richard Wright's house: Paris conferees Darlene Roy, Amritjit Singh, Julia Wright, and Ben Davis gather following the dedication of Richard Wright's house. Scene was the closing ceremonies of the February 1992 "African-Americans in Europe Conference." Julia, daughter of the late novelist, and Davis, a friend of the Wright family, helped organize the dedication program.

IN MEMORIAM. . . IN TRANSITION . . .

Alvin Ailey - Marian Anderson - Arthur Ashe - Pearl Bailey -

Chet Baker - James Baldwin - George Houston Bass - Vivian Baxter -

James "Cool Papa" Bell - Roseann P. Bell - Wayne Bennett -

Mary E. Brown - Honey Coles - Miles Dewey Davis III -

Sammy Davis Jr. - Nadine DeLawrence - Melvin Dixon -

Thomas Dorsey - Billy Eckstine - Redd Foxx - Addison Gayle -

John Burks "Dizzy" Gillespie - Jim Henson - Audrey Hepburn -

David Hines - Clyde C. Jordan - Eddie Kendricks -

John Oliver Killens - Albert King - Etheridge Knight - Cleavon Little -

Audre Lorde - Bobby McClure - Arthur Marshall - Leo Maitland -

Thelonius Sphere Monk - Craig Moore - Rudolph Nureyev -

Leothy Owens - Singleton Palmer - Joseph Papp - John Pratt -

Byron Robertson - Gerard Sekoto - Johnny Shines -Garth Tate -

Sarah Vaughn - Harold Washington - Valerie Wellington -

Chancellor Williams - Frank Yerby - Ruth B. Younge - Mimi Zanger

NOTES ON CONTRIBUTORS

JEANETTE ADAMS is a poet on the staff of the Department of Special Programs at City University of New York. Adams studied with Gwendolyn Brooks and has published her poetry in *Essence* magazine as well as in individual collections: *Sukari, Picture Me in a Poem*, and *Love Lyrics*. **MAYA ANGELOU**, who read her poem, "On the Pulse of Morning," at President Bill Clinton's inauguration, has authored more than a dozen books of diverse writings including *I Know Why the Caged Bird Sings* and *I Shall Not Be Moved.* She is Reynolds Professor of Amerian Studies at Wake Forest University in Winston-Salem, NC. **B. J. ASHANTI**, New York poet, editor and jazz enthusiast, also writes cultural criticism and fiction. Ashanti's poems have been published in *Essence, Greenfield Review, Presence Africaine*, and *Pan-African Journal.* His latest book of poetry is *Nova.* A critic called him the "John Coltrane of poetry." **JABARI ASIM** is Editorial Page Copy Editor of the *St. Louis Post-Dispatch* and is editor of *Eyeball.* His poems have appeared in **In the Tradition**, *Catalyst, Shooting Star Review, Black American Literature Forum*, and *Literati Internazionale.* During the fall of 1992 he was a lecturer in African-American literature at the University of Missouri-St. Louis. **ALVIN AUBER**, the founding editor of *Obsidian: Black Literature in Review,* currently teaches creative writing and African-American literature at Wayne State University in Detroit. His books include *Against the Blues* and *South Louisiana Poems*, and his poems have been published in *Callaloo..*

AMIRI BARAKA, poet, playwright, jazz critic, and cultural architect, helped define and shape the Black Arts Movement of the 1960's. He lives in Newwark, NJ. His books include *Blues People* and *The Amiri Baraka/Leroi Jones Reader.* **GEORGENE BESS**, a teacher at Georgia Southern University, has published articles in *Literati Internazionale* and *Clashing Harmonies and Universal Particulars: A Workshop Report on the Third National Black Writers Conference.* **GWENDOLYN BROOKS** is Poet Laureate of Illinois and was the first Black to win a Pulitzer Prize for literature (1950). *Children Coming Home* is her most recent work. She currently holds the Gwendolyn Brooks Chair of Black Literature at Chicago State University. **MICHAEL CASTRO**, poet, critic, and scholar, directs the River Styx at Duff's Poetry Series in St. Louis and teaches creative writing at Lindenwood College. *(US)* is his latest book of poems. **DR. E. PELICAN CHALTO** and Amiri Baraka, who suggested that *Drumvoices* publish Chalto, met on a U.S. Airforce base in Puerto Rico in the 1950's. Pelican lives, writes, and plays his clarinet in Louisville, KY.

HENRY DUMAS was born in Sweet Home, Arkansas in 1934, raised from the age of 10 in Harlem, and had lived in East St. Louis for one year at the time of his shooting-death in New York City in 1968. Though only a few of his writings were published during his lifetime, Dumas's posthumous literary reputation has grown steadily. His recent works, edited by Eugene B. Redmond, include *Goodbye, Sweetwater* (fiction, 1988) and *Knees of a Natural Man* (poetry, 1989). **KOFI L. DUNBAR** is a free-lance writer and poet living in East St. Louis (Il.). He is a frequent contributor to the *Monitor* Newspaper. New York poet **CORNELIUS EADY** has read his poetry on NPR's "Morning Edition," at Tougaloo College, and at State Community College in East St. Louis. A winner of the American Academy of Poets Lamont Poetry Prize, Eady's books include *The Gathering of My Name* and *Victims of the Latest Dance Craze*. **MARI EVANS** lives, writes, composes music, and oversees numerous good projects in Indianapolis. She has taught at Cornell University, Purdue, and the State University of New York at Albany. *I Am a Black Woman* and *A Dark and Splendid Mass* are among books of verse by this former writer-in-residence at Spelman College.

LEON FORREST, professor of English and chair of the African-American Studies Department at Northwestern University, writes novels--with titles like *Two Wings to Veil My Face* and *Divine Days*--that are set in his native Chicago. His fiction has been praised by Ralph Ellison and Toni Morrison. *Relocations of the Spirit*, a collection of essays by Forrest, will be published by Mayer Bell in June 1993. **J. e. FRANKLIN** is a Texas-born/New York-based playwright. Several of her dramatic works, including *Black Girl* and *The Prodigal Daughter*, have premiered in New York City. **BOB HOLMAN,** aka "The Plain White Rapper," is a mover and shaker on the New York City poetry--"slam"--scene. His work has appeared in *Literati Internazionale* and he has performed his poetry on film, radio (including NPR), and at Duff's Restaurant in St. Louis. **DARRYL HOLMES** is a young poet of commitment and strength who was awarded a B.A. in Creative Writing by Queens College, CUNY. His poems have been published in *Eyeball* and *A Gathering of Hands*, and his first collection, *Wings Will Not Be Broken*, came out from Third World Press in 1990. **JA JAHANNES**, a poet and critic, is dean of the College of Humanities and Social Sciences at Savannah State College. He participated in the International Conference on Black Women Writers and Magic Realism at Jackson State University (Mississippi) in October 1992. *Truthfeasting* is his latest book of poems. **IRA B. JONES** is publisher of *Eyeball*, a member of the Black Man's Think Tank, and active on the St. Louis poetry and cultural arts scene. His poems have appeared in *Front Lines*, *In the Tradition*, *Catalyst* and *Young Tongues*.

ETHERIDGE KNIGHT (1931-1991) helped advance a plain-speaking, gut-dazzling poetry pioneered by Zora Neale Hurston, Melvin Tolson, Langston Hughes, Sterling Brown, and the best bards of the 1960's Black Arts Movement. Born in Mississippi, he served with the U. S. Army in Korea and later did time (for armed robbery) in Indiana State Prison, the inspiration for his first book, *Poems From Prison* (1968), brought out by Dudley Randall's Broadside Press in Detroit. By the end of his short life, he had published several more books, such as *Belly Song*, and become writer-in-residence at places like Butler University in Indianapolis. In 1993 the state of Indiana awarded him a posthumous Distinguished Arts Prize. **EARNEST McBRIDE** is a Mississippi-based educator, activist, and free-lance writer who reports on social economics, arts, and civil rights issues. He has written articles on the Medgar Evers assassination and is a frequent contributor to the *Jackson Advocate*. **DEBRA F. MEADOWS,** a poet, playwright, actress, and former dancer, is a native of San Antonio, Texas. Now a New Yorker, she is the author of the choreopoem, *donkey face's soliloquies have arrived/& it's not just the poet/ but the poem itself*, and the one-act play, *Mama's Lil' Foxes*. Her poems have appeared in *PAX*, *The Thing Itself*, *Pegasus*, and *Third Woman*. **JANICE MIRIKITANI** lives in San Francisco where she writes, does cultural arts organizing, and publishes her poetry, fiction and drama. Active in multicultural communities and causes, she has published several volumes of her writings, including *Awake in the River*. She was one of the editors of *A Time to Greez!*, a collection of Third World Writings of the 1970's for which Maya Angelou wrote the introduction. **CARLA MOODY** is a St. Louis poet who teaches English and speech in Academic Support Services at Harris-Stowe State College. In 1990 she won second prize in the St. Louis Poetry Center's Annual Competition. **TESS ONWUEME**, Nigerian-born poet, playwright, and scholar, is currently an associate professor of English at Vassar College, though she has taught at other U.S. institutions: Montclair State College and Wayne State University. Her plays include *The Broken Calabash*, *Legacies*, and *Go Tell it to Women: An Epic Drama for Women*. She was the first woman president of the Association of Nigerian Authors. **RAYMOND PATTERSON**, poet, scholar, and editor, recently retired from City University of New York where he continues to direct the Annual Langston Hughes Festival. He is a widely anthologized and translated poet whose books include *26 Ways of Looking at a Black Man* and *Elemental Blues*.

ROBERT EARL PRICE is a poet, playwright, filmmaker, and novelist currently living in Atlanta. A former resident of Los Angeles, Price's awards include a *Black World* literary prize and a National Endowment for the Arts Creative Writing Fellowship. *Blood Elegy* is one of his volumes of poetry. **EUGENE B. REDMOND** is Poet Laureate of his native East St. Louis, founding editor of *Drumvoices Revue*, and associate publisher/poetry editor of *Literati Internazionale* and *The Original Chicago Blues Annual*. A professor of English at SIUE, he won a 1993 American Book Award from the Before Columbus Foundation for *The Eye in the Ceiling: Selected Poems*. **ISHMAEL REED**, multicultural literary pioneer and guru, is a journalist, poet, novelist, cultural organizer, editor, publisher, professor at UC Berkeley, and the driving force behind the Before Columbus Foundation and P.E.N. Oakland. Among his books are *Yellow Back Radio Broke Down*, *The Last Days of Louisiana Red*, *Secretary to the Spirits*, and *Japanese by Spring*. **LUIS RODRIGUEZ** is a journalist, poet, and former Los Angeles gang member now living in Chicago. The publisher of Tia Chucha Press, he has been anthologized in *Southern California Anthology*. His collections include *The Concrete Poems* and *Running in the Streets*. In the spring of 1992, he read his poems to an eager East St. Louis audience.

DARLENE ROY is a poet, essayist and administrator with the Illinois Department of Public Aid. An East St. Louis native who attended Lincoln Senior High School--Miles Davis's alma mater--Roy's work has appeared in *Black American Literature Forum*, *Break Word With The World*, *The Original Chicago Blues Annual*, *Black Bard's Digest*, and *American Poetry Anthology*. She is president of the

EBR Writers Club. **JEFFREY SKOBLOW**, a poet and essayist, grew up in New York and Baltimore. Currently a member of the English faculty at SIUE, Skoblow is also an actor. His first book, *Paradise Dislocated*, a treatise on socialism and romanticism, will be published in the fall of 1993. Skoblow is an assistant editor of *Drumvoices*. **CHRISTINA SPRINGER** is a mother, writer, and filmmaker living in Yellow Springs, Ohio. She co-founded Back Porch Productions: A Women's Media Collective whose first film was *Out of Our Time*. Her writings have appeared in *Shooting Star Review*, *Athena*, *Lavender Visions*, and *Piece of My Heart*. **CHRISTOPHER STANARD** is a 25-year-old engineer currently living in Columbia, SC. As a student at Morehouse College he edited *Literatus* and *Stentorian*. In 1986, his poem "Cold as Ice" won the Annual Clark College Writers Workshop Poetry Competition. His writings have appeared in *The Durham Sun*, *The Atlanta Inquirer*, *Woman Engineer*, and *The Christian Way*. **RICHARD STIMAC**, a graduate student in English at SIUE, is managing editor of *Tornado Alley* and an editorial assistant to *Drumvoices Revue*. In 1992, he won first prize in the Milly Southwood Poetry Competition for "Steel City Blues." **ERIC STINUS** lives in Copenhagen, Denmark where he does journalism, poetry, and translations. A human rights activist, he is married to artist Chittaprosad. Among his published works is the epic poem, *The Conquest of Ceuta*. He has traveled to Turkey, India, Nicaragua, Africa, and Yugoslavia.

Former and current Graduate Assistants and Student Assistants to Drumvoices Revue and Literati Internazionale gather on the campus of Southern Illinois University at Edwardsville during fall 1992. From left are Richard Stimac, Debjani Dasgupta, Christina Veasley, William Dorman, and Michelle Foster. Dorman and Stimac are publisher and managing editor, respectively, of Tornado Alley.

FRANCY STOLLER is a poet, mother, wife and cultural organizer living in Indianapolis. A member of the Free Peoples Poetry Workshop, she participated in the 1992 Etheridge Knight National Festival of the Arts. **ZOHREH T. SULLIVAN** specializes in the British novel, colonial discourse, and the postcolonial novel in English. A native of Iran, she is professor of English at the University of Illinois at Urbana-Champaign. Sullivan has written on Iris Murdoch, Joseph Conrad, E.M. Forster, V.S. Naipaul, and Chinua Achebe. Her book, *Narratives of Empire: The Fictions of Rudyard Kipling*, came out from Cambridge University Press in 1993. **CLYDE TAYLOR**, a member of the English faculty at Tufts University, won *Black World* magazine's Richard Wright Award for Literary Criticism and founded the African Film Society. Taylor has contributed articles to *Black American Literature Forum* and to *Griefs of Joy: Anthology of Afro-Amerian Poetry for Students*. The editor of *Vietnam and Black America*, he was also the recipient of a Ford Foundation Fellowship which he completed at Harvard University's W. E. B. DuBois Institute. **SENECA TURNER** , a St. Louis native, is a writer and educational consultant specializing in mediation and arbitration. He has lived and worked in Chicago and Los Angeles and currently resides in New York City. His writings have appeared in *Black American Literature Forum*, *Flare*, *Perceptions II*, and *Nommo*.

DEREK WALCOTT, winner of the 1992 Nobel Prize for Literature, is a native of St. Lucia in the Caribbean. Walcott has been publishing poetry and plays since 1948. Among his books are *Dream on Monkey Mountain*, *Collected Poems*, *Arkansas Testament*, and *Omeros*, an epic. He teaches at Boston University. **CHARLES WARTTS, JR.** is a journalist, teacher, novelist, and world traveler who spent two years in Tanzania. Currently on the faculty of the University of Missouri at St. Louis, Wartts is a former editor of *Muhammad Speaks*. His writings have appeared in *Black American Literatue Forum*, *Take Five* and *River Styx*. **TYRONE WILLIAMS** received a Ph.D. from Wayne State University in poetics. An associate professor of English at Xavier University in Cincinnati, Ohio, his poems have appeared in *River Styx* and *Kenyon Review*. **ANDREA M. WREN** is a poet, fiction writer, reviewer, and associate editor of *Eyeball*. She won the 1990 Zora Neale Hurston-Langston Hughes Literary Prize, awarded by Spelman College, her alma mater. Her writings have been published in *Catalyst*, *In the Tradition*, *Take Five*, *The Original Chicago Blues Annual*, and *Break Word with the World*. A graduate of Lincoln Senior High School in East St. Louis, she is a board member of the EBR Writers Club board of directors.